A JAPANESE RECONSTRUCTION OF MARXIST THEORY

A JAPANESE RECONSTRUCTION OF MARXIST THEORY

Robert Albritton

Department of Political Science
York University, Ontario

MACMILLAN

First published 1986

Published by
THE MACMILLAN PRESS LTD
Houndmills, Basingstoke, Hampshire RG21 2XS
and London
Companies and representatives
throughout the world

Filmsetting by Vantage Photosetting Co. Ltd
Eastleigh and London
Printed in Hong Kong

British Library Cataloguing in Publication Data
Albritton, Robert
A Japanese reconstruction of Marxist theory.
1. Communism
I. Title
335.4′0952   HX73
ISBN 0-333-39591-3 (hc)
ISBN 0-333-39592-1 (pbk)

Contents

Preface

Before he died in 1977, Kozo Uno expressed the wish that his theories should not remain entrapped within the insularity of Japan. This book in a way represents the fulfilment of that wish. It is the first book based on the ideas of Uno to be written by a non-Japanese. I did not have the honour of meeting Professor Uno before he died, but if he were alive I would hope that he would be pleased with this book.

The sub-plot of this book is East meets West. I have used my extensive knowledge of Western Marxism in order to develop Uno's ideas in the direction of the most important controversies in the Western tradition. I hope the result is a cross-fertilization which will strengthen the Marxian traditions in both the East and the West. In the past the language barrier has been a serious obstacle in the way of mutually stimulating exchanges. Perhaps this book will serve to encourage future dialogue between Japanese and Western Marxists.

In some ways it is most appropriate that Uno's ideas should first take root in Canada. The location of Canada as a Pacific rim country places Japan on its horizon. Further, Canadian Marxists maintain a certain distance from British, French and American Marxists while being exposed to their theories and debates. I feel that intellectually and geographically I am located in a position to encourage a critical confrontation of ideas from these somewhat diverse traditions of Marxist thought.

Of course, the main reason why Uno's ideas have taken root in Canada is because of the presence of his student Thomas Sekine at York University. Sekine's *Dialectic of Capital* is the primary inspiration for this book, and I owe him an immense debt for many of its ideas. We have worked closely together for the past eight years at York University.

Since this book has been about four years in preparation, I am indebted to many people for the development of my ideas along the way. The Uno study group consisting of Sekine, Stropple,

vii

Duncan, Bell, Weinstein, Maclean, Smardon and Maruyama has been continually stimulating in our exploration of all areas of Marxist theory. I have also received helpful comments on parts of the manuscript from Professors Chastain and Cunningham and from P. Hebert, J. Drydek and W. Secombe.

I am deeply indebted to Professor S. Mawatari for arranging a speaking/study tour of Japan. While there I met with Uno scholars at eight different universities. The comments of Professors Itoh, Nagatani, Kobayashi, Watanabe, Ouchi and Mawatari were especially helpful. Professor Mawatari organized a seminar at Tohoku University which discussed the entire manuscript chapter by chapter. Needless to say this was most helpful and special thanks are due to the graduate students who commented on various chapters: T. Okuyama, H. Shima, B. Maclean. Y. Tomita, K. Sasaki and J. Onishi.

Finally I am indebted to Linda Briskin for carefully editing the entire manuscript, for clarifying discussions of many points, and for sharing the pains and joys of such an undertaking as this book.

Department of Political Science   Robert Albritton
York University

1 Introduction

A theoretical system cannot be stronger than its foundations. Althusser was the most recent Western Marxist who attempted to give clear and consistent answers to the basic questions of Marxist theory. He explored the scientific character of Marxist theory and tried to specify the meaning of 'political economy', 'historical materialism' and 'dialectical materialism'. What is the relation between the laws of motion of capital first formulated by Marx in *Capital* and the study of history? What is the epistemological character of these laws? In the light of the answer to these questions, in what sense is Marxian political economy a science? Althusser did attempt to answer these questions and in doing so hoped to give Marxist theory a firm foundation. In the early 1970s Althusser's paradigm was influential and perhaps even hegemonic amongst Western Marxists, but its inability to deal successfully with a number of basic problems eventually led to its demise. Since its decline, no alternative has sparked wide interest; indeed I am not even aware of any attempts since Althusser to deal with the foundations of Marxist theory in anything like his scope and thoroughness. This book is an effort to begin to fill this vacuum. It is my belief that the work of the Japanese political economist Kozo Uno provides a framework for successfully solving many of the difficulties that cannot be solved within the Althusserian paradigm.[1]

Kozo Uno (1897–1977) is undoubtedly the most important and original Japanese contributor to Marxian political economy. His *Principles of Political Economy* was published in two volumes in 1950 and 1952. The *New Principles* was a condensed and revised version first published in 1964 and now available as Uno's only work translated into English.[2] Uno wrote books dealing with many areas of Marxian political economy, but his reconstruction of Marx's *Capital* in his *Principles of Political Economy* is considered his greatest contribution. In Japan Uno's work is widely known and read, and the influence of his writings has been

1

sufficiently strong to result in the creation of a Uno School of Political Economy. Today it is one of the largest and most significant schools of Marxian political economy in Japan.[3]

Though the Uno School has many professors at leading Japanese universities, it appears to have 'lost momentum' in recent years.[4] Though there are many reasons for this, the reason that I want to emphasize is a certain tendency towards scholasticism and intellectual conservatism. A very large portion of the combined energy of the Japanese Uno School has focused primarily on the most abstract level of political economy, what Uno called 'the theory of a purely capitalist society'. Thus instead of developing the mediations between the inner logic of capital and historical analysis, they have by and large generated overrefined debates on value-form theory or some other special area of the theory of a purely capitalist society. And instead of developing the epistemological foundations of Uno's framework in order to develop it as a general paradigm, they have focused too much on interpreting Uno's texts. As a result, Unoists who have engaged in more empirical levels of analysis often produce work that is indistinguishable methodologically from Marxists working within non-Unoist paradigms. In short, the power and distinctiveness of Uno's framework as a general paradigm of Marxist theory has not been sufficiently worked out in opposition to other paradigms. This book represents the first steps in overcoming these defects.

The translation of Uno's *Principles* into English has sparked a growing interest amongst Western Marxists, but this interest has also focused primarily on economic theory.[5] The result is a failure to understand fully the power of Uno's reformulation of Marx's law of value and a tendency to view his contribution as narrowly economic and not as what it potentially is – a complete paradigm.

My desire then is to present Uno's approach as a complete paradigm which gives clear and consistent answers to all the fundamental issues of Marxist theory, and offers guidelines for all areas of Marxian social science. Such an undertaking is perhaps too much for one individual in this age of specialization. I cannot be an expert in all areas of Marxian social science and cannot do justice to the body of literature that exists in each area. To deal with this problem, I want to distinguish clearly between the general principles which inform the Uno approach and the particular application that I work out in each area. What is most important to me is the general principles themselves, and not my particular application which may in some cases be inadequate because of my lack of expertise in a particular area of research. But even where my contribution may seem rather thin in relation to the rich body of literature that exists in a particular area, I feel it is important for me to indicate a way of applying the general principles that I have extracted from Uno's approach. Then at least an indication of how to proceed will be articulated for others to either reject or improve upon.

My knowledge of Uno's theory comes not from being able to read Japanese, but from working closely with his student Thomas Sekine for the past eight years. Since I do not have direct access to the voluminous literature produced by the Japanese Uno School, I only know Uno through Sekine. It would be presumptuous of me to speak of 'the Uno approach' as if I was trying to represent the entire Japanese Uno School. I shall therefore speak of 'the Uno/Sekine approach', not suggesting thereby that there are not many other important contributors to Uno theory, but only that for me it is through Sekine that I understand Uno theory. Further, I do not mean to suggest by the phrase 'the Uno/Sekine approach' that Sekine is Uno's equal in creating the approach. However, having visited Japan and spoken with many Uno scholars, I do think that Sekine's contributions are major even though the Japanese themselves are not generally familiar with them. In my view Sekine's most important contribution is his effort to clarify epistemological issues with the aim of developing Uno theory in the direction of a complete paradigm. Sekine has devoted himself to the most basic issues of Marxian economics which in the case of the Uno School means 'the theory of a purely capitalist society' and the epistemology implicit in it.[6] His monumental *Dialectic of Capital* improves upon Uno's pure theory by making its dialectical logic explicit, by using the latest mathematical techniques, and by engaging with some of the best economists in both the bourgeois and Marxian traditions.

Using the phrase 'the Uno/Sekine approach', then, is meant to imply two things: first, that it is through Sekine that I know Uno, and second, that I think Sekine has made important contributions to Uno theory. The Uno School is already divided into distinct tendencies or sub-schools, and I do not want to contribute to a further splintering by declaring a Uno–Sekine faction. Instead I claim that Sekine has opened debate on very fundamental issues which could serve to demonstrate that what Unoists have in common is more fundamental than the issues that divide them.

My purpose will be to present the basic principles and concepts of the Uno/Sekine approach, and then to develop its implications by critically analysing the work of various theorists in the tradition of Western Marxism. I shall be particularly interested in the most crucial, problematic and unresolved debates, because it is especially with these controversies that I can show the contributions that their approach can make to Western Marxism. Though in my view the Uno/Sekine approach represents a major advance in developing the scientificity of Marxist theory, it leaves many problems unresolved. Most of the work available in English deals with Marxian economics and especially with pure capitalism, but this work has profound implications for dialectical materialism, historical materialism and Marxist theory generally. As I move away from pure theory to stage theory and historical analysis, as I move from the base to the superstructure, and as I move from capitalism to non-capitalist modes of production, the Uno/Sekine approach is less and less well worked out, so that my analysis becomes both innovative and tentative. I do not view the Uno/Sekine approach as a completed doctrine with definitive conclusions, but rather as a new approach with great promise. The aim of this book is to present this promise not by a focus on one area of Marxist theory but by making brief but sharp forays into many areas of Marxist theory. This will result in short critiques of many thinkers in the tradition of Western Marxism. If at times my condensed characterizations of various thinkers do not do justice to the subtlety and profundity of their thought, it is not because I wish to be dismissive, but is rather a requirement of a book that is as synthetic and condensed as this one. While realizing that nearly every chapter in this book could itself be expanded into a book, it is my hope that in simplifying I do not distort too much.

Though Uno grounds his approach in a substantive theory, still Uno theory is in my view primarily a framework or methodology which can absorb any positive contribution to our knowledge of society and history. In this sense I believe that it is a theory which can unify Marxian social science. From the point of view of the Uno/Sekine approach many divisions in the history of Marxist theory are unnecessary. For example, in Western Marxism there has been a sharp division between those who emphasize the scientificity of Marxist theory and those who see it as a perspective of radical criticism. But Marxism must be both a science and a radical/critical ideology, and it is precisely the complementarity between these two aspects that is one of the great strengths of Marxism. This book primarily explores Marxism as science without implying for a moment that the moral/critical side is not important. Towards the end of the book I attempt to give some indications of how the scientific and moral sides fit together while leaving it to others to develop Marxism as an ethics of freedom, as a humanism, as a radical/critical ideology and as a transformative practice.

The structure of this book follows the logic of the Uno/Sekine approach. Since they view political economy as the foundation of Marxist theory, this is my starting-point and the major focus of the book. Dialectical materialism which is the basic epistemology of political economy comes next, and the book ends with a short section dealing with historical materialism. This final section is the most tentative and least well developed.

Sometimes 'political economy' is used loosely to refer to Marxian social science in general, but I want to use it to refer specifically to the theory of capitalism. According to Uno and Sekine the theory of capital is divided into three distinct levels of analysis: the theory of a purely capitalist society, stage theory and historical analysis. Part I of the book starts with a chapter which focuses on the relation of the logical and historical in Marx's *Capital* in order to show that the three levels of analysis are consistent with what Marx was trying to achieve. The next three chapters deal with the three levels of analysis, and the final chapter of Part I deals with how the theory of the capitalist superstructure is derived and developed in relation to the three levels of analysis. Part II on 'Dialectical Materialism' has two chapters: one dealing with the approach of Uno and Sekine and the other a critical analysis of various other approaches. Finally Part III on 'Historical Materialism' deals briefly with the relation between the dialectic of capital and historical materialism, with some basic concepts of historical materialism, with the relation between theory and practice and with the transition away from capitalism.

Part I
Political Economy

2 The Uno/Sekine Approach and Marx

The purpose of this chapter is to introduce some of the basic conceptions of the Uno/Sekine approach through a critical analysis of some texts by Marx and Engels. Central to the approach of Uno and Sekine is a conceptualization of the relation between the law of value and history, or, in other words, between the logical and historical in the theory of capital. I shall therefore focus primarily on Marx's inadequate resolution of this issue and on its resolution through the levels of analysis approach developed by Uno and Sekine. I also hope to show that the levels of analysis approach makes the best sense of Marx and that the critique developed by Uno and Sekine is an immanent critique. Finally this chapter is an introductory chapter because although it focuses primarily on the relation between the logical and historical, this is in my view what is fundamentally at issue throughout the entire history of Marxist theory. This will therefore constitute the basic thread running through this entire book. In this chapter the focus will be soft rather than sharp. This will facilitate making the chapter more introductory by enabling me to introduce a number of basic conceptions that are peripheral to the main focus of the chapter but that will be more fully developed in later chapters.

Marx saw *Capital* as his most important and most scientific work, and yet its scientificity and its centrality to Marxian social science has been disputed. In recent years the law of value, which is the core of *Capital*, has been rejected by many Marxists, and this attack on the scientificity of the theory has lent support to those who challenge the centrality of *Capital* to Marxian social science.[1] Those who celebrate the demise of the theory of value often do so because they see it as a major source of economic determinism, reductionism and dogmatism, which, it is generally agreed, have retarded Marxist theory and practice.[2] The levels of analysis approach to political economy developed by Uno has radical implications for the entire tradition of Marxist theory. The approach of Uno establishes the scientificity and centrality of the law of value much more firmly than did Marx himself while avoiding the pitfalls of economism. My entire book will expand upon how this is possible, but this chapter will briefly introduce the levels of analysis approach by explaining what it is in relation to Marx's texts.

According to Uno and Sekine, Marx's *Capital* contains three levels of analysis: the theory of a purely capitalist society, elements of a theory of the liberal stage of capitalism and analysis of capitalist history. Though *Capital* primarily contains a theory of a purely capitalist society, lacking any conception of levels of analysis, Marx occasionally mixes them. This weakens his aim which in the first instance is a rigorous statement of the law of value or 'laws of motion of capitalism'. Besides weakening the conceptualization of the law of value, this unconscious mixing of levels of analysis leaves the relation between the law of value and history indefinite and unclear. Since Marx left this relationship theoretically unspecified, other thinkers who followed in his wake have filled the theoretical silence with debate, confusion and inadequate resolutions to the problem. I contend that the levels of analysis approach developed by Uno and Sekine not only offers the strongest interpretation of the law of value, but also the most theoretically sound approach to the relation between the law of value and history.

1 THREE LEVELS OF ANALYSIS

According to Uno and Sekine our theorization of capitalism divides into three levels of analysis: the theory of a purely capitalist society, the theory of the mercantilist, liberal and imperialist stages, and the analysis of history. Let me start, then, with the theory of a purely capitalist society where the commodity-form comes totally to dominate socioeconomic life.

The commodity-form first develops historically in the external trade between communities; hence, from the point of view of community life it is an alien form. In pre-capitalist economies the commodity-form was generally peripheral to socioeconomic life, and to the extent that it did from time to time penetrate society, it tended to undermine or even dissolve the social order. Capitalism represents a radically new world-historic economy because with capitalism the commodity-form seizes control of production itself and attempts to regulate all of economic life by the 'commodity–economic principle'.[3] If the commodification of economic life were ever complete, society would be governed by a self-regulating market; and though this point is never reached in history, there is sufficient tendency in this direction for us to arrive at the idea of a purely capitalist society by allowing this historical process to complete itself in theory.

The spread of the commodity-form develops over centuries, but absolutely crucial and central for the development of capitalism is the commodification of labour-power, because, with this occurrence, the commodity-form has located its source of profit within a production process controlled by itself. This gives to capitalism a great dynamism since now that its source of self-expansion is internal, it can penetrate pre-capitalist economies and transform them together with itself into an economy that is more and more capitalist in a world that is also becoming more capitalist. The limit would be a global society in which all production is the production of commodities by commodified labour-power as regulated by the self-regulating market. This is what Uno calls 'a purely capitalist society'.

A purely market-governed society is a reified society in the sense that the human subject becomes determined by the independent movements of commodities, money and capital. Marx frequently refers to this reification throughout the three volumes of *Capital*, as when he writes: 'production relations are converted into entities and rendered independent in relation to the agents of production',[4] or 'value as capital acquires independent existence, which it maintains and accentuates through its movement'.[5] In the theory of a purely capitalist society Uno and Sekine allow this reification to become total, so that by letting capital have its own way at the level of theory, they entrap it into exposing itself for what it really is. It is reification that enables them to theorize the laws of motion of capitalism in the abstract and in general as distinct from all the concrete contingencies of their actual operation in Britain in 1859 or Germany in 1900. The self-purifying and self-abstracting tendencies inherent in reification mean that they can theorize the laws of motion of capitalism as laws working with 'iron necessity'.[6] Total reification achieves a level of abstraction that sheds all contingencies associated with the historical concrete so that capital can be theorized as having an inner logic of necessary relations. It is reification that enables them to treat 'the characters who appear on the economic stage' as 'personifications of the economic relations that exist between them'.[7]

But if reification is total at the level of pure theory, and if the law of value works with iron necessity at this level, how does Uno relate the law of value to history where class struggle and all sorts of contingent phenomena must deflect and alter the workings of the law of value? What happens when reification is not total as it never is at the level of history, and as a result, characters on the economic stage actively intervene in economic relations as opposed to being mere personifications of them? As E. P. Thompson has argued:

no worker known to historians ever had surplus value taken out of his hide without finding some way of fighting back . . . by his fighting back the tendencies were diverted and the 'forms of development' were themselves developed in unexpected ways.[8]

Some theorists have attempted to overcome this antimony between necessity at the level of theory and contingency at the level of history by placing contingency and class struggle within the law of value itself. But this is self-defeating because the law-like character of the law of value is bound to be undermined by such a move. The solution to the problem is not to mix these two levels of analysis, but to develop a third level of analysis that can mediate the two. We can then maintain the necessity of the law of value at the level of pure capitalism while taking account of agency and contingency at the level of history. Uno refers to this mediating level of analysis as stage theory. Stage theory is a meeting-ground for the law of value and concrete history and it results in theorizing the dominant form of capital accumulation and accompanying political and ideological forms for the stages of mercantilism, liberalism and imperialism.[9]

The commodity-form has two aspects, value and use-value. The production of use-values is universal to all societies, but the generalized subsumption of use-value production to the motion of value is only characteristic of capitalism where the commodity-form tends to become universal.

At the level of pure capitalism the motion of value is allowed to overcome all use-value obstacles including the special use-value labour-power. That is, the reifying force of capital securely commodifies labour-power with the implication that class struggle is temporarily quieted at this level of theory (the working-class and capital are simply personifications of economic categories). This produces a clear and precise understanding of how capital secures the commodification of labour-power, the centrality of this commodification, the tenuousness of this commodification, the precise relation between capital and labour, and why class struggle is likely to occur and at what points. With this knowledge firmly established at the level of pure capitalism, it can be used to orient stage theory where use-value production and the motion of value in subsuming it are concretized in the form of modes of accumulation dominant in different stages of capitalist development.

The following example will illustrate the relation between the three levels of analysis. At the level of pure theory we grasp the abstract tendency for capital to concentrate and centralize; at the level of stage theory we can understand the main dynamics of the very rapid centralization of capital that occurred in the last quarter of the nineteenth century (i.e. in the stage of imperialism), and at the level of historical analysis we can understand how Rockefeller achieved control of the oil industry in the United States. Clearly this last level of analysis cannot be deduced from the first, but rather pure theory and stage theory serve to guide and inform the analysis of history. Marxists are freed from being tossed back and forth between economism which wants to apply the law of value directly to history and voluntarism which wants to see everything in terms of class struggle, power and subjective will. We can overcome these equal and opposite errors by developing three levels of analysis which mediate the objectivity of pure theory and the subjectivity and spontaneity of history.

Since in a purely capitalist society socioeconomic life is completely governed by the self-regulating market, the political and ideological superstructures can only be conceived of as passive forms that do not interfere with the self-regulation of the law of value. At the level of pure capitalism it is therefore accurate to say that the superstructure is a passive reflection of the base, and for this reason we can only theorize the basic superstructural forms (as opposed to content) at this level of theory. The materiality of the state and ideology as real social forces are theorized at the level of stage theory and historical theory. At these latter levels of analysis the superstructure may play an active and interventionist role up to and including the nullification of the law of value altogether. Thus the conception 'base and superstructure' is only completely realized at the level of pure theory, since even at the level of stage theory the economic base cannot do without the support of the state and ideology, and at the level of historical analysis this support is always extensive. The closer a particular economy comes to pure capitalism, the less it needs the active support of the state and ideology and the more possible it becomes to realize a policy of *'laissez-faire'*. The fact that no historical economy ever comes very close to total *laissez-faire* only goes to show that in reality use-values are not so docile or easily subsumable to the motion of value. A firm grasp of this point helps to clarify the great distance between pure theory and historical theory, so that the reductionism of looking for the law of value directly in historical theory is avoided.

The purity of the theory of a purely capitalist society means that social relations have become objectified, and this makes it possible to theorize economic relations as necessary relations. It is primarily Sekine who has made explicit the dialectical logic embedded in Marx's *Capital* and Uno's *Principles*, and who has worked out the very close parallel between Hegel's *Logic* and the theory of a purely capitalist society.[10] Sekine shows that pure theory has a necessary beginning and necessary unfolding of categories generated from the basic contradiction between value and use-value. Being self-conscious about the dialectical logic of pure theory, Sekine is able to make pure theory more rigorous and at the same time offer a resolution to the debate over the nature of dialectical materialism. Sekine argues that dialectics is a method of arriving at objective knowledge, and the fact that it is possible to construct a rigorous dialectic of capital has great import for objectively grounding Marxian social science.[11]

Though the dialectic of capital and levels of analysis pertain only to capitalism, the theory of a purely capitalist society serves to ground and to help interpret the hypotheses, maxims and concepts of historical materialism. Thus for example 'class', which has a clear, precise and objective meaning in a purely capitalist society, is not always clear at the level of capitalist history, and can be yet less determinant in pre-capitalist social formations. The pure theory can serve as a guide in sorting through this complexity to make the best sense we can of historical reality.[12]

Having presented this very brief outline of the Uno/Sekine approach, I shall proceed to engage with Marx and Engels on the basic question of the relation between the logical and the historical.

2   THE LOGICAL–HISTORICAL METHOD

Sometimes the method used by Marx in *Capital* has been called the 'logical–historical method' as if a hyphen would allow us to slide easily from the theoretical to the historical and back.[13] Unfortunately, as we shall see, this hyphenated expression is only a verbal solution to a very real problem, a solution that lulls us into feeling at ease precisely where we should sharply and intensely focus our analytic and critical powers.

An important textual source of the 'logical–historical method' is Engels's review of Marx's *A Contribution to the Critique of Political Economy* written in 1859. After discussing some of the problems with presenting political economy as a history, Engels writes:

The logical method of approach was therefore the only suitable one. This, however, is indeed nothing but the historical method, only stripped of the historical form and of interfering contingencies. The point where this history begins must also be the starting point of the train of thought, and its further progress will be simply the reflection, in abstract and theoretically consistent form, of the course of history, a corrected reflection, but corrected in accordance with laws provided by the actual course of history, since each moment can be examined at the stage of development where it reaches its full maturity, its classical form.[14]

We see that with this method, logical development need by no means be confined to the purely abstract sphere. On the contrary, it requires historical illustration and continuous contact with reality.[15]

These passages have been approvingly quoted by various Marxian economists as if they were definitive, requiring little else to be said on the matter; but unfortunately the relation between the logical and historical is one of the knottier problems in the entire tradition of Marxism. Engels is claiming 'the logical method is nothing but the historical method . . . stripped of the historical form and of interfering contingencies'. But this is a highly cryptic statement, that I can neither accept nor reject without some unpacking. Is the law of value simply an abstracted history following the historical development of capitalism? If so, why does the theory start with the commodity-form and end with interest? And if it is an abstracted history, how do we do the abstracting or in other words how do we distinguish the needed abstractions from the 'interfering contingencies'? Furthermore, though clarifying the logical development with historical illustrations may be non-controversial, what other kinds of 'continuous contact with reality' are called for? How can we maintain this 'continuous contact with reality' without having contingencies interfere with our abstract logic? Finally how can we reconcile the logical–historical method, as outlined here by Engels, with Marx's explicit arguments in the Introduction to *The Grundrisse* to the effect that the sequence of categories in the theory of capital does not follow a historical sequence? To shed more light on these issues let me turn to *The Grundrisse*.

3　THE LOGICAL AND HISTORICAL IN *THE GRUNDRISSE*

In *The Grundrisse* Marx explicitly rejects the sort of logical–historical method implied by the previous quotes from Engels. Marx argues that the correct method of political economy is to move from the most abstract categories to the more concrete categories. And in this instance by 'concrete' he does not mean the real or empirical concrete, but rather the synthetic concrete or concrete-in-thought which 'is concrete because it is the concentration of many determinations, hence unity of the diverse'.[16] Thus, for example, with the theory of a purely capitalist society, we start with the commodity-form and the opposition between value and use-value as the most abstract categories, and we move to ever more concrete categories. The money-form is more concrete than the commodity-form, and the capital-form is more concrete than the money-form. The sequence of categories 'commodity', 'money', and 'capital' moves from the abstract to the concrete. Marx is careful to differentiate his position from Hegel's which

conceives 'the real as the product of thought concentrating itself
. . . whereas the method of rising from the abstract to the
concrete is only the way in which thought appropriates the
concrete. . . . But this is by no means the process by which the
concrete itself comes into being.'[17] The concrete-in-thought is
simply the way the mind appropriates the real concrete which
'retains its autonomous existence outside the head'.[18]

Since the real concrete has a separate existence from the
concrete-in-thought, the sequence of categories in political economy does not have to correspond to the sequence of history. In
the theory of political economy 'money' is a more abstract and
simple category than 'cooperation', and though money appears
early in history, there have been societies in Peru and elsewhere
that developed cooperative labour processes and yet did not
develop money.[19] Thus we see cases where the theoretically more
concrete category exists historically before the more abstract.
Furthermore, money reaches its full development only in the
generalized commodity production of modern bourgeois society,
so that according to Marx, 'this very simple category, then, makes
a historic appearance in its full intensity only in the most
developed conditions of society'.[20] Though money may 'exist' in
an embryonic form very early in history, it only becomes a fully
developed economic form in modern capitalism.

An even clearer illustration is the category 'labour'. Men and
women have always laboured, so that historically this would have
to be the first category of a political economy that followed the
sequence of history; and yet it was only Adam Smith who first
formulated the notion of labour in general as wealth-creating
activity in general. This is because the notion of labour-as-such or
abstract labour could only arise in modern bourgeois society with
its very advanced division of labour and commodization of
labour-power. As Marx puts it:

Indifference towards any specific kind of labour presupposes a
very developed totality of real kinds of labour, of which no
single one is any longer predominant. As a rule, the most
general abstractions arise only in the midst of the richest
possible concrete development, where one thing appears as
common to many, to all. Then it ceases to be thinkable in a
particular form alone. On the other side, this abstraction of
labour as such is not merely the mental product of a concrete

totality of labours. Indifference towards specific labours corresponds to a form of society in which individuals can with ease transfer from one labour to another, and where the specific kind is a matter of chance for them, hence of indifference. Not only the category labour, but labour in reality has here become the means of creating wealth in general, and has ceased to be organically linked with particular individuals in any specific form.[21] ['Concrete' in this quote is being used in the sense 'real concrete' and not 'synthetic concrete'.]

Labour may be as old as humanity itself, but the concept of 'abstract labour' is a modern concept which requires the actual development of a labour-market and 'indifference towards specific labours'. Although labour-as-such is an abstract category, it is also a historically specific category in the sense that it is a product of definite historical relations and it possesses its 'full validity only for and within these relations'.[22] We can conclude from this that the economic categories of Marx's *Capital* are historical categories in the specific sense that they presuppose the historical existence of capitalism and in the sense that they remain valid only within this historically specific mode of production.

Of course, this historical specificity of the theory of capital does not mean that the theory is of no use in understanding pre-capitalist modes of production. Since 'bourgeois society is the most developed and the most complex historic organization of production',[23] the theory of its inner organization provides orienting concepts and guidelines for the investigation of various pre-capitalist modes of production. But in carrying out these investigations, we must be careful not to 'smudge over all historical differences and see bourgeois relations in all forms of society'.[24] In this way and in this sense, the theory of the most developed and complex organization of production can aid us in understanding the anatomy of less complex modes of production.[25]

Marx forcefully demonstrates that the method of political economy is in no sense an 'abstracted history'. The starting-point of the theory is not primitive accumulation or the transition from feudalism to capitalism, but fully developed bourgeois society. Fully developed bourgeois society is the given, and the sequence of categories of the theory aimed at understanding this given is determined by the necessary inner connections of capital. If we were to take a historical approach and start with the transition from feudalism to capitalism, then our starting-point might be with the categories of land and ground rent.[26] But this would violate Marx's claim that the scientifically correct approach is to move from the abstract to the concrete. The abstract is abstract relative to the given object of analysis – fully developed bourgeois society, and '. . . capital is the all-dominating economic power of bourgeois society'.[27] In Marx's view our theoretical object must therefore be capital. We must begin the theory with the most simple and abstract determinant of capital, the commodity; and not with some category suggested by the history leading up to capitalism. Marx is clear and unequivocal on this point:

It would therefore be unfeasible and wrong to let the economic categories follow one another in the same sequence as that in which they were historically decisive. Their sequence is determined, rather, by the relation to one another in modern bourgeois society, which is precisely the opposite of that which seems to be their natural order or which corresponds to historical developments.[28]

This sequence of categories, then, is determined by their inner connections within capitalist society and not by any sequence of historical development. The theory of political economy is essentially the theory of capital, and this theory is not genetic. The theory does not aim at explaining the origins of capitalism, instead the starting-point or the given is fully developed capitalism.[29]

Let me summarize the position I have reached. There is a determinant relation between theory and history in Marxian political economy. Nevertheless it is inaccurate to claim that the theory of capital is an abstracted history or that the sequence of categories follows history. The categories of the theory of capital are historical in the sense that they presuppose the historical development of capitalism and in the sense that they theorize a historically specific mode of production. The sequence of categories is determined by the necessary inner connections of capitalism, but the theory as a whole is useful in shedding light on pre-capitalist and post-capitalist modes of production as long as adequate attention is paid to their specific historical differences from capitalism.

In *The Grundrisse* Marx continually emphasizes the basic importance of arriving at a clear and precise concept of capital. This is because capital is 'the all-dominating power'[30] and the inner construction of modern society'.[31] 'The exact development of the concept of capital is necessary, since it is the fundamental concept of modern economics, just as capital itself whose abstract reflected image is its concept is the foundation of bourgeois society.'[32] It is clear that the 'exact development of the concept of capital' is the theory of the inner workings of capitalism, and that therefore the meaning of 'capital' cannot be encompassed in any sort of brief definition. While keeping in mind the limitations of any partial or brief characterization of capital, I shall turn to Marx's *Capital* in order to explore its theoretical object with a view to clarifying further the relation between the logical and historical.

4   THE LOGICAL AND HISTORICAL IN MARX'S *CAPITAL*

Reification

In Volume III of *Capital* Marx formulates a concise statement of capitalism's most fundamental or characteristic features.

> Capitalist production is distinguished from the outset by two characteristic features.
>   First, it produces its products as commodities. The fact that it produces commodities does not differentiate it from other modes of production; but rather the fact that being a commodity is the dominant and determining characteristic of its products. This implies, first and foremost, that the labourer himself comes forward merely as a seller of commodities, and thus as a free wage-labourer, so that labour appears in general as wage-labour. In view of what has already been said, it is superfluous to demonstrate anew that the relation between capital and wage-labour determines the entire character of the mode of production. *The principal agents of this mode of production itself, the capitalist and wage-labourer, are as such merely embodiments, personifications of capital and wage-labour* . . . the entire determination of value and the regulation of the

total production by value results from the above two characteristics of the product as commodity, or of the commodity as a
capitalistically produced commodity. (emphasis added)

Furthermore, already implicit in the commodity, and even
more so in the commodity as product of capital, is *the
materialisation of the social features of production and the
personification of the material foundations of production*, which
characterise the entire capitalist mode of production.
(emphasis added)

The *second* distinctive feature of the capitalist mode of
production is the production of surplus-value as the direct aim
and determining motive of production. Capital produces
essentially capital, and does so only to the extent that it
produces surplus value.[33]

This passage proposes two essential features of capitalist production: generalized commodity production and production aimed
at expanding surplus value. It seems to me that the discussion of
fetishism of commodities or reification which Marx includes
under the first characteristic feature is so important that it should
be separated out and listed as a third essential feature. I shall refer
to this 'materialization of the social features of production and
the personification of material foundations of production' as
reification. Reification refers to the process whereby the expansion of value in the form of capital takes on an independent
existence such that the agents of production are simply used by
capital for its own self-expansion. The capitalist and the wage-
labourer are simply the 'ebodiments, personifications of capital
and wage-labour'. Throughout *Capital* Marx analyses the false
appearances that arise from reification. He penetrates the false
appearances that arise from viewing the economic categories as
standing for mere things externally related. Marx's constant
reminder that the economic categories are simply the dominant
social forms of bourgeois society is absolutely essential in
emphasizing the fact that capitalism is a historically limited mode
of production and that what has become reified can also become
unreified. In *The Grundrisse* Marx writes:

The reciprocal and all-sided dependence of individuals who are
indifferent to one another forms their social connection. This
social bond is expressed in exchange value.[34]

> The social character of activity, as well as the social form of the
> product, and the share of individuals in production here appear
> as something alien and objective, confronting the individuals,
> not as their relation to one another, but as their subordination
> to relations which subsist independently of them and which
> arise out of collisions between mutually indifferent individuals.
> The general exchange of activities and products, which has
> become a vital condition for each individual – their mutual
> interconnection – here appears as something alien to them,
> autonomous, as a thing.[35]

Commodity exchange is the all-pervasive socioeconomic connection between individuals, so that individuals become externally
related very much like matter in motion and the only thing that
ties them all together in mutual dependency is the motion of
value. As a result, interpersonal relations become materialized
and objectified, so much so that economic categories appear to
theorize things alone. In order to demystify this false appearance,
Marx takes great pains continually to demonstrate that the
economic categories, though objective, are in fact *objectified
social relations*.

The existence of reification is what makes it possible rigorously
to theorize the motions of capital, since it is precisely reification
that enables us to speak of the dynamic of capital as self-
expanding value which prevails over and shapes social interaction
to fit the needs of capital. Capitalism is self-reifying in the sense
that it tends to spread and entrench the commodity-form as the
governing principle of socioeconomic life. Thus, for example,
labour-power becomes increasingly commodified with the development of machine production, and at the same time labour-
power becomes more homogeneous and deskilled. Increasingly
capital can go to the labour-market and hire not this or that type
of labour, but labour as such to produce any use-value whatsoever with absolute indifference to anything but profit criteria.
But this self-reifying, self-simplifying, self-abstracting and self-
purifying tendency answers a question that I posed earlier:
namely, how do we distinguish the essential abstractions for
theorizing the law of value from the interfering contingencies?
The answer is that the self-purifying tendencies at work in
capitalist history, though never completed, develop sufficiently to
enable us to allow them to complete themselves in theory. Smith

and Ricardo are able to proceed quite far in arriving at the fundamental abstractions of political economy by being guided by the self-abstracting tendencies of capitalism even though these tendencies were far from maturity when they wrote. Writing 40 or 50 years after Ricardo, gives Marx a much better vantage-point since the self-abstracting tendencies are much more developed, and with them, an emerging socialist movement which adds to Marx's vantage-point. Therefore the answer to our question is that capitalism itself proceeds quite far in shedding 'interfering contingencies'. By allowing this process to complete itself in theory, the result is a totally reified purely capitalist society. In the first instance, it is capitalism itself which distinguishes between the necessary and the contingent, so that our theoretical abstractions are helped along considerably by the development of reality.

Necessity

Following Marx's usage I referred to the law of value as 'the necessary inner connections' of capitalism. This implies that the law of value theorizes a totality with a clear distinction between inner and outer, and that the inner is characterized by necessary relations as opposed to the outer. Marx uses many different metaphorical expressions in trying to conceptualize this inner versus outer distinction, but he never arrives at the concept of a purely capitalist society or the concept of levels of analysis though he comes close in some passages. In my view the 'inner nature' of capital that he is trying to theorize is totally reified pure capitalism. Pure capitalism is a totality because as Marx puts it 'value as capital acquires independent existence, which it maintains and accentuates through its movement'.[36] The theory of the 'inner essence' of capital is the theory of value; it is the theory of how value through its own motion and without outside help can subsume and regulate capitalist socioeconomic life. As Marx puts it, 'capital is the self-expansion of value' without the aid of an outside 'other'.[37]

In the following quote from Volume I of *Capital* Marx makes it clear that value is the most abstract and universal category of bourgeois production:

The value-form of the product of labour is not only the most abstract, but is also the most universal form, taken by the product in bourgeois production, and stamps that production as a particular species of social production, and thereby gives it its special historical character. If we treat this mode of production as one eternally fixed by Nature for every state of society, we necessarily overlook that which is the *differentia specifica* of the value-form, and consequently of the commodity-form, and of its further developments, money-form, capital form, etc.[38]

This quote explains why Marx begins *Capital* with value-form theory. The basic capital-form is M–C–M′, but this means that the commodity-form and the money-form must be developed before we can understand the capital-form.

Further, since the money-form is logically derived from the commodity-form, money being a special commodity which becomes universal equivalent, it is clear that logically the commodity-form must come first in value-form theory. Value-form theory demonstrates that value must differentiate itself into commodities and money. In order to proceed dialectically, we must start with the most abstract category 'commodity' and then show that a full understanding of its nature requires the category 'money', which is logically derived from the commodity, and further, to understand fully both 'commodity' and 'money', we must logically derive 'capital'. In this fashion the dialectic of capital proceeds in necessary logical steps until the motion of value has subsumed all use-value obstacles and the dialectic of a purely capitalist society is completed. To explicate fully why the move from 'commodity' to 'money' is a necessary move, I would have to examine thoroughly the contradiction between value and use-value inherent in the commodity and show why the contradiction necessitates the generation of money, but this is beyond the scope of this book, and it is done in a very complete and clear way by Sekine in *The Dialectic of Capital*.[39] I shall have more to say on the issue of necessity in subsequent chapters.

Metaphorical Expressions of the Relation between the Logical and Historical

As I have already mentioned, Marx uses various metaphorical expressions or analogies to try to explain the relation between the law of value and history, but he never produces clear and precise theoretical concepts. The following quote from Marx's 'Results of the Immediate Process of Production' expresses one of these metaphors:

> The more highly capitalist production is developed in a country, the greater the demand will be for *versatility* in labour-power, the more indifferent the worker will be towards the specific content of his work and the more fluid will be the movements of capital from one sphere of production to the next. Classical economics regards the versatility of labour-power and the fluidity of capital as axiomatic, and it is right to do so, since this is the tendency of capitalist production which ruthlessly enforces its will despite obstacles which are in any case largely of its own making. At all events, *in order to portray the laws of political economy in their purity we are ignoring these sources of friction, as is the practice in mechanics where the frictions that arise have to be dealt with in every particular application of its general laws.*[40] (emphasis added)

Marx's discussion of the 'versatility', 'indifference' and 'mobility' of labour is simply using other words to talk about the abstractness of labour. Thus the tendencies that Marx is speaking of only complete themselves in the theory of a purely capitalist society where the reality and the concept 'abstract labour' coincide. But the analogy between the laws of pure mechanics and the laws of pure capitalism can be misleading.

The relation between the laws of mechanics and their application and the law of value and its application is far from parallel. The law of value is not simply like an ideal machine that in reality always has frictions. A machine involves the interaction of rigid parts that have definite and set motions. The law of value is like the theory of a self-constructing machine, where it is not us who abstract from the frictions but the machine itself in an effort to construct itself. The fact that it never actually becomes a smooth-running machine empirically does not prevent us from allowing it to complete itself in theory. But then we must remember that when we apply the law of value in a particular empirical context, we are not simply looking for 'frictions', but rather that we are looking at a partially deconstructed machine that is not very machine-like at all in its operation in the sense that it cannot operate without all sorts of outside supports, and in the sense that it loses some of its rigidity and becomes partially protean with unpredictable motions and motions that are altered by various and sundry outside interferences which are themselves not entirely predictable. The approach of Uno and Sekine would require us to interpret the metaphor in the following way: the theory of a purely capitalist society is like the theory of a self-constructing machine. The theory copies the principles of the machine's self-construction allowing the construction to complete itself in theory. This self-constructing machine tries to complete itself in history, and though it never succeeds, in attempting to do so, it passes through stages of development enabling us to develop a stage theory. Pure theory and stage theory then help to orient historical/empirical studies, where the efforts of the self-constructing machine to complete itself are further deflected or unfulfilled because of diverse contingencies, particularities and recalcitrant use-values.

The machine/friction metaphor could lead to an extremely economistic use of the law of value. Because the law of value is a purely economic theory, this metaphor would imply economic determinism at the level of history except for local frictions. But this is very inadequate because as Uno and Sekine point out, even at the rather abstract level of stage theory, the state and ideology play a significant role in supporting the law of value, and at the level of historical analysis the political and ideological become much more than simply oil to the frictions to the law of value.

Furthermore, contrary to Marx, it is not correct for classical economists to regard the mobility of capital and labour as 'axiomatic', since this blinds them to the fact that the economic relations are historically specific reified social relations. A dialectical as opposed to an axiomatic approach sees that this mobility is only achieved by allowing reification to become total *in theory*. This problematizes the mobility of capital and of labour by making it clear that this mobility is not simply given. It only partially exists in reality and only fully exists at the level of pure theory. We then understand how this pure mobility comes about: namely, through the theoretical extrapolation of the self-reifying tendency of capitalism. Furthermore, we understand the need to mediate pure theory and empirical reality where mobility is far from complete. Finally, the abstractions in a dialectical approach are arrived at with the aid of the self-abstracting tendencies of reality itself whereas this is not necessarily the case with an axiomatic approach.

In the following quote from Volume III of *Capital*, Marx uses the 'friction' metaphor coupled with the frequently used but vague notion of 'approximation'.

> This would assume competition among labourers and equalisation through their continual migration from one sphere of production to another. Such a general rate of surplus – viewed as a tendency, like all other economic laws – has been assumed by us for the sake of theoretical simplication. But in reality it is an actual premise of the capitalist mode of production, although it is more or less obstructed by *practical frictions* causing more or less considerable *local differences*, such as the settlement laws for farm-labourers in Britain. *But in theory it is assumed that the laws of capitalist production operate in their pure form.* In reality there exists only approximation; but, *this approximation is the greater, the more developed the capitalistic mode of production and the less it is adulterated and amalgamated with survivals of former economic conditions.*[41] (emphasis added)

Here Marx asserts that 'in theory it is assumed that the laws of capitalist production operate in their pure form', but this could be misleading since we do not simply 'assume' 'for the sake of theoretical simplification', rather we let capitalism purify itself. Now it is accurate to say that the law of value and pure capitalism 'is an actual premise of the capitalist mode of production' in the sense that the self-containedness of the law of value indicates the world-historic possibility of capitalism as a hegemonic economic system. The problem is how this 'actual premise' relates to history. Marx uses the settlement laws in Britain as an example of a 'practical friction', 'causing more or less considerable local differences' in the functioning of the law of value. He does not seem to think that these 'practical frictions' are problematic because the more developed the capitalist mode of production, the less the divergence between the laws of pure capitalism and empirical reality. Thus Marx seems to think that capitalism will become more and more pure, the more it develops. But this overemphasizes the ability of value to overcome use-value obstacles. Uno and Sekine show that the development of capitalism leads to the production of use-values that become more and more difficult to subsume to the law of value. Even the development of heavy industry requires finance-capital in order to be capitalistically managed, but finance-capital, which involves the development of monopoly and very active state intervention must already represent a step away from the continued self-purification of capitalism. According to Uno and Sekine, then, it is incorrect to say that as capitalism develops it becomes purer. It may be that it becomes less adulterated with pre-capitalist survivals as it develops, but this is not the same thing as becoming purer since with the stage of imperialism it is apparent that the obstacle in the way of further purification is generated by the development of capitalism itself in the form of heavy industry.

This is an important point because it explains in part why Marx would not see any need for stage theory. If capitalism in history becomes more and more pure until a brief period of revolutionary transition, then the tendency for capitalism asymptotically to approach pure capitalism would dispense with any need for stage theory. But this greatly overemphasizes the capability of the motion of value to subdue use-value obstacles. The ramifications of this are immense, making for a significant break between Marx's conceptions and those of the Uno/Sekine approach. According to Uno and Sekine, capitalism can only be historically viable for a limited range of use-value production (or what is the same thing a limited range of the development of productive forces), and precisely for this reason capitalism only achieves a partial and loose grip on history. This not only affects the way Uno and Sekine relate the law of value to history, but also it affects how they understand the transition away from capitalism. What needs to be emphasized at this point in the argument is that capitalism only becomes purer through the stage of liberalism, and that already with the stage of imperialism, the law of value must increasingly rely on monopolies and the state to help it capitalistically manage heavy industry.

In a final quote from *Capital* Marx uses the metaphor 'ideal average' to refer to the relationship between the law of value and empirical history:

> In our description of how production relations are converted into entities and rendered independent in relation to the agents of production, we leave aside the manner in which the interrelations, due to the world-market, its conjunctures,

movements of market-prices, periods of credit, industrial and commercial cycles, alternations of prosperity and crisis, appear to them as overwhelming natural laws that irresistibly enforce their will over them, and confront them as blind necessity. We leave this aside because *the actual movement of competition belongs beyond our scope, and we need present only the inner organization of the capitalist mode of production, in its ideal average, as it were.*[42] (emphasis added)

It is clear from this that any conjunctional phenomena such as the actual movement of credit, foreign trade, prices or boom/bust cycles must remain beyond the scope of the theory since these involve a host of particular contingent factors. The scope of the theory is 'only the inner organization of the capitalist mode of production, in its ideal average, as it were'. But the law of value is not an 'ideal average' in the sense of an abstraction averaged from a large number of particulars. This implies an empirical as opposed to a dialectical approach. The concept of pure capitalism does not come from averaging large numbers but from tracing the self-reifying tendencies of capitalism. Thus the development of economic theory from Smith to Ricardo to Marx achieves ever purer and more accurate categories by grasping the self-abstracting principles at work in capitalism and not by making empirical abstractions from conjunctural particulars.

Capital and the Logical–Historical Method

Earlier in this chapter I argued that the logical–historical method, which sees the law of value as abstracted history, is rejected by Marx in *The Grundrisse*. But the logical–historical method can be interpreted more broadly to refer to any approach which sees an unproblematic or overly close connection between the law of value and history. Where the relation between the law of value and history is not clearly and precisely theorized, it is almost natural to lapse into the logical–historical method. This is because lacking theoretical clarity on this relation, thinkers tend to move back and forth from the law of value to history as though such moves are unproblematic. Marx is no exception to this tendency.

Despite many passages in Marx's writings that seem to reject the logical–historical method, one can find other passages that support it, and this is because Marx himself was unclear about the relation between the law of value and history. For example, Marx begins *Capital* with the sequence 'commodity', 'money' and 'capital', and it seems that this parallels history where at first there is commodity barter without money, then there is the use of money to promote commodity trade, and finally there is the development of capital as a profit-making activity. Marx even gives examples that would support this interpretation. But when we look at other parts of *Capital* or at the work as a whole we find no such parallel, and we discover that the sequence of categories is a sequence of dialectical logic. *Capital* is primarily a theory of fully developed capitalism and of the law of value and not of the economic life of peoples from primitive society to the present.

Marx continually gives historical examples to illustrate the law of value, but sometimes the illustrations make it seem that there is no distance at all between the law of value and empirical reality but only minor frictions. Sometimes the historical illustrations give the impression that Marx is writing 'abstracted history' and not a theory of the necessary inner connection of pure capitalism. One reason that Marx included so much historical material was that he very much wanted *Capital* to be as readable and accessible as possible. Marx was also aware that a dialectical method of presentation might appear as an '*a priori* construction', and to avoid this he wanted to tie down the inner logic of pure capitalism to history.[43] For this reason he felt compelled to include a historical chapter on 'Primitive Accumulation' at the end of Volume I of *Capital*. As Marx puts it, 'The whole movement therefore, seems to turn in a vicious circle, out of which we can only get by supposing a primitive accumulation.'[44]

Despite many efforts to understand the relation between the logical and the historical, Marx remains vague and waivers back and forth between a dialectical approach and the logical–historical method, which as Althusser has argued may be either Hegelian or empiricist depending upon whether the logical or historical is accorded primacy.[45] Marx saw his theoretical object as being in some sense the inner logic, inner nature, inner essence, inner organization or necessary inner connections of capital in general. His aim was to present a complete theory of the law of value, and this he more or less accomplished; but where he remained completely vague was on the relation between the law of value and history. Thus in Chapter VI of Volume III of *Capital* Marx writes:

> The phenomena analysed in this chapter require for their full development the credit system and competition on the world-market, the latter being the basis and the vital element of capitalist production. *The more definite forms of capitalist production can only be comprehensively presented, however, after the general nature of capital is understood. Furthermore, they do not come within the scope of this work and belong to its eventual continuation.*[46] (emphasis added)

Unfortunately the 'eventual continuation' that Marx is here referring to was never written. Therefore it remains unclear just how Marx might have moved from the theory of the general nature of capital to its more definite forms. It is precisely to this problem that the levels of analysis approach developed by Uno and Sekine addresses itself.

Though Marx lacked the clear and precise concepts of 'a purely capitalist society' and 'levels of analysis', he generally avoided mixing levels of analysis because of his single-minded focus on the law of value. There are, however, a number of points in *Capital* where he does mix levels of analysis in ways that interfere with the conceptualization of the law of value.

Perhaps the clearest example is his discussion of the counter-tendencies to the tendency for the rate of profit to fall.[47] I contend that the only countertendency that needs to be discussed at the level of pure theory is the tendency for the rate of surplus value to rise, because this is the only countertendency that is generated by the inherent motion of capital in a purely capitalist society. I will not discuss all of the countertendencies that Marx mentions because two will be enough to indicate the problem of mixing levels of theorizing. First, Marx mentions foreign trade, but this cannot be a countertendency because in a purely capitalist society there are no boundaries and hence there is no distinction between domestic trade and foreign trade. Second, Marx mentions the 'depression' of wages below the value of labour-power', but this cannot be a countertendency to a long-run tendency like the declining rate of profit because in general the depression of wages below the value of labour-power can only be conjunctural. In a purely capitalist society all exchanges are *quid pro quo*, so that such an unequal exchange could only be a short-run phenomenon occurring in the trough of a depression and counterbalanced by wages above the value of labour-power at the height of prosperity just before a depression. Since in the long run wages must approximate the value of labour in a purely capitalist society, depression of wages cannot be considered a countertendency at this level of theory.

Marx did not see the need for a separate level of stage theory because he seemed to assume capitalism would purify itself until it reached its point of demise. He died before imperialism consolidated itself as a distinct stage of capitalist development, and for this reason he tended to see the early signs of monopoly capitalism as signs of the transition to socialism. Monopoly capitalism was not conceived of as a stage of capitalism so much as the inauguration of a phase of transition. About the formation of joint-stock companies Marx writes:

> It is the abolition of capital as private property within the framework of capitalist production itself . . . the stock company is a transition toward the conversion of all functions in the reproduction process which still remain linked with capitalist property, into mere functions of associated producers, into social functions. . . . This is the abolition of the capitalist mode of production within the capitalist mode of production itself, and hence a self dissolving contradiction, which prima facie represents a mere phase of transition to a new form of production.[48]

Marx, then, saw this movement away from the self-purifying tendency of capitalism as a movement away from capitalism itself, rather than a move from a liberal stage to an imperialist stage of capitalism. It is only with Lenin, writing from the vantage-point of World War I, that it becomes possible to conceive of imperialism as a distinct stage of capitalist development, and therefore to intimate the need for stage theory.

Class Struggle and the Law of Value

Marx's *Capital* lives and breathes class struggle to such an extent that some interpreters have gone so far as to argue that the law of value directly expresses class struggle. But class struggle involves a political balance of forces which is conjunctural and always changing, whereas, according to Marx, the law of value implies that capital and labour are mere personifications of economic categories whose motion is one of iron necessity. Since the law of value is the inner logic of capital and class struggle is historical, the effort to integrate the law of value directly with class struggle tends to produce some form of the logical–historical method which itself tends towards economism or voluntarism. As I have already pointed out, Marx was not always clear on this issue and there are many passages in *Capital* which would support a logical–historical method. In the main though, Marx treats capital and labour as completely reified and secured commodities in working out the law of value, although he may use examples of class struggle to illustrate the law of value. The reason that he maintains total reification is because as soon as class struggle is introduced into the law of value, contingent conjunctural elements are introduced that undermine the necessary connections of the theory.

The one point at which class struggle seems to be crucial even to the law of value is on the length of the working day. But in a purely capitalist society there is no class struggle since it has been temporarily quieted by the completion of reification. At the level of pure theory, though we may say that the length of the working day is at least in part determined by class struggle, the analysis of class struggle itself is not a part of pure theory; only the result of class struggle, namely a working day of a particular length is part of pure theory. In other words, from the point of view of pure theory, the length of the working day is simply given. Thus pure theory looks at what variations in the length of the working day mean to the law of value without going into the conjunctural determinants of a working day of a certain length. Pure theory can certainly take note of the fact that class struggle is likely to play an important role in the historical determination of a working day of a particular length, but it does not step outside its level of analysis to carry out the historical analysis of such struggles without being very explicit about moving from one to another level of analysis.

In *Capital* Marx creates confusion and lends support to the logical–historical method because of the lack of any conception of levels of analysis. The move from the discussion of the law of value to the historical analysis of class struggle is all too often made without signalling the reader that he is moving from one level and type of analysis to another. With the approach of Uno and Sekine, it is clear that at the level of pure theory class struggle plays no role whatsoever in determining the law of value, though once we have this determinant law of value, we have an objective reference to guide and improve our historical studies of class struggle. Paradoxically, by allowing reification to complete itself and thus theoretically suppressing class struggle, we benefit by gaining a theory that can be a great aid in our studies of class struggle.

The inadequacy of Marx's *Capital* when it comes to theorizing the relation between the law of value and class struggle is one of the most serious weaknesses of the theory. Lack of clarity on this point has produced both confusion and controversy. How can the law of value operate with iron necessity when it is at least partially dependent on the contingencies of class struggle? The law of value is the inner logic of capitalism as such and in general, but the outcomes of class struggle are conjunctural in the sense that they are the result of conflict between groups in a particular political system. The ten-hour day or the eight-hour day is primarily the result of class struggle constrained by a particular level of development of the productive forces. Thus the ten-hour day cannot be determined by the law of value itself. Rather the law of value helps us to understand why, at a historical level of analysis, it is possible for the length of the working day to be shortened and why also it cannot be shortened too much. Because the understanding of the outcomes of class struggle is always primarily conjunctural, it should in the main be studied at a historical level of analysis. This does not mean that the law of value cannot serve to inform this analysis. But to say that the law of value directly reflects class struggle or vice versa must either undermine the necessity of the law of value or undermine the subjective factor that is essential to class struggle. The recent debate between Thompson and Althusser is one example of the kind of controversy generated by Marx's failure to arrive at a more determinate conceptualization of the relation between class struggle and the law of value. The Uno/Sekine levels of analysis approach can in principle resolve this issue.

5   CONCLUSIONS

In this chapter I have introduced some of the basic ideas of the

Uno/Sekine approach to Marxist theory and have tried to show that these ideas offer a solution to problems around the relation between the logical and historical with which Marx and Engels were struggling. I have indicated that Marx was groping in the direction of the concept of a purely capitalist society and a dialectical method but never achieved a clear and determinant conceptualization of the relation between the logical and the historical. In *Capital* Marx uses such vague terms as 'friction', 'approximation' and 'ideal average' to discuss the relation between the law of value and history. Also because of the way Marx mixes in historical illustrations with the law of value, many passages suggest a logical–historical method. But, I have argued, the logical–historical method is incorrect because it sees too close and direct a connection between theory and history. The law of value is either seen as an abstracted history or capitalist history is seen as the concretization of the law of value. The result is weakened theory, reductionist history or both. I have in this chapter begun to outline the way in which the Uno/Sekine approach solves the problem of the relation between the logical and historical and between the law of value and history. In what follows of Part I, I shall develop the levels of analysis approach and bring out its implications by critically analysing theorists in the tradition of Western Marxism and by offering new perspectives on current debates. I shall turn next to the theory of a purely capitalist society.

3 Theory of a Purely Capitalist Society

In the previous chapter I argued that the Uno/Sekine conceptions of 'pure capitalism' and 'levels of analysis' represent reasonable extensions of Marx's efforts in *Capital*. Because Marx's understanding of the relation between the law of value and history was not well worked out, he fell back on the use of metaphors and vague expressions and failed to achieve a determinant theoretical conceptualization. 'The theory of a purely capitalist society' and 'levels of analysis' are determinant concepts that can solve the problems Marx was wrestling with in a way that is most in keeping with his aim to construct a scientifically adequate theory of political economy. In this chapter I shall move from the focus on the relation between the logical and historical to a focus on the law of value itself. My main concern will be to indicate some of the improvements that Uno and Sekine make on Marx's formulation of the law of value – improvements that flow primarily from a more determinant conceptualization of the theoretical object and from a more rigorous dialectical approach.

In some ways this is the most difficult chapter to write, and that is because of the richness, fullness and immense scope of the theory that it attempts to convey. Uno and Sekine have made their greatest contributions at the level of the theory of pure capitalism, and one is tempted simply to refer the reader to their writings. Uno's *Principles* is available in English, and the interested reader is encouraged to read this work. However, it is extremely condensed and really represents notes that Uno never expanded because of declining health. The work that enlarges and refines Uno's *Principles* and brings it up to date is Sekine's monumental *Dialectic of Capital*. It is this work which makes the dialectical logic of the theory explicit, which debates with some of the best economic theorists both Marxist and non-Marxist and which offers mathematical proofs where needed. I shall not try to summarize this theory in its entirety in this chapter, but instead shall discuss some of the differences between Uno and Sekine's theory and Marx's *Capital* and shall consider some current controversies from the point of view of the theory of pure capitalism. My aim is to give the reader some indication of the implications of the Uno/Sekine approach by presenting very condensed pieces of it in connection with familiar literature and debates. The defect of this is that the theory of pure capitalism constitutes a dialectical totality. Extracting pieces from it is bound to do some violence to the theory by leaving out logical steps and mediations behind certain conclusions.

Marx's three volumes of *Capital* contain in rough and incomplete form the foundations of a theory of a purely capitalist society. At the centre of this theory is the law of value which reveals the necessary socioeconomic relations that are attendant upon the capitalist expansion of value. Anyone who seriously studies Marx's *Capital* is bound to be impressed by the great scope and depth of its explanatory power. I am inclined to agree with Louis Althusser when he claims that Marx's *Capital* is the founding work of sociohistorical science on the same order as the work of Euclid for mathematical science or that of Galileo and Newton for natural science; and yet what is peculiar about Marx's *Capital* is how little attention has actually been devoted to improving the theory and building upon it.[1] Not only would one expect the founding work of a new science to have a groping and incomplete character, but also *Capital* was left in a very unfinished state (only Volume I was completed). It would be unrealistic to expect a perfected science to spring fully formed out of Marx's head. One would expect to find in *Capital* the rough-hewn basics that others would refine, enlarge and perfect: but this is not in general the way that successors have related to Marx's text. Often interpreters have either defended the text as it stands or have rejected it as it stands. Though some have reconstructed pieces of it, few have undertaken to reconstruct the theory as a whole with a view to clarifying and sharpening its arguments. But this task is of pressing importance given the penchant for various schools of Marxism to find the law of value wanting and therefore either to abandon it or to gut it. And it is to this task of reconstructing the whole that Uno and Sekine have directed their considerable abilities.

According to Sekine, the idea of a purely capitalist society presupposes an ideal environment in which the motion of value is allowed to prevail over use-value obstacles.[2] Such a concept is unlike a subjective analytic construct or model because in this case thought is guided by the self-purifying tendencies inherent in capitalism. Historically value does increasingly subsume and neutralize use-value production, at least up until the stage of finance-capital (roughly 1875). Though at a historical level capital never approaches very close to pure capitalism, yet the tendency in that direction enables us to conceptualize a purely capitalist society where all production is production of commodities by means of commodified labour-power. By extending in thought the self-purifying tendencies of capitalism, the idea of capitalism is purged of all local particularities and contingencies which might confuse our grasp of capitalism's inner logic. With the concept of a purely capitalist society, it is possible to understand the working of capitalism entirely in accord with its own economic principles without any interference of extra-economic force or other alien forces (either non-capitalist or non-economic). The theory of a purely capitalist society reveals what capitalism must be or how it must operate when it is allowed to be most fully itself. With this knowledge of what capitalism necessarily is, we can begin to understand actual capitalist societies which are always impure. We can begin to distinguish clearly the capitalist from the non-capitalist and the economic from the non-economic, and thus we can grasp the degree to which particular societies are capitalist and how they operate in the light of various 'impurities' which interfere with the motions of capital.

The previous chapter demonstrated that Marx's *Capital* is only possible because capital is self-purifying. Economic categories such as 'value' and 'abstract labour' would be subjective and formal unless capital had some tendency to make itself more homogeneous and pure. If capital did not have an inner coherence resulting from the tendency towards a self-regulating market and was continually and primarily determined by external forces, no such theory as contained in Marx's *Capital* could be written. If the motions of capital were determined at every moment primarily by political policies or some other contingent set of influences, then surely there could be no sense to 'laws of motion of capital'. And since at a historical level this is to some extent true, the only rigorous theory of capital that can be written is a theory of a purely capitalist society. Uno and Sekine make explicit this concept which is only implicit in Marx's *Capital*.

We can only clarify what capitalism really is by allowing it in our minds to be totally victorious over its social–historical environment. We know, however, that in reality its victory is never more than partial, and even this partial victory requires allies (e.g. the state and ideology). Use-values in reality are never so docile as we must assume in the pure theory. For example, labour-power always resists being commodified, resulting in class struggle. The effort totally to commodify nature also creates severe problems for capitalism and treating money as a pure commodity to be regulated only by the market seems often to contradict the needs of real economic life. These problems and others at the level of concrete history require that capital receive the support of state policies. The fact that use-values are not so docile at the level of empirical history necessitates levels of analysis where we move from pure theory, where use-value obstacles are neutralized, to stage theory, where the constraints of dominant forms of use-value production give rise to a dominant form of capital accumulation and accompanying state policies, and finally to historical theory, where use-value obstacles have to be considered in their specificity. As we move towards the historical concrete, necessity becomes increasingly constrained and interfered with by contingency.

1   THE DIALECTIC OF CAPITAL

Marx was neither explicit not systematic in developing the dialectical logic embedded in the law of value; and yet, following Sekine, I shall argue that this is the key to understanding the epistemology of the law of value and to understanding the precise meaning of the 'theory of the necessary inner connections of the capitalist mode of production'. Once we become fully self-conscious of the dialectical logic of the theory of a purely capitalist society, we can state the theory in a much more rigorous fashion than did Marx.

Western Marxists have not made a great deal of headway in discovering the dialectical logic embedded in the law of value. In *The Making of Marx's 'Capital'* Rosdolsky brings to our attention some of the dialectical qualities of Marx's theory of value, but this is mostly because in arriving at an interpretation of *Capital*, he relies heavily upon *The Grundrisse*, where dialectical modes of expression are more on the surface.[3] Some essays in the collection edited by Diane Elson attempt to deal with the dialectical logic of the law of value but only with limited success.[4] David Levine, in *Economic Theory* Volume I, brings out some aspects of dialectics but falls far short of reconstructing the law of value as a whole as a rigorous dialectic.[5] Perhaps the dearth of dialectical readings of *Capital* stems in part from the predominance of positivist and empiricist approaches to social science in the West, whereas in Japan Marxian economics was established as the predominant academic discipline of economic theory when Japanese universities were first developing in the 1920s. For this reason it was easier for Japanese Marxists to explore the logic of the theory of capital without being diverted by a hegemonic positivist tradition.[6] It is not surprising then that Japanese Marxists are the first to reconstruct the theory of value as a whole as a dialectical logic.

Sekine has demonstrated the very close parallel between Hegel's *Logic* and the dialectic of capital. Just as the basic contradiction in the *Logic* is between 'Being' and 'Nothing', so the basic contradiction of the dialectic of capital is between value and use-value. The *Logic* is divided into the Doctrines of Being, Essence and Notion and parallel to this the dialectic of capital is divided into the Doctrines of Circulation, Production and Distribution. Furthermore, the logical structure of each of these doctrines parallels the logical structure of the corresponding doctrine in Hegel's *Logic*. More will be said about this parallel in Chapter 7, but suffice it to say now that the theory of a purely capitalist society does have a dialectical logic.[7]

The reason that the theory of a purely capitalist society can have a dialectical logic is that it is a theory of a self-determined totality. The logic of that self-determination can fully express itself at the level of pure theory. By allowing reification to complete itself in theory, the tendency for commodity-economic logic to discard all extra-economic contingencies is completed. This means that the personal and interpersonal become objectified by the operations of the self-regulating market, and social life becomes essentially objectified economic life. A purely capitalist society is essentially a purely economic society. Whereas in Hegel's philosophy the concepts are made pure and free from the contingencies of everyday imagistic discourse by a philosophic abstraction which finally rests upon the assumption that the inner logic of the mind corresponds to the inner logic of the universe, in the case of the materialist dialectic of capital, the effort to arrive at pure concepts free from contingency is aided by the self-abstracting tendencies of capitalist reality itself.

The sequence of categories in a dialectical logic has a necessary beginning, a necessary unfolding and a necessary completion determined by the logic of the totality being theorized. The beginning must be the most abstract, empty and unspecified category of the totality being theorized. This initial emptiness is then filled in by a dialectical contradiction which moves by necessary steps to overcome this initial emptiness until the theoretical object is filled out, completely synthesized or becomes 'concrete'.

Let me illustrate the dialectic of capital by briefly outlining its first few steps. The starting-point of the dialectic of capital is the commodity with its basic contradiction between value and use-value. Sekine argues that 'this contradiction reflects the fact that the commodity-economic principles that bring capitalist society together are alien to the material aspect of its economic life which is common to all societies'.[8] The value of the commodity can only free itself from the particularity of its own use-value by suppressing that use-value in the process of expressing its value in the use-value of another commodity. When the social connectedness of a commodity is expressed in the use-value of another commodity, this phenomenal form is exchange-value. Value-form theory shows the necessary steps in moving from this initial expression of exchange-value to the point where the use-value of one commodity becomes set aside as the universal value reflector of all other commodities. Through this 'universal equivalent' or money, value has achieved an external unifying standard that makes all commodities immediately equatable with each other. Thus the dialectic has shown how money is necessarily generated out of the imminent contradiction between value and use-value within the commodity.

Money makes the exchange of commodities C–M–C possible, and through this establishes a market where exchanges become interconnected so that the sale by one person is the purchase by another, who in turn had to sell something to make the purchase. But this social world of value connections is constrained by the use-value wants of the exchangers who sell commodities they do not want to get those that they do. When they get what they want, the exchange stops so that the motion of value is constrained by the consumption of use-values in C–M–C. With the formula M–C–M', or buying in order to sell, money is withheld from the market not to save up for some article of consumption needed by the saver, but to buy commodities not needed and to resell them for a profit. Now value expands itself without the use-value constraints of C–M–C, and we have arrived at the primitive circulation form of capital (using money to make more money).

Thus the necessary beginning of the dialectic is the commodity-form and it is out of its inner contradiction between value and use-value that the necessary sequence commodity, money and capital unfolds. And although this sequence parallels that of Marx in *Capital*, Marx does not make the dialectical logic explicit.

As already stated, Uno divides the theory of a purely capitalist society into three basic doctrines: the Doctrine of Circulation, the Doctrine of Production and the Doctrine of Distribution. In the Doctrine of Circulation, commodity, money and capital are examined as circulation-forms without reference to their substantive content. In the Doctrine of Production, commodity, money and capital as circulation-forms are shown to be the phenomenal forms of an underlying labour and production process. All societies must have a labour and production process, but when this is integrated with the commodity-economic principle of the circulation-forms, a specifically capitalist production process is formed. In the Doctrine of Production the contradiction between value and use-value becomes a contradiction between the historically specific capitalist circulation-forms and the labour and production process which is the suprahistorical substantive base of all societies. The overcoming of this contradiction generates the specifically capitalist production process. The key to understanding this integration is the commodification of labour-power and the economic processes that maintain this commodification. In the Doctrine of Production we investigate the capital–labour relation that forms the substantive base of the capitalist mode of production. In order to grasp clearly this relationship we must assume that capital and labour are homogeneous.

In the Doctrine of Distribution, Sekine shows that capital can maintain its unity while differentiating itself and reaching a *modus vivendi* with alien elements. Capital is now grasped as a heterogeneity unified by the rate of profit. Technical differentiation requires price categories, while reaching a *modus vivendi* with landed property generates the theory of rent, and finally capital's functional specialization in order to save on circulation costs generates the theories of commercial capital and interest-bearing capital. With the category of interest, capital itself becomes a commodity and the dialectic achieves closure.

Sekine's Doctrine of Circulation roughly corresponds to *Capital* Volume I, Parts I and II. The Doctrine of Production corresponds to the remainder of Volume I and all of Volume II, while the Doctrine of Distribution roughly parallels Marx's Volume III. But within this overall correspondence there are many differences stemming from the much tighter logical development made possible by Sekine's self-conscious dialectical logic. I shall turn now to explore some of these differences.

2   THE BEGINNING

In a dialectical theory the beginning is crucial since not only must it be a necessary beginning relative to the object being theorized, but also it contains the basic contradiction the unfolding of which constitutes the dialectic. The beginning is the foundation upon which the dialectic is built. If the foundation is not firm, the entire theory built upon it will be weak. As Marx himself admitted, all beginnings are difficult and are decisive for what is to follow.[9] In referring to the presentation of value-form theory in Chapter 1, Marx writes that 'the analysis of these forms seems to turn upon minutiae. It does in fact deal with minutiae, but they are of the same order as those dealt with in microscopic anatomy.'[10] In other words, since the beginning constitutes the foundation of the theory, minute differences can make a momentous difference in our understanding of the theory based on this foundation. A small mistake at the beginning can reverberate through the entire theory and undermine it as a whole. In what follows I shall try to indicate some of the momentous consequences of minute differences between Marx and Uno (and Sekine), and show how Uno and Sekine's formulations help to resolve ongoing confusions in the interpretation of the theory of value.

As I have already discussed, the dialectic of capital presupposes a purely capitalist society. Marx was correct to start *Capital* with the concept of 'commodity', because this is the most abstract and simple form of capital. According to the dialectical logic of Sekine and Uno, a commodity must be conceived as something that can become capital in the same way that a primitive or embryonic form of capital has the potential of synthesizing itself into the adequate fully developed form of capital. Sekine emphasizes that to arrive at a clear and precise conception of capital, we must begin by grasping the very sharp contrast between mere goods or products and commodities. The slightest dulling of this contrast at this early stage of the dialectic can produce a great deal of confusion and misunderstanding (as we shall see Marx does dull this contrast). The concept of 'commodity' locates the totality to be theorized since it is the most abstract form of capital, but the contradiction that actually begins the movement of the dialectic is the contradiction between value and use-value. Initially we can only say of value that it is the quality of homogeneity that makes all commodities exchangeable, as opposed to use-value, which initially is the quality of heterogeneity in commodities.[11] A commodity must be exchanged because it has no use-value to its owner. Goods may sometimes be exchanged, as when a farmer with excess eggs exchanges them for another farmer's excess tomatoes. This sort of exchange between consumers each with an excess wanted by the other is a barter. Barters are occasional and sporadic deals between consumers and have nothing to do with the commodity, which is always and from the beginning produced for exchange. Commodities therefore cannot be bartered but must be exchanged for money, because it is only with the development of money that they can express their value, that is, their homogeneity or their commodityness. It is therefore the value aspect of commodities that differentiates them from goods or products and that becomes the defining feature of capitalism, to the extent that Marx often writes of capital as 'the self-expansion of value'. Indeed the dialectic of capital itself is the unfolding of this value aspect as it subsumes or prevails over successive use-value constraints. It is only with pure capitalism that all products necessarily become commodities.

Marx's presentation of the form of value or exchange-value is confusing, because it suggests the possibility of an exchange between commodities without the mediation of money – in other words a barter. Marx starts his value-form theory with the expression 'x commidity A $= y$ commodity B', suggesting that his 'elementary' or 'accidental' form of value is an actual exchange ratio, or a barter.[12] But exchange-value cannot be a barter exchange ratio if commodity exchanges do not take place without money, and money has not yet been generated in the dialectic of capital. In fact it is precisely through the theory of exchange-value or value-form that we show the logical generation of money. Sekine shows that the elementary form of value is a subjective expression of value. The owner of commodity A expresses the value of the commodity that he does not want in terms of the use-value of a commodity that he does want. No actual exchange, only a proposal for an exchange, takes place. The elementary form of value, then, takes the form 'I am willing to exchange 100 bales of cotton for 10 ingots of iron.'

This mode of expressing the elementary form of value has immense ramifications for the entire theory. I shall therefore pause to note some of its important features. First and most significant, it is not simply the equation of two commodities, but is a *subjective* expression beginning with 'I am willing . . .' Thus the dialectic begins with an active subject proposing an exchange.[13] In the course of the dialectic this active subject is converted into a passive subject or in the words of Marx into a mere 'personification' of economic categories. It follows that the subject, though made passive, does not disappear. As I shall argue later, this point is particularly important to emphasize in the face of the Neo-Sraffian tendency to equate the value of labour-power to a fixed basket of wage-goods in their theory of 'the production of commodities by means of commodities'. Furthermore, this latter expression can be misleading because the subjective element, though made passive, does not disappear. Being clear on this point is also important in developing the mediations between pure theory and historical analysis which involves reactivating the subjective factor. Marxian economics differs from classical subjective theories of value which see the economy purely as a resultant of individual decisions. But it also differs from Neo-Ricardian accounts which tend to leave out the subject altogether. Reification leads to the domination of the commodity over the economic life of society, but the 'passification' of the subject that results is tenuous and must be shown step by step at the level of pure theory. Without such a dialectical approach economic theory becomes excessively formalistic and the subject can only be reintroduced in *ad hoc* ways in the move from theory to history.

The second point that needs emphasizing about the elementary expression of value is that it is only a *proposal* for an exchange. This is important in emphasizing the distinction between commodity exchange and barter. A commodity can only be exchanged for money, but money does not yet exist, and in fact value-form theory is precisely a theory which demonstrates the necessary derivation of the money-form from the commodity-form. Actual exchanges can only occur after the generation of the money-form and the price-form.

Finally, I use 'bales of cotton' and 'ingots of iron' instead of 'linen' and 'coats'. The reason is that the exchange is being proposed by an incipient capitalist and not by a consumer. The elementary value-form must be a form that can dialectically generate the capital-form. Since 'bales of cotton' and 'ingots of iron' are not normally commodities for immediate consumption, my usage makes it clearer that we are dealing with merchant traders or embryonic capitalists and not consumers bartering excess goods.

The elementary form of value is a unilateral expression of the value of cotton by the cotton owner in terms of iron. This subjective and isolated expression of value must express the homogeneity of commodities whereby they can be treated as qualitatively the same and differing only quantitatively and thus immediately equatable with each other. The expression '10 ingots of iron' is already money in embryo. In the expanded form of value all commodity-owners express the values of their commodities in terms of the use-values of commodities they want. In this form the isolated character of the first value-form is overcome and the generally implicit in value is brought out; but this form of value is chaotic because there is potentially an infinite list of proposed exchanges without any unifying factor. This form generates an indefinite number of small monies. The necessity for money as universal equivalent now becomes apparent. It is only with the generation of money that any commodity becomes equatable with any other, so that commodities can be universally exchanged and a system of normal prices can be established. With the development of prices, the initial proposed exchange is either socially confirmed or rejected. For example, my initial proposal to exchange 100 bales of cotton for 10 ingots of iron may not have been realistic, and according to normal prices I may have to offer 150 bales for 10 ingots.[14] According to Sekine: 'it is only when all commodities reflect their value in the use-value of a single commodity called "money" that the expression of value becomes the universal, social act of pricing'.[15]

By showing that barter has no role in value-form theory, it becomes clear that the theoretical object is capitalism, and that we are proceeding dialectically from the abstract-in-thought (commodities in contrast to goods) to the more synthetic concrete in order to show that the commodity-form must necessarily generate the money-form. Many interpreters of *Capital* have incorrectly viewed the elementary form of value as a barter and have followed this by positing a historical parallel to the logical derivation of money. Value-form theory ends up being a synopsis of history beginning with primitive barter and ending up with the money-form.[16] Often Parts I and II of Volume I are seen as a pre-capitalist or a fictional mode of production called 'simple commodity production', which later is impinged on by capitalist production relations.[17] But the theory of capital traces the necessary inner connections of *the capitalist mode of production*. No rigorous or dialectical theory of capital can be derived from the specifically non-capitalist modes such as barter or simple commodity production. In the expression of the elementary form of value, 20 yards of linen = one coat, orthodox economics is inclined to see a barter between two consumers, but 'the consumer cannot possibly develop into a capitalist'.[18] Only by adopting the point of view of the seller are we adopting a point of view that can develop into an adequate conception of capital by developing the form of value. Value only concerns the seller since to him his commodity is useless, while use-value 'is not simply the use-value of an object of consumption, but a use-value from the point of view of the purchaser of the commodity which still belongs to its seller'.[19] Sekine argues that 'in order to fix value in a determinant form the expression of value must, therefore, not be studied in an actual process of exchange, but from the point of view of the seller exclusive of the point of view of the purchaser'.[20] For this reason Uno and Sekine substitute 'I am willing to exchange 20 yards of linen for one coat', for the expression '20 yards of linen = one coat', because this latter expression makes it seem that an exchange has actually taken place. This is important because the coat does not represent a use-value consumed by the linen owner, but instead it is the elementary form of money, and 'money is the direct value-reflecting object since the consumability of its use-value is irrelevant'.[21] Money 'is no longer demanded for its own material use-value but for the social and abstract use-value in that all commodity-owners wish to have it, not for its direct use or consumption but for its having an immediate purchasing power of all other commodities'.[22] So we see that it is very important to conceive of the owner of the 20 yards of linen as a merchant who eventually becomes a capitalist rather than a consumer who wants to barter a commodity that is not needed for one that is.

3   THE LABOUR THEORY OF VALUE

Marx's introduction of the labour theory of value in Chapter 1 of *Capital* has perhaps been the most serious source of confusion in the entire theory of capital. The work of Uno and Sekine demonstrates that the labour theory of value can only be firmly grounded in the dialectic of capital after the circulation-forms and their logic have subsumed the production process. The premature introduction of the labour theory of value confuses the meaning both of the Doctrine of Production and of the Doctrine of Circulation. Here Marx unwittingly violates his own stricture. In a letter to Engels defending postponing the treatment of the transformation of values into prices until Volume III, Marx writes: 'If I were to cut short all such doubts in advance I would spoil the whole method of dialectical exposition.'[23] By treating the labour theory of value in advance of its proper location according to the method of dialectical exposition, that is by introducing it in the theory of circulation instead of in the theory of production, the meaning of the labour theory of value is confused, its theoretical grounding is severely weakened, and the method of dialectical presentation is spoiled.

In *Capital*, Volume I, Chapter 1, Marx argues that in order for two commodities to be exchangeable they must contain some common property or substance that makes them equatable. By a process of elimination, Marx concludes that they have only one property in common – that of being products of labour. Having argued this, he must introduce the distinction between abstract and concrete labour, skilled and unskilled labour, and finally the concept of socially necessary labour-time. But in this context none of these concepts can be properly theoretically grounded. The labour theory of value is thus vulnerable to attack and has been rejected by many economists from Bohm-Bawerk to Steedman.

Instead of demonstrating the necessity of the labour theory of value, Marx simply posits it. It is thus very easy for Bohm-Bawerk to put forward another theory: namely, that what two commodities have in common that makes then exchangeable is utility. In a similar vein, Steedman argues that the labour theory of value stands as an obstacle in the way of an adequate theory of prices and profits.

Uno and Sekine correct this weakness by demonstrating the necessity of the labour theory of value to the dialectic of capital. The Doctrine of Circulation, which begins the dialectic of capital, only reveals the inner logic of the circulation-forms or the operation of the *form* of value. Thus capital first appears as the circulation-form M–C–M′ and is in the first instance a method of using money to make more money.[24] It is only in the Doctrine of Production, after the circulation-forms have subsumed the production process, that we can arrive at an adequate conception of the capitalist production process. First and foremost a capitalist production process requires the commodification of labour-power, because only then can capital produce any commodity whatsoever in accord with social requirements. According to Sekine 'Just as money measures the value of all commodities because it can buy any commodity regardless of its use-value, labour forms value because it can produce any commodity indifferently to its use-value.'[25] In all economies there must be some more or less efficient allocation of the total social labour-time to produce the goods or commodities required by society. In capitalism it is the commodity-economic principle that allocates total social labour so that only that amount that is socially necessary is applied to the production of each type of commodity. It is through the exchange of commodities that social labour is allocated in socially necessary amounts and it is the law of value that regulates the exchange of products so that in a state of equilibrium no labour is wasted. If too much labour relative to social demand is devoted to a particular branch of industry, then that does not count as part of the total value forming and augmenting labour. In this way, social demand acts as a passive constraint on value formation. Many interpreters of Marx fail fully to appreciate the role of demand in value theory.[26]

This is an important point since without a full appreciation of the role of social demand in the formation of value, the entire labour theory of value is misconceived. The realm of circulation and social demand acts as a passive constraint on value augmentation, and those who fail to grasp this point arrive at a theory of value that is essentially productivist and Ricardian.

The Doctrine of Circulation can only generate the *form* of value (i.e. the commodity-form, the money-form and the capital-form); the *substance* of value or the labour theory of value must be developed in the context of the Doctrine of Production (since it is here that we understand the creation of value). The Doctrine of Production shows how the labour and production process common to all societies operates under capitalism, according to the circulation-forms and their logic. The only real social cost in any economy is labour. In order to be viable, capitalism must be able to reproduce itself by channelling total social labour efficiently to meet social demand. Human labour is always abstract, in contrast with the labour of bees, in the sense that it is not pre-programmed and can produce many different things. But this quality of abstractness is only perfected under the regime of capital, where labour is used by capital to produce any commodity whatsoever with total indifference to its use-value. It is this indifference which enables capital to move in response to price changes so as to ensure that only the amount of labour that is socially necessary is devoted to the production of each type of commodity. In short, it is the perfection of labour's abstractness in a purely capitalist society that makes the labour theory of value hold, or as Sekine puts it: 'socially necessary labour forms value because it is the only factor of production that is not specific to the production of any particular use-value'.[27]

In his article 'The Necessity of the Law of Value', Sekine shows that the tendency towards the perfection of labour's abstractness or indifference to use-value flows from the basic condition for the existence of capitalism, namely the commodification of labour-power. In order to be viable any society must guarantee that the direct producers receive the product of their necessary labour since otherwise the continued existence of the direct producers will be jeopardized. In the case of capitalist society, this means that the working-class must be able to buy back the product of their necessary labour with their money-wage. 'The workers must receive real wages just enough to reproduce their labour-power, neither more nor less, because in either case its supply diminishes.'[28] In other words the perpetuation of labour-power as a commodity must be secured, but if this is the case the labour theory of value tends to hold; 'hence it follows that the validity of the labour theory of value is equivalent to the viability of capitalist society'.[29]

The following quote from Sekine will help to situate what I have just argued in the larger context of the law of value:

> The law of value exhibits various properties arising from the fact that in capitalist society all commodities are produced as value indifferently to their use-values. The dialectic of capital treats this fundamental law by virture of which capitalist society hangs together in three particular aspects: they are *the necessity, the absolute foundation, and the concrete mode of enforcement* of the law of value. The necessity of the law refers to the proposition that the historical existence of capalist society is equivalent to the validity of the labour theory of value, i.e., to the determination of value as the embodiment of socially necessary labour. The absolute foundation of the law of value establishes that its operation presupposes a feasible set of technologies, the adoption of which guarantees positive values. The concrete mode of enforcement of the law of value shows how the law specifically enforces itself through the motion of prices once a feasible technology is adopted, i.e., not necessarily proportional to values and a general rate of profit often different from the ratio of surplus value to the value of total capital advanced.[30]

This makes it clear that the labour theory of value does not imply production prices proportional to values, but does imply that '*all capitalistically produced commodities have positive equilibrium prices, whether or not proportional to values, because they embody value* (emphasis added).[31]

4 CIRCULATION, PRODUCTION, DISTRIBUTION

By introducing the labour theory of value, implying production, very early in his discussion of circulation, Marx's presentation tends to undermine not only the labour theory of value as argued above, but also the importance and integrity of circulation. In recent years there has been a continuing debate between those who emphasize circulation and those who stress production.[32] Those who emphasize the primacy of production tend to overemphasize the active production of value in the production process and to neglect the passive constraint of social demand on value formation. A one-sided stress on the primacy of production sometimes produces an economics closer to Ricardo than to Marx, in the sense that the undialectical emphasis on production produces a system of interconnected errors, including an underestimation of the autonomy and importance of circulation, a failure to grasp value-form theory and hence the nature of capitalist money, a failure to understand the specificity of variable capital and the commodity labour-power and a failure to grasp the relation between value and price. Larger methodological errors, such as adoption of the logical–historical method, an abandonment of dialectics and a failure to theorize the historical specificity of capitalism, also arise. The outcome of these errors is usually to abandon the theory of value altogether or to collapse it into a sociology of class struggle.

Those who overemphasize circulation and neglect production make some of the same errors. In its extreme form this tendency is simply mainstream bourgeois economics, which ignores the class relation, denies crisis (or has a most superficial explanation of it), and develops formal models that completely ignore the historical specificity and uniqueness of capitalism. Placing too much weight on circulation can also lead to underconsumptionist economic theories.

It is correct to insist upon the primacy of production in the sense that this is where value is produced, but only within a dialectical totality that grasps the necessary interconnection of production with circulation. Perhaps one of the best antidotes to all these one-sided approaches is a careful reconsideration of the discussion of the three forms of the circuit of capital at the beginning of Volume II of *Capital*. I shall not attempt this here, but shall instead note that our understanding of the Doctrine of Distribution (Marx's Volume III) depends very much on a prior grasp of the relation between circulation and production.

Those who one-sidedly emphasize distribution tend to focus single-mindedly on 'the transformation problem' or on the falling rate of profit. Instead of carefully reconsidering circulation and production from the point of view of the inadequacies of Volume III (i.e. the Doctrine of Distribution), they use these inadequacies as an excuse to reject value theory in favour of completely alien doctrines of price and profit. But a theory of prices and profits, no matter how logically and formally worked out, is useless unless it is part of a theory of the inner organization of the capitalist mode of production. Distribution must be grounded on an accurate rendering of circulation and production and their interrelation.

Before leaving this discussion, it is important to comment briefly on the much-disputed Section 4 of Chapter 1 of *Capital* on the fetishism of commodities. In many ways the 'fetishism of commodities' is a key concept in understanding the capitalist mode of production; and yet its location and manner of presentation in *Capital* have given rise to confusion. The 'fetishism of commodities' refers to all the cognitive confusions which arise from the peculiar character of the commodity-form. Fetishism first appears with the money-form which is a particular commodity made universal equivalent. Marx discusses the 'enigmatic' appearances that result from a particular use-value becoming the universal value-reflector. He also refers to the tiresome debate over whether money has value by nature or by convention. It becomes clear that neither of these alternatives is quite adequate when we come to understand that money has value because of the deep structure of the capitalist economy – a structure that is both material and social. The reason why the money-form gives rise to fetishism is because of its abstractness, or in other words its loose connection to its underlying material and social reality. This peculiarity of the money-form generates fetishism throughout the theory of the purely capitalist society. For example, the wage-form makes it appear that a definite quantity of labour is being paid for. Circulation-forms often obscure the extraction of surplus value as do the different forms of surplus value (rent, interest, profit).

Besides discussing fetishism all through the three volumes of *Capital*, Marx devotes Section 4 of Chapter 1 to an extended discussion of it. But if there is to be a separate section on fetishism this is not where it belongs. This is because fetishism becomes most clear only after we have before us both the form *and* substance of value. The fetishism of commodities is precisely all the ways that the circulation-forms obscure the formation and augmentation of value. Thus this concept is most clearly understood when we return to the circulation process within the Doctrine of Production only now with the process of production fully specified and embedded in the circulation process. $M-C-M'$ is now altered to $M-C \ldots P \ldots C'-M'$, so that we must take into account that which is momentous for the entire theory, namely that the capitalist circulation process is interrupted by the capitalist production process. Marx can only make sense out of the fetishism of commodities in Chapter 1 because he has already introduced the labour theory of value, but if he were not to violate his own dialectical method of presentation, then both would have been developed within the Doctrine of Production.

5 THE LAW OF POPULATION

Uno and Sekine formulate the law of population differently from Marx. They make it clear that the law of value must be supplemented by the law of population because labour-power is a peculiar commodity that cannot be reproduced by capital itself. Like Marx they see that a surplus population is a necessity in order for capital to expand because it does not have the capability of producing more workers on demand. Capital can expand its production even when the labouring population is given and fixed by introducing labour-saving technology, or what is the same thing, by raising the organic composition of capital.[33] But where they differ from Marx is in their understanding of the introduction of new labour-saving techniques. Major innovations involve sizeable new investments in fixed capital, and such investments are usually too costly unless the old fixed capital (old technique) is close to being fully depreciated or the new investment is forced upon capital by the intensity of competition in a depression. Uno argues:

> Although capital is generally motivated by the production of relative surplus value to improve upon the existing method of production, it is not directly concerned with the propagation of improved techniques. The general adoption of new productive methods must, therefore, in principle, be forced upon capital by the severity of competition that it faces in the phase of industrial depression.[34]

Thus in a purely capitalist society a widening phase of capital accumulation alternates with a deepening phase. In the widening phase the scale of capitalist production is expanded on the basis of a particular fixed capital compliment and technique. As long as surplus population is available capital can expand on the basis of the old techique while the capital investment fixed in that technique depreciates. As the reservoir of labour dries up, wages begin to rise and an excess of capital relative to surplus population develops. As the marginal profitability of capital investment approaches zero, the interest rate rises because of a shortage of loanable funds resulting from the slow-down of capital expansion. The result is the periodic crisis characteristic of capitalism. The severity of competition that results forces capital to reorganize and to introduce new labour-saving methods of production. The reserve army of labour is replenished and a revolution of value takes place reconstituting the basic capital–labour relation. Furthermore, Sekine argues:

> The law of capitalism that brings about this renewal of value relation by forcing capital to innovate its technological base in the event of the excess of capital is called the law of surplus population or that of the falling rate of profit depending on the way the same thing is looked at from different angles.[35]

This conception of the law of population ties in with the notion of 'surplus population' or 'industrial reserve army' with the deepening and widening phases of capital accumulation, which are in turn tied in with the increasing difficulty of maintaining the rate of profit as organic composition rises in each deepening phase. As a result the law of value and the law of population come together at the most basic point, namely the necessity to secure the commodification of labour-power, and they show that periodic crisis is needed both to secure labour-power as a commodity and to bring about renewal and innovation of productive technology. Periodic crisis reveals that both labour-power and fixed capital are difficult to manage capitalistically.

According to Uno and Sekine, Marx's discussion of accumulation in Volume I of *Capital* is misplaced and should be discussed in connection with the reproduction schema at the end of Volume II. This is because it is only in Volume II that Marx develops the concept of 'fixed capital', but this concept is crucial to understanding the widening and deepening phases of accumulation and an adequate conceptualization of these phases is crucial to the whole theory of periodic crisis. There are passages in the Volume I discussion of accumulation that suggest that the rising of organic composition is a continuous process, but this completely ignores the problems of fixed capital replacement. Even in Volume II where Marx suggests that fixed capital replacement is the material basis of periodic crisis, this fruitful idea is never really developed and integrated into the theory.

6   ACCUMULATION AND REPRODUCTION

Marx's reproduction schema have been much abused by subsequent interpreters. They have been used to generate crisis theory, to generate a theory of imperialism, and to generate an equilibrium model of capitalism. Both Rosdolsky and Mandel argue against these misuses of the reproduction schema and in favour of a highly limited use – namely to demonstrate the possibility of capitalism.[36] The work of Uno and Sekine agrees in general with the position outlined by Rosdolsky and Mandel, only Uno and Sekine go much further in specifying the precise character and function of the reproduction schema in the dialectic of a purely capitalist society.

Within the dialectic of capital the reproduction schema have a very specific and limited use. What they demonstrate is only that capitalism while producing all products anarchically as commodities can reproduce and expand by maintaining an appropriate division between basic and non-basic goods. The reproduction schema look at the capitalist process of accumulation in a one-sided and highly abstract and schematic way. Department I produces means of production or basic commodities, and Department II produces means of consumption or non-basic commodities. In simple reproduction all the surplus value is consumed by capitalists and in expanded reproduction some surplus value is reinvested.

Since neither department is self-sufficient, an exchange must take place between them, such that the constant capital in Department II must be less than or equal to the sum of variable capital and surplus value in Department I. Sekine argues that this exchange relation is not an equilibrium condition, but is an intersectoral constraint that capitalism must meet in order to reproduce itself.[37] The reproduction schema are not an equilibrium model but are a circular flow model at a high level of abstraction. According to Sekine, 'The theory of the reproduction-schemes, therefore, does not demonstrate whether a capitalist economy can or cannot maintain an equilibrium; the theory shows whether or not the capitalist economy would continue to be viable, if it always maintained its equilibrium.'[38]

All the variables within the reproduction schema are values. This is because at this stage of the dialectic, we have not yet introduced the concrete capitalist market which in dealing with technical heterogeneity gives rise to prices of production. It is appropriate that the reproduction schema should be expressed in value categories because we are still considering capital and labour to be homogenous. That is, we are still focusing on the basic capital–labour relation that underlies the capital market, and this relation is articulated in value categories. Value categories do not deal with differences in technique, so that we must assume a constant organic composition of capital within the reproduction schema. Furthermore, as Sekine has convincingly argued, socially necessary labour is only that labour that is necessary to meet social demand, so that labour which is unrealized or wasted does not count as part of value-forming labour. Value categories imply an equilibrium, and there cannot be any unrealized value. Therefore there cannot be any such thing as a 'realization problem' in connection with value categories. Since the reproduction schema are expressed in value categories, they assume an equilibrium, and therefore cannot be used to show any sort of disequilibrium, disproportion or underconsumption.

The reproduction process of capital is first of all the reproduction of workers and capitalists.[39] But from the point of view of the reproduction schema, we cannot fully grasp how the reproduction of labour-power as a commodity is maintained. This is because the schema simply assume that adequate labour-power is always available as a commodity, and hence only view the reproduction of labour-power from the point of view of wage-goods.[40]

It now becomes clear that the reproduction schema in their one-sided abstractness must be supplemented by the theory of accumulation with its law of population and widening and

deepening phases. The reproduction schema are too abstract and
formal to deal with the problem of fixed capital replacement and
with the reproduction of labour-power as a commodity; and
therefore the reproduction schema are also not the appropriate
place from which to derive a theory of crisis. To deal with these
issues, we need the theory of accumulation which shows that the
difficulties that capital has in securing labour-power as a
commodity and in replacing fixed capital are deep problems that
are interrelated and that require periodic crisis for their resolution.

From the standpoint at which we have arrived, we can now see
that the reproduction schema can only deal with capital accumulation in its widening phase, because a schema that is so abstract
and formal is too restrictive a format for the full development of
the law of population and the problem of fixed capital replacement.[41] The reproduction schema simply show that capitalism can fulfil a basic technical constraint common to all
economies; namely, that basic and non-basic goods must be
produced in appropriate quantities if the economy is to reproduce
itself or to expand.

Some Marxists have used the reproduction schema as models
for capitalist accumulation as a whole.[42] If what I have argued is
correct, then this is clearly an error. Though the capitalist mode of
production tends towards equilibrium, it does this only in the
course of passing through cycles, so that it is most likely to
approach equilibrium in the prosperity or widening phase before
the excess of capital sets in. The urge to fit the entire capitalist
mode of production into such a formalistic system as the
reproduction schema is not Marxian but neoclassical. We cannot
fit the law of population and fixed capital replacement into such a
framework, much less the subtleties associated with market price,
rent and interest. There is a reason why the reproduction schema
occur at the end of Volume II and not the end of Volume III of
Capital, that is, because Marx never thought such schema could
possibly serve to encapsulate the capitalist mode of production as
a whole.

7 THE TRANSFORMATION PROBLEM

My discussion has indicated some of the confusions that arise
from Marx's lack of precision in his presentation of 'value

categories'.[43] In particular I have tried to show how seemingly small details in the presentation of value-form theory in Chapter 1 place the entire theory on shaky foundations. This shakiness becomes most obvious in Marx's discussion of the relation between values and prices, particularly in Volume III with the so-called 'transformation problem'. The difficulty in mathematically transforming value magnitudes into price magnitudes has been the Achilles heel of Marx's *Capital*.

Uno and Sekine point out that values do not present any insurmountable difficulties to the theory of price determination if the dialectical nature of the theory of capital is kept in mind. Because many interpreters have been trained in the positivist or empiricist tradition or have been influenced by the hegemony of this tradition, they fail to grasp the dialectical logic of *Capital*. Marx himself helps these interpreters by not being explicit and clear about his dialectical method or rigorous enough in his presentation of the theory of capital as a dialectic. Because Marx continually gives quantitative examples to illustrate value relations, he gives the impression that a system of value quantities exists quite independently of the system of price quantities and that the price system must be derived mathematically from the value system. This impression is wrong. Once it is understood that the theory of capital is a dialectic, it follows that the sequence of categories must move from the abstract to the concrete. In this way, the movement from one level of abstraction to another may be considered a 'conversion' or 'transformation'. Thus the commodity-form is 'transformed' into the money-form, which is 'converted' into the capital-form.[44] The reason why value categories are used exclusively in Volumes I and II is that the motion of commodities and money is being examined from the point of view of the workers-versus-capitalist production relation. At this stage of the dialectic both capital and labour are treated as homogeneous so that the basic production relation can be examined in its purity. As we move through the dialectic, value becomes ever more concrete, or, what is the same thing, ever more capitalistically specified. In Volume III value reaches its most concrete expression in the form of market prices, which converge upon market production prices. It is only in Volume III that value expresses itself in a quantitative form that approaches the actual prices in the market of a purely capitalist society. In order to reach this point, values must be modified to account fully for the price effects of the actual technical diversity of capital and for the price effects of supply and demand. This degree of concreteness in use-value production can be suspended earlier in the dialectic because it has no place at a level of abstraction that is exploring the necessary connections between circulation-forms and between circulation-forms and basic production relations. In a dialectic the sequence of categories is a necessary sequence so that a more concrete category cannot be posited before its time has arrived – all categories necessary for its full understanding must already have been derived, and the step to the more concrete category must be shown to be a necessary step. Thus the quantitative expression of values earlier in the dialectic must not be read to represent some independently determined quantitative system, but rather simply to be more theoretically abstract or more theoretically primitive representations of price where the technical differentiation of capital has not yet been introduced and the capitalist market is held implicit. The basic confusion, then, around the 'transformation problem' comes from seeing as a mathematical transformation the dialectical movement from one level of abstraction to another. What is essentially a conceptual transformation is seen as a mathematical transformation.[45]

Another source of confusion on the relation between values and prices flows from Marx's misleading presentation of the labour theory of value. By simply positing labour-value in Chapter I of *Capital*, Marx gives the impression that value is simply the addition of units of labour. But as I have previously argued, the labour theory of value cannot be clearly stated and defended until after the circulation-forms have been developed. It then becomes clear that circulation acts as a passive constraint on value formation and augmentation, so that labour expended on commodities in excess of social demand is wasted and is no part of value. This understanding of the passive constraint placed by supply and demand on value formation is essential to understanding the theory of market value and market price, which Marx left in a very unfinished state. Supply and demand play a crucial role in our understanding on how market value resolves issues involving choice of technique. This point will be expanded later.

According to Uno and Sekine the movement from values to prices is a movement within the dialectic of capital from one level of abstraction to another. To be more specific, prices are the way that values express themselves in the capitalist market, or in the words of Sekine 'prices are simply the capitalistically more congenial form of values'.[46] In the Doctrines of Circulation and

Production where the basic worker-versus-capital relation is developed, capital remains homogeneous and use-value production is treated in its generality without reference to diversity of techniques. In the Doctrine of Distribution we must reconsider value from the more concrete perspective of the capitalist market and the technical heterogeneity of capital. Because of the technical diversity of capital and because of supply and demand conditions in the market, prices diverge from values, but this divergence is never arbitrary.

According to Uno and Sekine, a society is viable 'if and only if the direct producers have a guaranteed access to the product of their necessary labour'.[47] When it comes to calculating prices this fundamental necessity of viability constitutes the '*basic constraint*' on the capitalist market that constitutes the direct role of the law of value in constraining price formation. According to the basic constraint 'the money value of wage goods currently produced must not differ from the money value of labour-power presently employed; for if this condition were violated for long, labour-power would not remain as a commodity and the capitalist market would be deprived of its own foundation'.[48]

Value categories grasp the reified social relation or the workers-versus-capitalist relation that is the foundation of the capitalist mode of production, while price categories conceptualize the thing-to-thing relation among commodities in the capitalist market as if value categories did not exist. The determining of prices as if values did not exist is made possible by reification, and the conclusion made by some economists that therefore values are irrelevant is one example of what Marx calls 'fetishism of commodities'. According to Sekine, prices are calculated from technical data and the basic constraint and not from values. But since there is a determinate relation between prices and values, once prices are determined values are as well. The transformation of values into prices is basically a conceptual movement from a more abstract to a more concrete level of analysis, but once having made this move, prices and values are simultaneously determined quantitatively by technical data and the basic constraint. We do not transform mathematically the value system into the price system or the price system into the value system, rather the two systems are quantitatively determined simultaneously.[49]

The relation between value and price is still not completely specified with the determination of production prices. Production prices explain prices from the standpoint of technical differences between different branches of industry. But there may also be technical differences within an industry, and the determination of the technique that determines price requires the theory of market value.

> The market value of a commodity is not necessarily equal to the quantity of labour actually expended even in equilibrium on its production, but is equal to the quantity of labour that 'society in its capacity of consumer' is obliged to spend for the marginal production of that commodity.[50]

According to this doctrine then, it is the social labour necessary for its marginal production that determines the market value of a commodity and the market production price is determined by the technique that supplies the marginal commodity. According to supply and demand conditions and technical factors it may be the more productive or less productive technique that supplies the marginal commodity. Thus it is only with the formation of the optimum allocation of social labour that all commodities are produced in socially required amounts and only that labour that is socially necessary is devoted to the production of all commodities. It is characteristic for capitalism, which is a reified economy, to achieve this allocation of social labour in an indirect manner.

> Thus capital in its individual pursuit of a higher profit-rate by reducing the labour-cost per unit of the commodity unknowingly maximizes the production of both absolute and relative surplus value. The rate of surplus value which is the ratio of surplus to necessary labour will then tend to be both maximized and equalized throughout the economy, apart from the extra surplus value that may be earned in the process of introducing a new technology.[51]

8   SRAFFIAN MARXISM

Ever since Bohm-Bawerk some people have argued that it is not possible mathematically to derive prices from values and that therefore Marx's value theory is at best unnecessary and at worst metaphysical or in some sense mystifying. Though such attacks have often come from bourgeois economists, recently such arguments have come from Marxists themselves. Sraffian Marxists in particular have gained a following and appear to be convinced of the correctness of their position. Referring to the work of Sraffa and Garegnani, Marco Lippi states: 'We owe to these authors the complete and definitive solution of the problem of prices in the theory of Marx and of the classical economists.'[52] Steedman writes: 'The Sraffa-based critique of Marx cannot be met head on and rationally rejected, for the simple reason that it is correct.'[53] Or Steedman again: 'Some Marxist economists will, of course, be reluctant to concede the irrelevance of the "labour theory of value", but it is now generally recognized that the demonstration of that irrelevance is logically impeccable.'[54] Hodgson uses Kuhn's theory of scientific revolutions to picture those Marxists who still cling to the labour theory of value as 'normal scientists' still clinging to the old 'paradigm' very much as some clung to the Ptolemaic view of the universe in the face of the Copernican revolution.[55]

The self-confidence of the Sraffian Marxists seems to be based on a supposedly rigorous theory of price determination. Generally they have done well in the debate with orthodox Marxists because orthodox Marxists have held too closely to the text of *Capital*, instead of immersing themselves into the logic of capital. As a result, some orthodox Marxists have been caught up in fruitless attempts to solve the transformation problem (as formulated by Marx) while others have retreated to philosophical defences of the labour theory of value, having been driven from the terrain of economic theory by the Sraffians.[56] And yet the orthodox Marxists are much closer to the truth than the Sraffians and have good instincts in coming to the defence of the labour theory of value. The power of the Sraffians is the power of mathematics and formal models, and they are correct in rejecting the effort to derive prices from values. The problem is that their theory of price determination is not a theory of *capitalist* prices and their understanding of the law of value is entirely inadequate. The Sraffians are far too ready to abandon value categories in favour of their formally correct theory of price determination. Instead of trying to correct the flaws in Marx's formulation of the law of value, they play up the flaws and reject the theory

altogether. Their need to be unchallengably correct has backed
them into formalism and into largely abandoning Marx's *Capital*
as the foundation of Marxian social science. They fetishize the
theory of price determination, so that the inadequacy of Marx's
Capital on this score is sufficient cause to reject value theory
altogether. Their project is to try to reconstruct Marxian
economics by grafting a sociology of exploitation onto a Sraffian
theory of price determination. But this approach completely
conflates the logical and the historical while destroying the inner
coherence of the dialectic of capital. The result is that the
objective foundation of Marxian social science is completely
undermined.

The strength of the dialectic of capital is that it conceptualizes
the thing-to-thing relations of the capitalist market as objectified
social relations. The dialectic of capital is objective because it
theorizes social relations that are not simply intersubjective but
are reified or objectified by being subsumed to the motion of
commodities. If we restrict economic theory to commodity-as-
thing, we can produce formally rigorous mathematical models,
but it is no longer clear how they related to the substance of
socioeconomic life. If social relations are not reified it is possible
to construct a sociology of exploitation using analytic constructs
in the mode of Weber, but such an approach is fundamentally
subjective and can at best yield conjectures. The falling apart of
the material and the social undermines the possibilities of an
objectively grounded social science; and in its place yields
formalistic economics and subjectivist sociology. Unfortunately
this is the trend of Sraffian Marxists; their tendency is to abandon
any effort to theorize the necessary inner connections of the
capitalist mode of production in favour of a formally 'correct'
model of prices and profits attached to a sociology of exploitation.

In a recent article, Sekine demonstrates that problems posed
for the labour theory of value by choice of technique, heterogeneous labour (the problem of skilled labour) and joint production
can all be solved by an adequate development of the theory of
market value, which Marx left in an unfinished and unsatisfac-
tory state.[57] Sekine also points out some of the difficulties of
Sraffian formalism. Some Sraffians have relied upon Steedman's
article 'Positive Profits with Negative Surplus Value' to argue

that value categories are not just futile but error-laden.[58] But Sekine argues convincingly that the technology upon which Steedman bases his argument cannot be capitalistically operated. From the point of view of capitalism, Steedman's technology is economically meaningless, so that his mathematically correct proof proves nothing about capitalism, or about value categories.[59]

Besides failing to see the dialectical logic of the theory of capital, the major error of the Sraffians is to give the value system no other significance than as a quantitative base for deriving prices and profits. But value categories rigorously theorize the necessary inner connections of pure capitalism that must underlie the capitalist market and thus lay the institutional base and *modus operandi* for deriving a specifically *capitalist* theory of prices and profits.

In the *Dialectic of Capital* Sekine argues that all transformation theories which, following von Bortkiewicz, try to solve 'price equations by means of the physical wage-rate or . . . the commodity-complex which forms the real wage-rate are invalid'.[60] This includes Morishima, whose effort to arrive at a 'labour-feeding input coefficient' amounts to reducing the consumption of workers to a technology as if 'capitalism possesses an unseen agency that prescribes the physical wage-rate' like a medicine.[61] This also includes von Neumann and the Sraffians, for whom the reproduction of workers is no different from the reproduction of horses and cows. Sekine aptly calls this method of wage determination 'the fodder method', and argues that such a technological reduction of workers' consumption, though mathematically neat, produces a fundamental distortion of how capitalism operates and therefore produces false production prices based on a fixed basket of wage-goods. In capitalism the reproduction of labour-power is achieved by individual consumption outside the production process. The reproduction of labour-power cannot therefore be collapsed into the production process. 'Capitalism possesses no Stalinist authority prescribing the consumption-basket.'[62] The law of value must preserve the basic capital–labour relation despite the complete freedom of each worker to buy wage-goods. This is why Sekine's theory of price determination uses the 'basic constraint' as opposed to the fodder method. This is also why the Sraffians, who reduce the reproduction of labour-power to the reproduction of cattle, arrive at prices of production that are capitalistically meaningless

> For suppose indeed that all workers are paid the physical wage. That would mean that every week they are forced to convert their money wage into, say, fifty cigarettes whether they smoke or do not, a bottle of vodka whether they drink or not, a lipstick and two razor blades whether they are male or female, some school supplies and a box of disposable diapers regardless of the age of their children, etc. . . . Even if this were the case in the first instance, the existence of the free capitalist market would surely not prevent the workers from actively retrading their commodities among themselves in an effort to achieve a more satisfactory assortment of consumable goods. In that process, however, not only must the prices of wage-goods but also the rate of profit and through it all other prices must change from those that would prevail in the absence of retrading. What then is the point of studiously calculating false production-prices first on the Bortkiewiczian assumption of a fixed complex of wage-goods, only to discover that real production prices deviate not only from values but also from false production prices.[63]

From the point of view of the operating principles of capitalism, the Sraffian theory produces false production prices. An extended mathematical demonstration of this is contained in Sekine's *Dialectic of Capital.*[64]

Besides producing wrong production prices, the fodder method also makes it impossible to generate an economically rigorous notion of exploitation. This is because, according to the fodder method, there is no reason to limit exploitation to living labour-power since animals and machines can also be exploited. Exploitation then becomes a totally meaningless concept. This explains why Marxian Sraffians who want to maintain the concept 'exploitation' must resort to sociology to supplement their formalistic economic theory. The result of this is a 'logically impeccable' price theory that in substance is wrong, supplemented by a sociology of exploitation which, lacking any grounding in the objectified economic relations of capitalism, must necessarily be Weberian and subjectivist. This amounts to a substantial improverishment of the Marxian theoretical project.

9   CRISIS THEORY

Crisis theory is another area where there has been a good deal of debate, and where inadequacies in Marx's formulations have led some Marxists to abandon Marx's theory of crisis. Uno and Sekine have important contributions to make in firming up Marx's theory of capital on this issue as well. To begin with, it must be understood that it is somewhat artificial to speak of Marx's theory of crisis as if it were a separate theory, since in a sense all three volumes of *Capital* constitute Marx's 'crisis theory'. Crisis theory, then, is an analytical separation of certain elements from the dialectic of capital for the sake of focusing on this special issue. With this important qualification, I shall proceed to discuss Uno and Sekine's dialectical reconstruction of Marxian crisis theory.

It is often stated that the periodic crisis of capitalism most fully exposes the contradictions of the capitalist mode of production. Now to review the discussion so far, the basic contradiction of the dialectic of capital is between value and use-value, or in other words between the commodity-economic principle and the concrete requirements of real economic life. The dialectic of capital moves from the abstract to the concrete by value 'overcoming' successive use-value constraints in order to secure within its own motion the basis for its continuing existence and expansion. The use-value that offers the most resistance to commodification is labour-power and at the same time the commodification of labour-power is the most important foundation of the capitalist mode of production, since it is this commodity that secures for capital the basis of value expansion within its own motion. And, because labour-power cannot be capitalistically reproduced in response to increased demand, the law of value must be supplemented by the law of surplus population in order to ensure the continued reproduction of this key commodity. Because of the central importance of labour-power and the difficulty in securing its continued reproduction as a commodity, we would expect the contradictions of capitalism and particularly capitalist crisis to centre around the commodification of labour-power.

The continued commodification of labour-power is only secured through periodic crisis produced by the joint operation of the law of value and the law of population. In its widening phase of accumulation, capital can expand by expanding production on a given technological base thus avoiding expensive new investments in fixed capital. This phase is typically without the large advances in productivity that come with new labour-saving technology so that as capital expands more and more workers are needed until the reservoir of surplus population tends to dry up. At this point wages rise, reducing the rate of profit and with it investment outlets. At the same time as capital expansion slows, the rising wage bill places pressure on loanable funds so that the interest rate goes up. The lack of productive investment outlets fuels speculative pressures which maintain artificially high prices and interest rates. As the interest rate rises and the profit rate falls a point is reached where new investment is not worth while and capital contraction occurs with a vengeance leading to a sharp reduction in economic activity with accompanying bankruptcies, unemployment and excess capacity. In the trough of depression wages and prices fall and excess capital is destroyed. Severe competition between firms leads to a massive reorganization of capital involving centralization and the introduction of new more productive technology. As a result, the surplus population is replenished and a new value relation is established between capital and labour that serves as the basis for a new widening phase of accumulation.

This account of crisis differs from Marx in clearly centring the theory of crisis on the law of surplus population and the renewal of fixed capital consequent on revolutions in the methods of production. Capital could in principle continue to accumulate without periodic crisis but for the difficulty of securing the commodification of labour-power and the 'lumpiness' of technological innovation and fixed capital investment. According to Sekine, fixed capital has two aspects: it is firstly a reproducible means of production and secondly a temporarily irreproducible means of production comparable to land.[65] This is because no firm can afford to abandon a major investment in fixed capital that is supposed to depreciate in ten years after only 2 years, even if a much more productive technique has been discovered and introduced by a few firms. Disequilibriums that occur between capitalistically produced commodities can generally be overcome by the price mechanism. The basic source of disequilibrium that underlies capitalist crisis must be related to commodities that the price mechanism cannot so easily regulate. These two commodities are labour-power and fixed capital, and it is precisely the difficulties in the regulating of these two commodities by the price mechanism that calls forth periodic crisis. The approach of Uno and Sekine is more radical than Marx in firmly rooting the necessity of crisis in the process of accumulation prior to any discussion of the falling rate of profit, and by demonstrating the periodic radical change in production techniques that must take place to secure the continued availability of labour-power as a commodity:

> The fall in the general rate of profit indicates that this fundamental adjustment involves a whole revision of the workers-versus-capitalists relation rather than mere changes in capitalist-to-capitalist relations observable on the surface of the commodity-exchange market . . . the excess of capital issues from the fundamental chasm between the products of capital as a whole and labour-power which capital cannot directly produce . . . nothing short of a structural reform in the technological base of society can save capitalism from the peril of destruction.[66]

Marx relies too heavily on the rate of profit alone and does not root his discussion of the declining rate of profit in the alternate widening and deepening phases of accumulation, so that it becomes easy to treat the rate of profit formally and argue that it has no tendency to fall. Uno argues that:

> there exists no inherent limit to the expansion of capital except the availability of additional labour-power. It is the incapacity of the capitalist method of production directly to regulate the supply of labour-power that determines the underlying cause of industrial cycles. Indeed, relative surplus population is formed in the phase of depression so as to allow an expanded reproduction in the subsequent phase of prosperity.[67]

When the theory of crisis is not firmly rooted in the law of surplus population it is easy for formalists to argue that the rate of profit has no more tendency to fall than to rise.[68]

According to Sekine, the law of the falling rate of profit holds in a purely capitalist society because the higher the organic composition of capital, the more difficult it is for increases in the rate of surplus value to offset the rising organic composition of capital. To be more precise, the higher the organic composition of capital, the less effective is the rise in relative surplus value during the deepening phase in offsetting the rise in organic composition of capital.

Marx's discussion of countertendencies to the falling rate of profit also leads to confusion because most of the countertendencies that he mentions do not even belong to the level of analysis that we are concerned with. The only countertendency that logically stems from the accumulation of capital as such is the tendency for the rate of surplus value to rise due to an increase in the production of relative surplus value. As argued in the previous chapter, countertendencies such as foreign trade or pushing wages below the value of labour-power cannot be part of pure theory.

The issue of countertendencies brings up again the issue of the relation between the logical and the historical. Much of the discussion of crisis theory has been seriously hampered by confusions around this issue.[69] The levels of analysis approach of Uno and Sekine can help resolve many of the confusions. The theory of crisis that is developed by the dialectic of capital for a purely capitalist society cannot be directly applied to the current crisis since we do not live in a purely capitalist society. The society that we live in today is in fact far removed from pure capitalism. Though pure theory cannot be directly applied to the current conjuncture, an understanding of pure capitalism can help us to clarify what is happening today. In so far as the state manages the reproduction of labour-power and the circulation of money and credit, labour-power and money have become de-commodified (i.e. not regulated by the market principle). It seems as though the current crisis cannot be rigorously theorized in value categories; and yet value categories can help us clarify the empirical situation and understand its structural necessities and range of possibilities. The debates between various schools of crisis theory such as underconsumption, declining rate of profit, disproportionality, profit squeeze, etc. at the level of a purely capitalist society are often confused with considerations of which one best explains the current conjuncture or which one is the least reformist in the current conjuncture. But these are very separate issues and should not be thrown together. Crisis theory must be modified depending on the level of analysis. Thus in the stage of imperialism, part of the function that crisis performs for pure capitalism is performed by imperialist war. Crises in the stages of mercantilism, liberalism and imperialism are different, and at the level of historical analysis a particular crisis may display all sorts of peculiarities.[70]

If the contemporary economy is becoming de-commodified, then to that extent it represents capitalism in a state of dissolution. Of course closely connected to this de-commodification is the growing manipulation of the economy by monopolies and the state. The current crisis cannot be grasped as a direct manifestation of the theory of crisis embedded in the theory of a purely capitalist society. Pure theory can provide an orientation and clues about what to look at, but a great deal of historical and conjunctural material is necessary to understand our present crisis. Furthermore, given the extent of political manipulation of contemporary economic life, any theory that purports to explain the current crisis in purely economic terms must be inadequate.

10 CONCLUSION

Over much of its history Marxian thought has suffered from an economism that is too ready to reduce the complexity of capitalist history and social life to being a direct function of the law of value. In recent years the reaction against this tendency has made Marxist theorists in the West too ready to abandon the objective guide that the law of value offers to our research and strategy. This combined with a veritable renaissance of Marxian social science has created a situation where Marxist studies have a great deal of sail but little rudder. Much of the energy being devoted to Marxist studies is being dispersed without the theoretical effectiveness that it might have precisely because the theoretical infrastructure of Marxian social science is weak and as a result eclecticism is rampant. This also means that Marxian social science lacks a clear and definite identity that would distinguish it from other approaches. We can certainly see these tendencies at work with the Sraffian Marxists.

In this chapter, I have attempted to give the reader an indication of the reconstruction of the law of value offered by Uno and Sekine. In my view Sekine's *Dialectic of Capital* is an impressive theory and this is achieved primarily because Sekine has fully exposed the dialectical logic embedded in Marx's and then in Uno's theory of value. In future chapters I shall indicate how it is possible for the theory of a purely capitalist society to serve as the objective foundation for Marxian social science without falling into the errors of economism and reductionism. It is the levels of analysis approach that makes this possible, and in what follows I shall develop this approach in at least outline form.

4   Stage Theory

The foundation of the Uno School is Uno's theory of a purely capitalist society. It is this theory that sets forth the necessary inner connections of capitalism in the abstract and in general, and hence establishes the foundation of political economy. The distance between the inner logic of capitalism and its historical development is great. To apply the law of value directly to history would therefore produce an economistic and reductionist history. The gap between the highly abstract theory of pure capitalism and concrete history must be addressed by developing mediations. There are many ways of doing this, but in Uno's view the most effective way is to develop a distinct level of theory. Following Lenin, Uno refers to this mediating level of theory as 'stage theory'.

Uno did not write a great deal on stage theory, nor has the Japanese Uno School as a whole.[1] There are many unresolved methodological issues about precisely how stage theory should be formulated and how it relates to both pure theory and historical analysis. I have attempted to outline an approach to stage theory. What is important, however, is not my particular version of stage theory, but the general principle that some sort of stage theory is required and that its construction should be guided by the theory of a purely capitalist society and history. Unfortunately the writings of the Japanese Uno School that deal with stage theory have not been translated into English. I therefore offer this outline of stage theory in English as a first attempt which will be improved on by others. What is especially needed to develop stage theory is its use to help understand the history of capitalism. It will then become increasingly clear what the logical status of stage theory is.

In this chapter I shall first elaborate on the general principles of stage theory based on the work of Uno and Sekine. Next, I shall consider the stage of imperialism through a critical analysis of some of the classical works and recent efforts at theorizing

73

imperialism. I shall conclude by reiterating the guidelines for constructing effective stage theory while noting issues that are controversial.

1 THE THEORY OF PURE CAPITALISM AND STAGE THEORY

The theory of a purely capitalist society completely exposes the law of value because it allows the commodification of socioeconomic life to complete itself. But this assumes ideal use-values that the motion of value can completely subsume and manage capitalistically. 'A capitalistically produced commodity is reproducible and hence can, in principle, be supplied in any quantity. It is widely and frequently traded in an impersonal market in which a large number of unidentified sellers face a large number of unidentified buyers.'[2] Further, a capitalistically produced commodity should be producible by a combination of machines and commodified labour-power in a factory or factory-like industrial process. This is really a corollary to the previous statement since it is precisely the industrial organization of the labour and production process that enables capital to supply a use-value in any quantity in response to the market. A use-value such as a shirt fits these requirements perfectly and hence may be considered an 'ideal' use-value. Other types of use-values may not be so capitalistically manageable. For example, consider grapes grown for vintage wine. Only certain soils and climates can grow such a commodity; the success of each crop is very dependent on the weather; the growing season cannot be significantly shortened by technological advances as can the production process of other commodities; a great deal of labour is needed for the harvest but at other times little labour is needed (unlike the steady supply of labour-power required by an industrial factory); and finally the fragility of the commodity limits the effective application of machinery. In this case, then, the use-value is rather difficult to manage capitalistically.

Agricultural commodities are generally difficult to manage capitalistically and this is one reason why petty commodity production has generally prevailed in agriculture, even in the most fully developed capitalist economies. The general reason for this is that ideal commodities must be producible by capital concerned only with quantitative value criteria. Where use-value and qualitative factors impinge, the motion of value is interfered with. In a purely capitalist society, even though landed property is an alien element, it is subsumed to the motion of value through the category 'rent'. But the dialectic of capital demonstrates that the relation between industrial-capital and landed property is tenuous because landlords may interfere with accumulation by charging monopoly rents. Furthermore, the existence of a separate landlord class collecting rent discourages industrial-capital from improving the productivity of the land by sinking fixed capital into it. Finally there is a strong tie binding farmers to the soil and this is a further qualitative factor that blocks the operation of the commodity-form. In short these qualitative or use-value obstacles make agricultural production far less flexible than industrial capitalism where capital can in principle move entirely in response to quantitative criteria. If flexibility is essential to the operation of value, then farms must be expanded, contracted or shut down in response to market forces. But this situation seldom exists. In fact industrial agriculture first developed on a large scale in the Third World under conditions of monopoly and primitive accumulation, that is under conditions that are not very capitalist.

Marx himself was only partially aware of the obstacles in the way of developing agrarian capitalism.[3] But if the law of value never directly regulates agricultural production to any significant extent, that does not mean that capitalism does not have a very large impact on it. The point that I want to emphasize in this discussion is the necessary tension between capitalist production and agrarian production because of the use-value characteristics of agricultural production.

If the motion of value has difficulty subsuming agriculture at a historical level, it also has difficulty subsuming other types of use-value production, not to mention services. Many of the fine arts seem to be inherently petty commodity production under capitalism. A large part of the price of a Van Gogh painting derives from the fact that it is produced by this particular individual. More interesting because more central to our modern economy are use-values such as spaceships, battleships or thermonuclear weapons. Clearly such products do not fit the criteria of being commodities since they are not supplied in any quantity for an impersonal market and hence do not fall under the regulation of the law of value. Here use-value overwhelms value. These examples show that not all commodities are equally manageable capitalistically. One could give other examples such as telephone systems, hydroelectric systems and other 'natural monopolies'.

Capitalism is a historically limited mode of production because the law of value can only subsume a limited range of use-value production. Value must be impersonal and only concerned with quantitative criteria; where personal or qualitative constraints are important, value has difficulty operating. The motion of value has difficulty subsuming agriculture or other areas of production where the qualitative aspects of nature loom large. It cannot fully subsume services because they are interpersonal. It can only partially subsume large and complex social products especially when they are only produced in a limited quantity for specific buyers. Capitalism only achieves a partial grasp on historical reality because of these difficulties that value has in managing purely according to commodity-economic principles the production of the use-values and associated technologies outside of a certain range. The more that an actual economy is made of ideal use-values such as shirts, pencils, bread and candles – i.e. commodities that can be produced in any quantity and are frequently traded in an impersonal market consisting of large numbers of buyers and sellers – the more the law of value can hold sway and the closer the economy approaches pure capitalism. As I have already mentioned, a purely capitalist society is entirely made up of ideal use-values in the sense that we let value overcome all use-value obstacles so that commodification becomes complete. Although this enables us to formulate the law of value as a set of necessary relations, it leaves us with a pure theory of an impure world. The question then becomes how to develop appropriate mediations so that the theory of pure capitalism can help to understand history where capitalism is always impure?

When we look at pure theory we see that the basic contradiction of the dialectic is between value and use-value, and that the law of value can only emerge fully when value is allowed to subsume use-value. But my previous analysis has shown that this requires ideal use-values, and that when considered concretely all use-values are not equally subsumable to the motion of value. That the motion of value has only limited success in taming use-values explains the limited grasp that capitalism has on history (i.e. historical capitalism never becomes pure). That value can successfully manage only a limited range of use-values explains the limited duration of capital's passage on this planet (i.e. capitalism only holds sway over a limited period of history). The demarcation of the capitalist epoch as a whole as well as of the stages of development within it should be based on the degree to which and the ways in which the motion of value subsumes use-value production.

In developing stage theory we need to look for the type or types of use-value production which are most representative of how capital accumulates for that particular stage of capitalist development.[4] According to Uno and Sekine, British wool manufacturing is most characteristic of the stage of mercantilism (roughly 1650–1755), British cotton manufacturing of the stage of liberalism (roughly 1775–1875) and German steel manufacturing of the stage of imperialism (roughly 1875–1917). Uno and Sekine see the periods before 1650 and after 1917 as phases of transition.

The law of value is active in all three stages of capitalist development, but in the stage of mercantilism it only has a very minimal grasp on economic reality. It is latent as opposed to being manifest. Here the motion of value does not directly control the labour and production process as in the case of industrial-capital, but rather the motion of value in the form of merchant-capital partially and indirectly subsumes production through a putting-out system of cottage workers. In this mode of capital accumulation the law of value is not manifest. Nevertheless since this putting-out system represents a world-historic movement towards industrial capitalism, it is already latent in this stage. The law of value is most manifest in the stage of liberalism because the dominant type of production is the sort of light manufacturing of use-values that are closest to the ideal use-values of a purely capitalist society. In the stage of imperialism dominance of the law of value is weakened as heavy industry requires the development of monopoly and state intervention that systematically distorts its operation.

The law of value represents the inner law of the capitalist mode of production, in the sense that it represents a purely capitalist society where the completion of reification means that the law of value is totally self-regulating and is not interfered with by any outside other. But as we move towards history, this inner law, which assumes ideal use-values, must now be modified in the light of the concrete imperatives of actual modes of capital accumulation. This is what I mean when I say that stage theory is the 'externalization' or 'concretization' in history of the basic value/use-value contradiction of the dialectic of a purely capitalist society. This basic contradiction is conretized in a dominant mode of accumulation, which includes all aspects of the dominant form of capital accumulation.

Stage theory is a distinct level of analysis arrived at neither by a deduction from pure theory nor by an abstraction from history. The concepts of stage theory are essentially abstract 'material-types' arrived at by using pure theory and history to help determine the main structures and processes of the dominant mode of capital accumulation in that historical stage.[5] Stage theory is essentially static since it aims to grasp the dominant type of capital accumulation and not actual historical change and development. The analysis of history constitutes a third level of analysis where agency and contingency operate within the general constraints of the stage-theoretic dominant type of accumulation. At the level of historical analysis we see to what extent and in what ways the dominant type of capital accumulation impacts on the world where capitalism always develops very unevenly. Actual historical change, including the transition between stages, must be analysed at the level of historical analysis, albeit historical analysis guided by stage theory and pure theory.

A stage implies some coherence to the law of value in the sense of a dominant type of use-value production and corresponding organization of value expansion to produce a mode of accumulation. In other words a stage implies a dominant type of capital accumulation that has internal integrity and coherency and that can be essentially understood as a self-expansion of value which is only secondarily dependent on outside forces, such as the state. The stage of mercantilism represents the first halting appearance of the law of value as a subsumption of the labour and production process to the motion of value in a putting-out system. The stage of liberalism represents the maturity of the law of value as it secures the commodification of labour-power and develops factory production. The stage of imperialism represents capital-ism in decay as the development of monopoly and state interven-tion begins to undermine the market. I use 'phase of transition' to demarcate the period before mercantilism and after imperialism.

A phase of transition as a transition away from feudalism or away from capitalism must be theorized differently from stage theory. In the case of the transition away from capitalism, the law of value can no longer be applied to arrive at a dominant form of capital, but rather we must carry out our analysis at a historical level, and we must understand history as an unravelling or disintegration of the law of value. The law of value is still useful as a reference-point for understanding what it is we are moving away from, but a phase of transition does not have the same sort of inner logic based on the law of value that a stage has. This does not mean that in the transition away from capitalism anything is acceptable, only that the law of value increasingly does not apply and that therefore the world must be understood primarily in terms of socioeconomic forces and power relations and not in terms of value theory. It is still possible to try to determine the tendencies manifested in relations between persistent structures, but it is not possible to understand these structures as manifestations of the law of value. Instead we need to understand structural developments as a movement away from or as a historically specific case of the unravelling of the law of value. Both the law of value and the theory of the imperialist stage serve to guide the analysis of the phase of transition away from capitalism.

Since in pure capitalism, society is governed by a self-regulating market, the state and ideology can only be conceived of as embryonic forms lacking materiality and interventionist capability. Furthermore, a purely capitalist society has no geographic or territorial location, but must be assumed to be a global society without boundaries and without foreign trade. But in history capital always develops within and between territorial states, and the development of capital and of the nation-state are up to a point mutually supporting. Also capital develops very unevenly when viewed spatially on a global scale. So in constructing stage theory we look for the form or forms of use-value production that most characterize the stage, forms that are always located in a particular territorial state and are supported by state policies. This is because when the total reification of pure capitalism no longer holds, then capital cannot do without the support of the political and ideological superstructure. Thus at the level of stage theory, we look for the dominant form of capitalist accumulation, we look for its geographical location and we look for the types of ideology and state policy that support it. Knowledge of the inner logic of capital achieved at the level of pure theory helps to interpret the historical material in constructing a stage theory, but stage theory is in no sense a deduction from pure theory. Rather, stage theory represents an externalization of pure theory, such that the use-value obstacles become more concrete and historical as do the motions of value in overcoming these obstacles. In its more concrete mode of organization and operation, value as capital is no longer self-supporting, but instead requires the support of determinant ideologies and state policies. Stage theory is no longer a purely economic theory. Transitional phases must be analysed at an historical level of analysis where the political and ideological are even more integrated with the economic or where the economic has less of a logic of its own.

2   MERCANTILISM, LIBERALISM, IMPERIALISM

In this section my purpose is to outline briefly the stages of capitalist development according to the approach of Uno and Sekine. I shall do this in a descriptive fashion without much reflection on the methodology employed since I will deal with this in the next section. Only the theory of the imperialist stage will be developed to any extent, and that will be done in later sections through a critical analysis of both classical and recent literature on capitalist development in the late nineteenth and twentieth centuries. This section, then, will outline the stages of mercantilism, liberalism and imperialism; and it will also discuss the problem of theorizing the period from 1917 to the present which I view as a phase of transition away from capitalism.

Mercantilism refers to the early development of capitalism in the seventeenth and eighteenth centuries. It is British capital that becomes predominant in this stage so that it is to Britain that we should turn in looking for the dominant form of use-value production. According to Uno, it is British wool production in particular that represents the form of use-value production most characteristic of this stage. Why wool rather than coal or iron, or why a type of use-value production as opposed to the triangular trade that initially involved slaves and sugar? The answer to these questions comes from combining the knowledge of precisely what capitalism is and how it operates with historical knowledge. We know that capitalism is essentially the commodity-economic operation of the labour and production process and that this depends crucially on the commodification of labour-power. In this stage of capitalist development merchant-capital is dominant and labour-power has not yet become substantially commodified, but in fully developed capitalism the circulation of value, here represented by merchant-capital, comes to dominate the production process. So we look for a type of use-value production that represents substantial inroads on the agrarian base of pre-capitalism and that represents a significant step towards the capitalist management of the production process. British wool production is precisely such a form of use-value production.

Merchant-capital organized wool production as a putting-out system. The growth of wool production made the raising of sheep more profitable and this stimulated the enclosure movement which separated the direct producer from the land. The cottage spinning and weaving of wool began to separate manufacture from agriculture, and the putting-out system was a major step towards capital's gaining control of the production process. The expropriation of the agricultural producer which was the basis of the gradual commodification of labour-power was 'accomplished *in concerto* by the establishment of the wool industry as independent of, rather than directly subordinate to, agriculture'.[6] The domestic handicraft production of woollen articles organized as 'a putting out system by merchant capital interested in international trade typifies the industrial activity of this stage'.[7] The dominant form of capital in the mercantilist stage is merchant-capital, and merchant-capital accumulates by organizing manufacturing as a putting-out system that gradually becomes separated from agriculture and is subordinated to international trade. Wool production is the type of use-value production that is most characteristic of the activities of merchant-capital in so far as it directly lays the foundations for the development of capitalism. This mode of accumulation was supported by the mercantilist policies of the absolute/constitutional monarchy which chartered trading companies and adopted policies such as the Navigation Acts and Corn Laws which directly supported merchant-capital. Mercantilism is the economic policy of the monarchy as it enforces the primitive accumulation of merchant-capital. Most crucial to this process of primitive accumulation is the separation of the direct producer from the land and the separation of manufacture from agriculture, for it is these processes that lay the foundations for the commodification of labour-power. This first stage of the birth and infancy of capitalism is appropriately called 'mercantilism', and it is English wool production organized by merchant-capital that most represents the evolution of the capitalist method of production in this stage.

The triangular trade may have lead to the accumulation of great fortunes, but this was essentially a system of unequal exchanges that did not involve merchant-capital in subsuming the domestic production process in the way the putting-out system did, nor did it involve merchant-capital directly in social processes leading to the commodification of labour-power. Perhaps a case could be made for some other use-value such as coal, but coal production seems minor in comparison with wool and involves various forms of impressed labour (at least in its earlier stages). It is not so directly tied in with the large socioeconomic processes that lead to the commodification of labour-power and the eventual subsumption of the production process by capital, nor does it play so important a role in foreign trade and in the growing national economy. In any case the important point here is not to insist on wool as the most characteristic form of *capitalist* production in the stage of mercantilism, but to show that the dominant type of use-value selected depends both on our knowledge of the law of value and on our grasp of capitalist history.

The stage of mercantilism represents an externalization of the law of value in a situation where labour-power is not yet substantially commodified and where the production process is only indirectly and partially controlled by capital through a putting-out system. But this means that the law of value can only manifest itself in the most embryonic and minimal ways, and to a large extent it is not manifest but is only latent in this stage. This is still primitive accumulation that depends substantially upon extra-economic force and various types of plunder and direct 'rip-off'. However, the beginnings of the law of value can be seen in profit-making based on the exploitation of labour, not through the wage-form but through a system of selling raw wool at a high price to the cottage weavers and buying back the finished cloth cheaply. This was possible because of the monopolistic position of the merchants who were price-makers *vis-à-vis* the cottage weavers who were price-takers. Of course, the exploitation of the cottage weavers was limited by the need to keep a sufficient number alive to do the weaving.

Liberalism, the second stage in the development of capitalism, is firmly established through the industrial revolution that results in factory production and the securing of the reproduction of labour-power as a commodity.[8] According to Uno, the most representative form of use-value production in this stage is English cotton manufacturing, and the form of capital that most successfully operates this sort of light manufacturing of consumer commodities is industrial-capital. With industrial-capital we see the fullest development of a competitive, market-governed economy and along with it the periodic crisis. This mode of capital accumulation is supported by economic policies aimed at overcoming restrictive practices in favour of free trade. This is the stage of classical liberalism with ideas such as *laissez-faire* or 'the least government is the best government' increasingly reflecting faith in the market to regulate the economy in an optimum fashion. The stage of liberalism with its *laissez-faire* tendencies most closely approximates pure capitalism, since in a purely capitalist society the total regulation of real economic life by the market means the disappearance of state economic policies. Total reification or pure capitalism is of course never closely approximated at the level of concrete history, but still it is approached most closely in the industrial capitalism of mid-nineteenth-century England. Thus according to Uno and Sekine capitalism reached its fullest maturity in mid-nineteenth-century England.

In summary, the typical form of use-value production of the liberal stage is cotton manufacturing; the dominant form of capital is competitive industrial-capital; its political location is Britain; and the dominant state economic policies and ideologies revolve around free-trade liberalism.

Because the stage of liberalism is closest to a purely capitalist society it is possible to assume mistakenly that pure theory is simply abstracted from this stage or that this stage somehow represents a varification of pure theory. The liberal stage is closest to pure theory because the sort of light manufacturing represented by cotton manufacturing is closest to the ideal use-values assumed by pure theory. Thus the dominant type of use-value production in this stage is the most conducive to pure theory because it is closest to the ideal use-values needed for the purely competitive market of pure capitalism. But it must be emphasized that at the level of stage theory these use-values are not considered ideal and abstract, and hence active support by the superstructure is necessary. Thus there is an active state during the stage of liberalism, only the dominant type of capital accumulation makes it more and more possible for this state to adopt free-trade and *laissez-faire* policies. Also a note of caution needs to be added that stage theory is still quite abstract and only aims to grasp the dominant *type* of capital accumulation as an abstract material type. Even at the height of this stage in Britain in the 1860s, significant parts of the economy were not even capitalist, or if capitalist, not necessarily the competitive industrial capitalism represented by cotton manufacturing. I will expand further on these points later in the chapter when I give examples of how to use stage theory. The point I want to emphasize here is that there is a great distance between the theory of the liberal stage and pure theory, because it is a distinct and more concrete level of analysis, and that cotton manufacturing is a concrete form of use-value production even though as a type it is closest to the type of ideal use-value production required by pure theory.

The reign of this form of use-value production came to an end in the late nineteenth century with the development of heavy industry and the Great Depression. The most characteristic type of use-value production then became iron and steel.[9] The economies of scale associated with large fixed capital investments in steel production required the long-term mobilization of large amounts of capital and credit. The development of the limited-liability joint-stock company accompanied by the development of the banking system facilitated the rapid centralization of capital in the late nineteenth century. Large banks became very interested in the operations of heavy industry since the banks committed large amounts of credit to the fixed capital investments of heavy industry. The resulting merging of industrial-capital and banking-capital is referred to as 'finance-capital'.

Finance-capital creates various types of monopolistic organization so as to protect its investments from the vagaries of the market. The result is chronic excess capacity which stimulates aggressive expansionism. The state economic policies necessitated by finance-capital are protectionism at home and aggressive expansionism abroad. The protectionism is needed to protect high monopoly prices from international competition in the domestic market, and expansion is needed to take up the slack of chronic excess capital relative to the home market. The development of monopoly and the consequent declining capacity of the

market mechanism successfully to regulate the economy necessitates more aggressive and interventionist policies on the part of
the state in order to support the operations of finance-capital.
Typical policies involve dumping and tariff wars, aggressive
colonial policies and a *'sozialpolitik'* (welfare state) which develops to stem the socialist menace and secure the reproduction of
labour-power as a commodity.[10] All of this results in a rapid and
large growth in the scope of state activities and in the public
expenditures needed to support these activities. Taken together
the state economic policies of finance-capital are referred to as
'imperialism'.

According to Uno and Sekine the German steel industry is the
material-type most representative of finance-capital. Perhaps a
case could be made for the American steel industry, but I do not
want to enter this debate. The point is to derive stage theory from
the dominant and most classical example of a type of capital
accumulation associated with a type of use-value production.
Everyone would agree that the paradigm case of finance-capital is
not any kind of British use-value production; and yet Britain was
the dominant (though declining) world economic power in this
stage. The fact that the dominant type of capital accumulation
does not reach its classical form in the dominant world economic
power is no doubt one reason why this stage of capitalism is
rather more short-lived than the others.

The first successful socialist revolution in 1917 marks the
world-historic start of the transition away from capitalism. In this
phase a dominant form of capital accumulation based on
externalizing the law of value can no longer be constructed. We
cannot, therefore, construct stage theory, but instead must
develop historical theory based upon a unravelling of the law of
value. Whereas in the stage of imperialism, state interventions
were mostly limited to influencing market forces, now state
intervention increasingly substitutes for the market, blocks
market forces and manipulates the market.[11] Markets in land,
labour, capital and money become manipulated and less regulated by commodity-economic principles.

Referring to the period from 1917 to the present as a
transitional phase does not mean that exploitation or the
production for profit cease, but only that the structural dynamics
of economic life can less and less be understood by the law of
value. The law of value loses its inner coherence as the market is

undermined by monopoly and by the state. Theorizing this period as a transitional phase rather than a capitalist stage proper is very important if we are to understand the character of the period and theorize it correctly. It is necessary to understand both that the law of value has failed and why it has done so in order to understand the statified economies that have developed. It is necessary to see that this is a transitional stage in which increasingly the world is becoming socialist, albeit at first with often rather primitive forms of socialism. The world-historic failure of the law of value must be fully grasped if the Left is effectively to criticize the tragically inappropriate 'free enterprise' ideologies still put forward by some of the most powerful economic powers.

The transitional phase from 1917 to the present can be divided roughly into two periods: the inter-war period and the post-World War II period. In the inter-war period the aim was to re-establish finance-capital and the gold standard; the result was depression, fascism and eventually World War II. The post-World War II period was based on an American-dominated international monetary system and American international policies aimed at keeping as much of the world open to American investment as possible. This was combined with quasi-Keynesian policies domestically and the internationalization of production. Some of the contradictions of this system are now becoming all too manifest, as the world teeters on the brink of financial crisis and governments everywhere begin to adopt wrenching austerity policies.

This view of twentieth-century capitalism has very important theoretical consequences. It is all right to speak of the dominant world economy in the 1980s as 'capitalist' if we are speaking loosely, but in our theorizing this might lull us into using inappropriate categories since we need to understand the senses in which the current conjuncture is not capitalist or is disintegrating capitalism that is in the process of becoming something else. For example, in the approach I am advocating fascism is not a capitalist superstructural form but a transitional form in the sense that it develops in the world-historic phase of transition away from capitalism. The transitional character of our age helps us to understand both the potentialities and dangers that we face. I have intentionally used 'transition away from capitalism' and not 'transition to socialism' since I think other outcomes than socialism are possible. The only way that we can achieve socialism, and its achievement is a real possibility, is radically to democratize the societies we live in, but I do not think any one will claim at this juncture that this will be an easy task.

3 THE LOGICAL STATUS OF STAGE THEORY

It should be clear from the preceding argument that stage theory is a disctinct level of analysis that cannot be directly deduced from pure theory but involves the concretization of pure theory in a historical epoch. If stage theory is not deduced from pure theory, neither is it abstracted from historical data. It may appear at first glance that 'merchant-capital', 'industrial-capital' and 'finance-capital' are Weberian ideal-types. I want to emphasize their differences by referring to the type concepts of stage theory as 'material-types' as opposed to 'ideal-types' or 'average-types'. Let me start by exploring the contrast between ideal-type and material-type.[12]

Take Weber's ideal-type 'charismatic domination' and compare it with the material-type 'finance-capital'. 'Charismatic domination' is constructed by a process of selective abstraction that eventually arrives at an extreme case which represents the most purified and abstract picture of a type of domination in contrast with other types of domination. The pure type of charismatic domination may never exist and in this sense it is a 'utopia', but real examples of domination may be sorted out according to whether they manifest charismatic domination to a greater or lesser degree. Such a concept is subjective in the sense that the knowing subject uses imagination and abstraction to create an extreme-type for the sake of highlighting and emphasizing some aspect of empirical reality. An indefinite number of ideal-types can be generated given the emphases placed upon reality and given the particular point of view and interests of the knowing subject. Not only is subjective imagination used in constructing the ideal-type but also it is used in applying it, as in the case of trying to figure out to what extent and in what ways the domination of President Ronald Reagan is charismatic.

The material-type concept 'finance-capital' is very different from the above description of a Weberian ideal-type. It is arrived at by concretizing the basic contradiction of the dialectic of capital between value and use-values. We look for the type of use-value production that is most characteristic and dominant in each stage and abstract from that our material-type concept. Thus German steel production most represents the dominant form of production in the stage of imperialism. In order to be capitalistically managed, mass production of steel requires that value organize itself in the form of limited-liability joint-stock corporations. The massive long-term fixed capital investments of heavy industry require the mobilization and centralization of society's saving and lending power, and hence the merging of banking-capital with industrial-capital to form finance-capital. Thus though 'finance-capital' is an abstraction it is an abstraction based upon a material-type of production which is in fact dominant in a particular stage of capitalist development. The dialectic of capital gives us an objective grounding so that our task is limited to finding the ways in which the dialectic concretizes itself. According to Weber's three-fold typology of domination, any empirical example of domination must involve a mix of charismatic, traditional and legal–rational domination. But I am not saying that any empirical case of capitalist production must be a mix of merchant-, industrial- and finance-capital; rather I am saying that these types of capital succeed one another in being historically dominant and that they have a determinant relationship both to the dialectic of capital and to history.

In summary, then, it is my contention that: first, unlike an ideal-type, a material-type does exist, and is not a one-sided utopia constructed for analytic purposes. Second, there is not an unlimited number of material-types, but only one that serves as the paradigm case. Third, the material-type is not transhistorical but instead is hegemonic only in a specific stage of capitalist development. Fourth, the construction of a material-type is guided by the objective reference-point of the dialectic of capital and not by a particular emphasis desired by the knowing subject.

'Finance-capital' is a pure-type concept in the sense that the historical reality of finance-capital always involves local peculiarities. Although German steel may be the purest example, in its empirical concreteness it involves its own peculiar details and irrelevant contingencies. So we theorize the German steel industry as a *type* of organization and operation of capitalist accumulation and not as a detailed descriptive history. Thus though finance-capital really does tend to dominate the stage of imperialism, its concrete working in France, Britain and the United States is bound to display considerable diversity.

It is important to emphasize that I do not arrive at the concept of finance-capital by abstracting from Germany, the United States, France and Britain to see what they all have in common in this stage. Such an approach is empiricist and does not produce an ideal-type or a material-type but rather an average-type. If the concept 'finance-capital' is an average-type abstracted from these 'four pillars of world finance capital', then we must abstract from their differences and find what they all have in common.[13] It may turn out that protective tariffs play a much bigger role in Germany than in Britain so that the protectionism falls away from our concept of finance-capital. Or it may be that banks play a bigger role in Germany than in the United States, so the role of banks must be made secondary. The stock-market may play a bigger role in the United States than in Germany, thus either making it secondary or requiring some more abstract concept that would combine both banks and stock-markets. What do France, Germany, Britain and the United States all have in common? The answer is monopoly. An average-type analysis produces an overly abstract concept that does not bring out the interplay of political policy and capital accumulation in its dominant form. Because political policies are likely to be different between nations, this dimension is likely to precipitate out so that the conception ends up being not only overly abstract but also economistic. The Uno/Sekine approach enables us to see why finance-capital developed later and less completely in Britain and France, so that we do not allow these cases to water down our abstraction based on the purer German case.

The material-type concepts of stage theory are based on a dialectical approach in contrast to the abstract impressionism of empiricist average-types or of Weberian ideal-types. Material-type concepts theorize the type of capital that is actually dominant in each stage of capitalist development, and thereby represent the externalization of the dialectic of capital in history. They are not mental constructs or analytic models with indeterminant relations to empirical reality, rather they display a determinant relationship between the inner logic of capital and its historical development.

The sequence of categories in the dialectic of capital is a

necessary sequence and this necessity derives from the overcoming of use-value obstacles by value in its effort to subsume an entire economic society to its motion. One necessary component of the dialectic of capital is periodic crisis, but this necessity is different from the necessity of imperialist war that emerges from the stage theory of imperialism. This is because the sequence of stages represented by the production of wool, cotton and steel is not a necessary sequence in the sense that we cannot show that the dialectic of capital must be externalized in these and only in these dominant types. It is true that capitalism has a tendency to produce more complex and more socialized use-values as it develops, and that these use-values are less and less amenable to being managed purely by the motion of value. Capitalism therefore has a limited life span, limited by a historical range of use-values that it can manage. Outside this range large chunks of use-value production begin to escape its grasp. With the development of heavy industry, which is the underlying material reality of the stage of imperialism, we already see a distinct weakening of the law of value. Thus although capitalism necessarily has a limited life span, it is not possible to show that the life span must take exactly the form that it does through the three stages. In other words the stage of imperialism cannot be deduced from pure theory because the historical environment in which it is externalized includes elements that are contingently given outside the operation of the law of value. But once these elements are given, we can say that the law of value will tend to operate in a particular way. Given the stage of imperialism, imperialist wars are a necessary outcome, but this stage itself cannot be shown to be necessary because it in part rests upon contingent givens (e.g. heavy industry and certain technological inventions). Therefore the necessity for imperialist wars in the stage of imperialism is a weaker necessity than the necessity for periodic crisis in a purely capitalist society, because it is a necessity based on a state of affairs that is itself based in part on contingent givens. To mark this difference it is perhaps more accurate to say that in the stage of imperialism strong pressures are created that make imperialist war a likely outcome.

4 APPLICATIONS OF STAGE THEORY

What I mean by 'stage theory' will become clearer if I examine some possible uses of it to clarify controversial issues concerning crisis theory and class struggle. Further applications of stage theory will be developed in later chapters.

First, I shall look at the question of crisis theory. At the level of pure theory I argued that crises arise first from the difficulties of maintaining the commodification of labour-power and second from the commodification of fixed capital. Capitalist crisis is rooted in the alternating widening and deepening phases of accumulation, and the result of crises is to restructure the basic capital–labour value relation on a new basis that permits another round of expansion. Crises force capital to renew its technological base and to replenish the reservoir of surplus population. But all of this assumes the total reification and complete commodification of a purely capitalist society. At the more concrete level of stage theory crisis will take different forms depending on the dominant type of capital accumulation. Because the dominant type of use-value production in the stage of liberalism is closest to the ideal use-values of pure theory, we would expect crises in Britain in this stage to conform most closely to the periodic crises of a purely capitalist society.[14]

In the stage of mercantilism crises are another matter altogether. Neither labour-power nor fixed capital are yet extensively commodified so that crises would not be generated by the logic of the law of value. Crises in this case are generated by external factors (external to the law of value) or by the extremely imperfect working of the law of value. Crises would likely be produced by sudden price changes due to speculation, new discoveries, new markets, monopolistic price manipulation, political price manipulation or by class struggle in the form of popular resistance to price changes or to the commodification of labour-power. Thus we would not expect general periodic crises in the stage of mercantilism but rather crisis of an occasional and partial character associated with the growing pains of capitalism in its early development.

This approach shows the need to reconsider the whole question of capitalist crises in the stage of imperialism. Because of the size and monpolistic character of firms in this stage, they have greater capabilities to stave off full-blown crises and indeed such crises become less and less tolerable the larger the units of capital. Protectionist policies guard against international price competition, and aggressive expansionism and support for finance-capital on the part of the state can forestall crises by exporting the problems that give rise to them, or by shifting those problems onto the non-cartellized sector or onto the backs of workers. When crises do finally occur, recovery is likely to be slower because cartellized industries will attempt to maintain high prices even in the face of a depression and this of course makes recovery much more difficult for non-cartellized industries, and creates a situation of stagnation or prolonged depression.[15] Even when high cartel prices finally do collapse, the crises will not necessarily bring about a renewed technological base and value proportion which will ensure another round of expansion, and this is because the health of the economy depends increasingly on aggressive expansionism, protectionism and nationalism. But this requires a strong state and aggressive imperialist policies, so crisis theory can no longer be theorized in purely economic terms. In fact it is precisely because crises in the imperialist stage can no longer perform all the functions that they perform in a purely capitalist society, and because each core state tries aggressively to export it economic problems that imperialist wars become likely. Periodic crises in the stage of imperialism cannot be theorized as a direct expression of the law of value and cannot be theorized in purely economic terms. Indeed the existence of finance-capital deflects the law of value significantly in this case altering the nature of crises and requiring significant state intervention. The partial inffectiveness of periodic crises in this stage of capitalist development must be considered a primary underlying cause for imperialist war.

Next let me briefly consider the issue of class struggle from the point of view of stage theory. In the stage of mercantilism, class struggle cannot take the form of capital versus proletariat since the proletariat does not yet exist in the putting-out system. What is possible is the rebellion of cottage weavers against the prices that the merchants pay for their cloth, or a revolt of consumers in general against high prices, for example, bread riots, or the uprising of peasants uprooted by enclosures, or other reactions of populations that are unsettled by primitive accumulation. These resistances against the commodification of socioeconomic life and particularly against the commodification of labour-power may be seen as class struggles in embryo, but in reality the groups in question, to speak strictly, are not capitalist classes and in part their rebellion is against being made into a class – in particular into a landless industrial proletariat. In the stage of mercantilism, the global expansion of capital generally relies upon slavery and forced labour and this is because not enough people have yet been pushed off the land to provide immigrant labour in the new territories. Even in the core states capital only manages partially to subsume the labour and production process through the putting-out system, so that it is not surprising that in the new territories pre-capitalist modes of forced labour are used.

This sort of struggle against being made into a class continues well into the stage of liberalism, but in this stage the victory of industrial capitalism and the commodification of labour-power take place. With these events, the industrial proletariat becomes a reality and we see the beginning of class-consciousness with various movements putting forward demands that clearly represent the interests and the point of view of the industrial proletariat. In the stage of liberalism we see the beginnings of class struggle in its classical form – that is capital versus the industrial proletariat.

In the stage of imperialism class struggle takes further new forms. The cartellized sectors give rise to strong unions and a socialist movement, while the existence of cartellized and non-cartellized sectors stratifies the working-class. Furthermore, the relation between centre and periphery creates a further stratification with many colonial workers suffering the violence and superexploitation of primitive accumulation. The growing power of the working-class in the core states and the need of finance-capital for a more stable labour force give rise to the beginnings of the welfare state and to political parties in the modern sense. The dangers of a growing socialist movement are offset by concessions and by a nationalist and inter-imperialist rivalry that finally issues in world war.

This analysis shows that strictly speaking capitalist classes do not even exist (except possibly in embryo) in the stage of mercantilism, and in the stage of imperialism class structure becomes complex both within the core states and even more so when viewed globally. The self-purifying tendency that takes historical capitalism closer to pure capitalism in the stage of liberalism is reversed in the stage of imperialism so that historical capitalism begins to move away from further purification. Starting with the stage of imperialism, there is no longer a historical tendency towards two homogeneous and polarized classes (of course there may be conjunctural tendencies towards polarization). Class struggle is increasingly overlaid with national struggles and struggles of particular strata and fractions within classes or even intermediate strata between classes. In fact the strong state required by the imperialist stage with its welfare state policies is the beginning of the modern service sector with its intermediate strata that have fuelled so much controversy within Marxist discourse on class.

5 CLASSICAL THEORIES OF IMPERIALISM

Since stage theory was really born with the theory of imperialism and since there is the most literature on this stage, I shall carry out a critical analysis of some of this literature to develop further the implications of the Uno/Sekine approach.

In his recent work *The Geometry of Imperialism*, Giovanni Arrighi claims that the Marxian theory of imperialism has become a 'tower of babel'.[16] This no doubt overstates the confusion, but it must be admitted that this particular body of literature displays a considerable proliferation of approaches and conceptual frameworks.

Classical theorists of imperialism such as Hilferding, Luxemburg, Lenin and Bukharin have often been analysed from a very politically motivated point of view. Because Lenin lead a successful socialist revolution, his text *Imperialism: The Highest Stage of Capitalism* has been most preferred and most influential. Because Luxemburg is often seen as a heroic and principled fighter against opportunism her *Accumulation of Capital* is also looked upon with favour. Hilferding's *Finance Capital* has often been written off because after he wrote the book he became a social democrat, so that interpreters look for the seeds of his revisionism in his earlier theoretical work. I shall argue that Hilferding's *Finance Capital* is the best of the classical works on imperialism.

So far the Marxian theory of imperialism does not have a clearly defined theoretical object or a theoretical approach with a firm scientific grounding. Lacking basic epistemological clarity, very often political or ideological criteria are substituted for scientific criteria in the development of reasons to accept or reject particular theories. Sometimes theories are accepted or rejected because they are branded as Third Worldist, reformist, economist or Stalinist and not because they have been shown to be valid or invalid, scientifically weak or strong. Some Marxists seem to think that Marx's *Capital* is a storehouse of scientific categories that can be borrowed free of charge. We find value categories being used directly to explain the latest twist or turn of history or to back up preconceived political positions. Unfortunately there is insufficient understanding of the internal integrity of the theory of capital, and of how its categories may best be used to help understand history.

A further problem of interpretation has been the tendency to apply these theories to post-World War II capitalism and to judge them by their ability to theorize the current conjuncture. In order to begin to clear away the confusion from the theory of imperialism, it is necessary to reconsider the scientific adequacy of these theories for the stage they were actually trying to theorize, namely the stage that begins around 1870 and ends in 1917, and then to determine their applicability to the current conjuncture. And we need to evaluate the theories according to their scientific adequacy and not according to the position of the author in the pantheon of Marxist heros or villains.

Although Marx had some awareness that the theoretical object of *Capital* was pure capitalism, he assumed that capitalism would become more and more pure. The early signs of the development of monopoly that he saw before his death in 1883 were interpreted as introducing a phase of transition away from capitalism that would rapidly be succeeded by socialism.[17] Marx could not foresee that finance-capital would, with the help of state policies, establish itself as a stage of capitalist development. It was only when the stage of imperialism was in decay with the advent of World War I that Lenin could first conceptualize it as a distinct stage of capitalist development.

Lenin correctly saw monopoly capitalism or imperialism as a stage of capitalism, and though his five-point list of essential features is a rough approximation, his pamphlet on imperialism as a whole is not a work of science so much as a popular polemic. Since Lenin's aims were primarily political and strategic, we cannot expect him to produce a scientifically rigorous theory. Lenin's recognition of stages of capitalist development is an important theoretical contribution, but his inability to arrive at a clear understanding of exactly what a stage is or of how the theory of capital in general relates to the theory of stages has been reproduced by all prior and subsequent Marxists in the Western tradition. In general these two questions about the character of the theoretical object and method of stage theory have not been focused on with sufficient theoretical intensity, so that they have either been ignored altogether or have been glossed over with simplistic solutions.

Hilferding

Hilferding's *Finance Capital*, first published in 1910, is the most theoretically sophisticated work dealing with imperialism.[18] Unfortunately this work has not been widely read, and it is the popularizers Lenin and Bukharin who are read and studied. But Lenin and Bukharin wrote polemical pamphlets on imperialism and not serious theoretical works. Their pamphlets were largely derivative and the greatest influence on both of them was Hilferding. Hilferding's *Finance Capital* is an impressive theoretical work, but it suffers from the logical–historical method which prevailed in all the classical writings on imperialism. Because Hilferding lacks a clear conception of pure capitalism and the necessity for levels of analysis, he has a tendency to move directly from the necessary inner connections of pure capitalism to more concrete levels of analysis, thus mixing levels of analysis that must be kept logically distinct. For example, he mixes the theory of money in pure theory with monetary institutions that are specific to the stage of imperialism and the theory of crisis in pure theory with considerations of crisis in the stage of imperialism.[19] Finance-capital is seen as the logical–historical outgrowth of capitalist development so that no conception of stage is necessary.[20] In this fashion pure theory and stage theory are collapsed together into a single logical–historical theory which treats the necessity for World War I as no different from the necessity for periodic capitalist crisis. Despite these theoretical weaknesses, Hilferding does make impressive strides towards an adequate conception of the dominant form of capital and accompanying state economic policies for the imperialist stage of capitalist development. Although his analysis of ideology and state policy is more developed than in other classical works, still this analysis is overly abbreviated.

Hilferding does recognize the primacy of the iron and steel industry to the stage of imperialism and seems to grasp intuitively that Germany represents the purest type or most classical example of finance-capital. However, he does not see the importance of the dominant form of use-value production as the link to the basic value/use-value contradiction of pure theory and therefore as the basis of stage theory. Also he does not argue systematically that the German case is the most typical, though he provides fuel for such an argument by considering some of the special and atypical characteristics of US finance-capital which would be the most obvious competitor for being the classical type of finance-capital.[21] It is because he intuitively focuses on the German case that his conception of finance-capital is as accurate as it is.

Unlike Bukharin and Luxemburg, Hilferding does not put forward a theory of economic collapse. Hilferding believes that imperialist war will 'unleash revolutionary storms'.[22] In this sense imperialism will tend to sharpen class struggle and polarize society. He also sees the 'tendency for finance capital to socialize production as facilitating enormously the task of overcoming capitalism'.[23] And though he uses the word 'collapse', the whole thrust of his argument is against an inevitable collapse. He makes it clear that for the proletariat to benefit from these tendencies, it must adopt a position of implacable opposition to the expansionist and militarist policies of finance-capital:

. . . victory can come only from an unremitting struggle against the policy, for only then will the proletariat be the beneficiary of the collapse to which it must lead, a collapse which will be political and social, not economic; for the idea of a purely economic collapse makes no sense.[24]

In other words victory comes not from the working of economic laws, but from a social and political mobilization which, though facilitated by objective conditions, has nothing automatic about it and indeed requires organization and leadership.

Hilferding is sometimes criticized for basing too much of his argument on the German case.[25] I have indicated that this is precisely the strength of his book. He does not neglect the internationalization of capital that occurs during the stage of finance-capital, but he sees this internationalization accurately as having a firm national base secured with protective tariffs. According to Hilferding:

> . . . international agreements represent a kind of truce rather than an enduring community of interest, since every change in the tariff defences, every variation in the market relations between states, alters the basis of the agreement and makes necessary the conclusion of new contracts. More solid structure can only emerge when either free trade more or less eliminates national barriers, or the basis of the cartel is not the protective tariff but primarily a natural monopoly, as in the case of petroleum.[26]

Lenin

Though Hilferding's conceptualization of finance-capital lays the basis for a stage theory of imperialism, Hilferding himself did not develop the concept 'stage'. In Hilferding's thinking finance-capital is simply an extension of Marx's *Capital*.[27] However, I have argued that the concept 'stage' is all-important if we are to escape the pitfalls of the logical–historical method. Lenin's *Imperialism* is of theoretical importance primarily because the concept 'stage' is for the first time brought to the fore. But because Lenin was under the influence of the all-pervasive logical–historical method, and because his intention was primarily polemical and not theoretical, the full theoretical implications of the concept were not developed by Lenin. In particular Lenin did not see stage theory as a distinct level of analysis, and therefore he did not clearly pose the problem of the relation between the theory of capital in general and stage theory.

Lenin argues that at a certain stage of development, concentration leads to monopoly.[28] This is clearly inadequate. First, he does not clearly distinguish concentration and centralization of capital. Concentration by itself (growth by reinvesting profits) would not necessarily ever lead to monopoly because it leads to larger but not necessarily fewer enterprises. The development of finance-capital in the late nineteenth century was primarily the result not of concentration but of centralization (merging existing units of capital). Though pure theory can outline the general tendencies towards both concentration and centralization, the more concrete analysis of stage theory is necessary to explain the extremely rapid centralization of capital in the late nineteenth century. The concept of finance-capital, the dominant form of capital, is necessary to grasp this rapid centralization of capital. I contend that neither concentration nor centralization at the level of a purely capitalist society can possibly explain the rapid centralization that occurred from 1890 to 1905. To understand this, we must move to the more concrete level of stage theory which brings in considerations of the type of use-value production that required this rapid 'merger movement'. It is not enough to know that capital has an abstract tendency to concentrate and centralize in order to explain this sudden and radical centralization that occurred at this particular time in history. For this we need stage theory and its concept 'finance-capital'.

Lenin centres his theory of imperialism on the concept 'monopoly-capital' as opposed to 'finance-capital'. The concept of 'monopoly-capital' is as applicable today as it was in 1900, but a concept so lacking in historical specificity that it masks over the extremely great differences between the pre-World War I and post-World War II economic epochs is not very useful. 'Finance-capital' as developed by Hilferding is a more concrete concept than Lenin's 'monopoly-capital' because it shows how the basic contradiction between value and use-value is concretized in a particular organization of capital in a particular epoch. Hilferding's concept of 'finance-capital' develops the *modus operandi* of the dominant form of capital and accompanying state policies; whereas 'monopoly' simply refers to the situation of a few large firms in each major industry.

At times Lenin slips into a empiricist rather than a dialectical approach. His concept of 'imperialism' is arrived at in part by abstracting from 'the four pillars': Germany, France, Britain and the United States.[29] Using this approach, he arrives at too high a level of abstraction, where the dominant form of capital and accompanying state policies lose their historical specificity and internal integrity. The result is looseness and abstractness. For example, tariff policy is much less important in Britain than in Germany, so when he abstracts from their differences to arrive at what they have in common, tariff policy precipitates out and becomes secondary. The dialectical method formulates stage theory by looking for the concretization of the dialectic of capital that is the purest or most representative type for the epoch. In this way we can study a concrete and coherent paradigm as the dominant type and be clear about how this type necessarily operates, and we avoid the abstract impressionism of empirical abstraction. Lenin's theory of imperialism is as good as it is because Lenin had read *Capital* and therefore had a grasp of the inner logic of capitalism, so that lurking behind what appears at times to be a method of empirical abstraction is a good grasp of the inner workings of capitalism. Also because of the influence of Hilferding on Lenin, Germany tends to become the paradigm case, though less explicitly so than with Hilferding, and occasionally compromised by the empiricism of the 'four pillars' approach.

The logical–historical method that permeated the work of all the classics dealing with imperialism tends to lead to economism. This is because the laws of motion of pure capitalism are purely economic, and if we see imperialism as the natural outgrowth of pure capitalism and see the analysis of imperialism as a simple extension of *Capital*, then our analysis of imperialism is likely to be formulated in purely economic terms. But at the level of stage theory the state plays an important supporting role to the dominant form of capital accumulation. In the case of finance-capital, politics and economics are so integrated that finance-capital is inconceivable without the collaboration of particular state policies. The variation of state policies from country to country is likely to be even greater than the variation of economic forms, so that Lenin's method of empirical abstraction from the 'four pillars' will precipitate out most of the political, leading to an analysis that is overly economic and overly abstract. Of all the classical writers, Hilferding deals most with the political dimension, but even he does not clearly trace the necessary connections between the dominant form of capital accumulation and state policy. His focus on Germany as the classical case of finance-capital enables him to get further than the other writers with this, and though a clear theory of state policy is not worked out, the raw material for such a theory is there.

Luxemburg

Both Rosa Luxemburg's *Accumulation of Capital* (published in 1913) and her *Anti-Critique* (published in 1915) were influential and controversial from their first appearance in print.[30] In order to understand her conception of imperialism, it is first necessary to look at her general views on the accumulation of capital. This is because for her imperialism is simply the accumulation of capital in the phase before its final collapse. After a lengthy reconsideration of the reproduction schema at the end of volume II of *Capital*, Luxemburg comes to the conclusion that:

> Marx's diagram of enlarged reproduction cannot explain the actual historical process of accumulation. . . . The diagram sets out to describe the accumulative process on the assumption that the capitalists and workers are the sole agents of capitalist accumulation.[31]

> From the aspect both of realising the surplus value and of procuring the material elements of constant capital, international trade is a prime necessity for the historical existence of capitalism – and international trade which under actual conditions is essentially an exchange between capitalistic and non-capitalistic modes of production.[32]

In Luxemburg's view the reproduction schema assumes a purely capitalist society, but such a society is impossible because neither capitalists nor workers can realize surplus value. A third party, the outside market, upon which capitalism is always dependent becomes necessary for accumulation. Since capitalism is not a self-dependent totality, it cannot be theorized dialectically. Instead, she argues, we must analyse the history of the exchange between capitalism and its non-capitalist milieu. She claims that there is a self-purifying tendency to capitalism since it does gradually absorb its non-capitalist milieu. As the non-capitalist milieu disappears, we approach pure capitalism, but since pure capitalism cannot accumulate, collapse becomes inevitable. The theory of a purely capitalist society, therefore, is not a theory of capitalism's inner workings but is a theory of an impossible utopia in the sense that capitalism as a mode of production must destroy itself to the extent that it becomes purely capitalist.

Luxemburg believes that the alternative to her view is that pure capitalism can create its own market, but the problem here is that 'capitalist accumulation becomes limitless once capitalist production has built a sufficient market for itself'.[33] and 'If we assume . . . the economic infinity of capitalist accumulation, then the vital foundation on which socialism rests will disappear.'[34] In other words, because it is impossible to generate a theory of crisis and collapse from Marx's reproduction schema, they are inadequate as explanatory models of accumulation. Apparently the idea of socialism is viable only if supported by a theory of collapse.

Since the theory of capitalist accumulation must, according to Luxemburg, focus on the exchange between capitalism and its non-capitalist milieu, what does Luxemburg have to say about this all-imporant exchange relation? Her answer is that the method of violence prevails, so that this all-important relation is not an economic exchange at all:

> The method of violence; then, is the immediate consequence of the clash between capitalism and the organizations of a natural economy which would restrict accumulation.[35]

> Only the continuous and progressive disintegration of non-capitalist organizations makes accumulation of capital possible.[36]

The method of violence that prevails in primitive accumulation continues unabated throughout the history of capital accumulation since primitive accumulation itself continues unabated. Capitalist accumulation is primarily and always primitive accumulation. Imperialism, then, is the final intense competition over the last remaining bits of non-capitalist milieu as capitalism reaches a purity that will ensure its collapse.

> Imperialism is the political expression of the accumulation of capital in its competitive struggle for what remains still open of the non-capitalist environment. . . . Though imperialism is the historical method for prolonging the career of capitalism, it is also a sure means of bringing it to a swift conclusion.[37]

Imperialism does not differ fundamentally from earlier accumulation based on the method of violence, it is simply the swan-song of capitalism as it reaches its historical zenith and finally divides up the entire globe prior to World War I. Therefore imperialism in the early twentieth century is the final expression of primitive accumulation.

Luxemburg is mistaken in her view that the disappearance of the non-capitalist milieu is the same thing as capitalism becoming more pure. Uno and Sekine demonstrate that during the declining stage, the stage of imperialism, capitalism becomes less pure even though it increases its hegemony over the world. This is because the development of both monopolistic practices and aggressive state interventionism are large steps away from pure capitalism. Thus capitalism does not become more pure as it absorbs the last of the non-capitalist milieu. If anything capitalism declines not because it becomes pure, but because it fails to become pure. The use-value obstacles of economic life are such that past a certain point capital must seriously compromise itself in order to increase its hegemony; hegemony increases, but the entire system becomes less capitalist.

By overemphasizing primitive accumulation and the method of violence, Luxemburg loses sight of the uniqueness of capitalism. Capitalism is the first mode of production in history that can even imagine '*laissez-faire*'. A purely capitalist society represents an economy that operates without the intervention of extra-economic force, and this is one of its most fundamental defining characteristics that differentiates capitalism from all other modes of production. No doubt at the level of history, capitalism continually resorts to the method of violence, but we should not allow this fact to blind us to the historical specificity of capitalism and lead us to collapse capitalism into an undifferentiated history of violence and struggle. For Luxemburg, not only is the specificity of capitalism lost, but also the specificity of stages of capitalist development. Imperialism is not so much a stage but just the latest manifestation of the method of violence.

Far from 'properly understanding' Marx, Luxemburg undermines the objectivity and scientificity of Marxist theory. If capitalism is basically parasitic, as Luxemburg claims, then it cannot be rigorously theorized as a mode of production that has internal integrity. The theory of a purely capitalist society and the law of value are completely undermined. Theory and history are collapsed together to the detriment of both: theory loses objectively and rigour, and history loses its specificity. A number of commentators claim that Luxemburg's greatest contribution is her focus on the interface between capitalism and its non-capitalist milieu, but to the extent that she abandons the law of value, she has no objective referent for arriving at criteria which would clearly distinguish capitalism from its non-capitalist milieu.[38] If we are not clear about what capitalism is, then neither can we be clear about the non-capitalist milieu.

In his critique of Luxemburg, Bukharin recognizes some of her errors when he writes:

> One has to know that abstract theory is a key to the knowledge of reality and one has to know how to handle it . . . between abstractions and their applications to empirical reality there are a whole lot of logical steps, which under no circumstances may be omitted. . . . Any analysis of the relation between the capitalist world and the 'third persons' has to be more concrete than theoretical constructions of *Capital*.[39]

Bukharin recognizes that *Capital* theorizes pure capitalism which must be mediated with the historical, but he himself is too caught up in the logical–historical method ever fully to draw the implications of this. Bukharin slides over the theoretical problem of precisely specifying these relations by use of a rather poetic metaphor. According to Bukharin, even in the stage of imperialism, the overwhelming majority of the world's population remain outside the capitalist mode of production; and yet capitalism 'is the conductor in the concerto of economic forms'.[40]

Like Luxemburg, Bukharin adheres to a theory of collapse, but for him the underlying contradiction is not the loss of a non-capitalist milieu but the contradition between the internationalization of productive forces and the nationally limited methods of appropriation.[41] Though his critique of Luxemburg is largely correct, Bukharin also slides into a theory of collapse which is the all-too-often economistic outcome of the logical–historical method.

Conclusions

I must conclude by emphasizing that even the best of the classics, Hilferding's *Finance Capital*, is far from being an adequate theory of the stage of imperialism from 1870 to 1917. All of the attempts to theorize this world-historic stage that I have considered are inclined towards economism because they attempt to derive their theory too directly from *Capital*. But stage theory must grasp the integration of the dominant form of capital accumulation with the political and ideological, and it is only Hilferding who proceeds any distance at all with this task. The levels of analysis approach developed by Uno offers us a much sharper conception of the inner essence of capitalism, and at the same time a method of relating this understanding in a systmatic way to more concrete organizational forms of capital. In this way we maintain the rigour of the laws of motion of capitalism at one level of analysis, and we can use this rigour to aid us in developing a more adequate conceptialization of stages of capitalist development. This in turn can serve to orient our study at a historical level where signposts are needed to guide our paths of analysis through dense and rapidly changing landscapes.

6 RECENT THEORIES OF IMPERIALISM AND UNDERDEVELOPMENT

Because the theories of imperialism developed since World War II are largely based upon the work of Lenin and Luxemburg, their errors tend to be further compounded. Lack of clarity about the relation between the theory of capital and capitalist history lead to eclectic borrowings from Marx's *Capital* coupled with ideas of monopoly capitalism which often produce a theoretical muddle.

There has been a mushrooming of Marxist literature on imperialism and monopoly capitalism in recent years. Most of this literatue has suffered from two major weaknesses: first, in seeing the post-World War II period as a continuation of the stage of imperialism or monopoly capitalism, it fails to understand the specificity of this period; and second, in following the logical–historical method, it tries to apply concepts of Marx's *Capital* directly to the current conjuncture. Out of these basic weaknesses flow numerous other shortcomings. For example, by applying the law of value to the current conjuncture, it arrives at economistic interpretations, which fail to emphasize the importance of the political and which see the law of value operating where it cannot. In unconsciously sliding back and forth between pure theory and the historical concrete, it tends to overgeneralize and undermine the integrity of theory and distort our understanding of history. As a result, it fails to grasp either the specificity of distinct stages of capitalist development or the peculiar features of the current conjuncture.

Most recent works on imperialism or monopoly capitalism are theoretically weakened by the failure to see the necessity for three distinct levels of theory. Capitalism has an inherent tendency to expand; this much is established clearly at the most abstract level of theory. The actual form that this expansion takes is delimited at the level of stage theory by the predominant structure of capital and accompanying state policies. Historically capital first takes root in certain areas, and it develops very unevenly on a world scale. At the level of stage theory, we can understand types and tendencies of expansion during a particular stage. Thus merchant-capital, small manufacturing capital and finance-capital foster certain types of expansion and place structural limits on the types of expansion that are possible. Actual forms of expansion such as the relation between Britain and India between 1750 and 1900 must be theorized at a historical level.

Baran and Sweezy

Monopoly Capital by Baran and Sweezy is an important and influential work.[42] They place a strong emphasis on the break between competitive and monopoly capitalism and argue for a separate theory of the laws of motion of monopoly capitalism in contrast to Marx's *Capital* which was based on competitive capitalism.[43] Their book focuses on the problems of excess capital in monopoly capitalism and is particularly strong in bringing out the irrational and reactionary character of post-World War II capitalism with its dependence on military spending. If the strongest part of the book is its underscoring of important features of post-World War II capitalism, its greatest weakness is its theoretic infrastructure.

Baran and Sweezy assume the theory of monopoly-capital is at the same level of analysis as the law of value, and this leads them into a number of errors. For example, they see only one stage from 1870 to the present. But the differences between the classical stage of imperialism from 1870 to World War I and post-World War II capitalism are very great. Although it is true that monopoly-capital and excess exist in both periods, the modes of operation of monopoly and the ways that problems of excess capital are dealt with differ greatly. Thus their theory is too abstract and too economistic to deal with the specific modes of accumulation and accompanying state policies that are dominant in these two periods. Let me consider some of the differences for a moment. In the classical period (1875–1917) the international gold standard was operative, and now the international monetary system is completely different. Then the internationalization of production was minimal, today it is not. Then the state lacked the capability to manage social demand, and now demand is managed as a matter of course. Then indebtedness was sharply constrained in comparison to the debt expansion now. Then the economic weight of the state was small and the welfare state was just beginning, and now the economic weight of the state is immense. Then there was a small service sector, and now there is a large one. Then no socialist movement had achieved power, and now half the world favours some form of socialism. The abilities of monopolies and of political forces to manipulate the economy are much greater today than in the stage of imperialism when the market was still basically sovereign. Baran and Sweezy's theory of monopoly capitalism is too abstract and economistic adequately to take account of these differences.

A levels of analysis approach and a recognition of the specificity of the stage of imperialism would greatly strengthen their book. The law of value is still operative in the stage of imperialism though weakened and distorted, but the period from 1917 to the present should be theorized as a transitional phase. Baran and Sweezy continually emphasize the dependency of monopoly-capital on exogenous factors, but this is precisely the situation in a phase of transition when the law of value has lost its internal integrity and coherence. In a transitional phase, it is correct to argue that the law of value does not apply, but then there are no laws of motion with the same logical status as the law of value. It is then possible to move away from an economistic single-factor analysis that places too much weight on the problem of surplus absorption to a recognition of the importance of political factors in their own right. The present conjuncture could then be understood as a movement away from the law of value in a phase of transition with a serious underconsumption problem as one factor in a complex which includes consideration of such things as the internationalization of capital, forms of state intervention, the international division of labour, international finance and the monetary system, class struggle and the spread of socialism, etc. As it stands their theory can be charged with being too abstract and too simplistic, even though in a one-sided way, like a Weberian ideal-type, they do bring out the underconsumptionist aspect of monopoly-capital.

It may be true that monopoly capitalism could not have survived without wars and epoch-making innovations, but this is not sufficient to understand the shifting contours of twentieth-century capitalism as an unravelling of capitalism.[44] As more and more of our economic life escapes market regulation and becomes de-commodified, to that extent our economic life becomes politicized and dominated by power-brokers. This unravelling is best understood as a complex of structures and processes that are both economic and political and that are moving ineluctably away from the regulation of the law of value, rather than as a simple counterposition of underconsumption with external stimuli.

Emmanuel

Imperialism seen from the point of view of the Third World has generated the theory of underdevelopment. The causes of underdevelopment that are most frequently mentioned are the draining off of surplus, the unfavourable international division of labour and unequal exchange. I do not want to enter into a full analysis of this literature, but a brief discussion of Emmanuel's *Unequal Exchange* will serve to develop some aspects of the approach to underdevelopment that flows from the work of Uno and Sekine.

According to Emmanuel the root cause of underdevelopment is the unequal exchange between the core and the periphery. Because of the lack of mobility of labour, the periphery develops into a low-wage area. Resulting from this is an unequal exchange in which more labour from the periphery is exchanged for less labour form the centre. Wages are the independent variable determining prices, so that commodities produced in the core have a high price and those produced in the periphery have a low price. Over time unequal exchange promotes the wealth of the centre and the poverty of the periphery. Emmanuel attempts to explain this unequal exchange in purely economic terms as an 'equalization of profits between regions where the rate of surplus value is institutionally different'.[45]

In a purely capitalist society all exchange is equal exchange. To the extent that a society is capitalist, systematic unequal exchange cannot take place. Unequal exchange can only take place to the extent that we move away from capitalism towards monopoly, political intervention, or lack of a unified market. We cannot therefore use the law of value to explain unequal exchange, and though we can introduce the concept of unequal exchange at the level of stage theory, its full development can only take palce at the level of historical analysis.

When we look at the history of the uneven development of capitalism on a world scale, Emmanuel's 'unequal exchange' appears to be an entirely inadequate explanation, especially when we give it his economistic interpretation and treat it as the basic cause of all underdevelopment. Of course, unequal exchange does take place, but it takes many different forms and usually requires the backing of extra-economic force. Unequal exchange contributes more in some times and places and less in others to underdevelopment, and in general is only one and not necessarily the most significant factor explaining underdevelopment. The reason for this is that Emmanuel's 'unequal exchange' focuses entirely on purely economic external trade relations, but these relations cannot be explained by the laws of motion of capital and therefore always lead one to look for deeper more basic causes, usually political, that make unequal exchange possible.

If we list some examples of unequal exchange, it will be apparent that the political dimension is crucial and that different types must be situated in different stages and phases of capitalist development. Take as an example the traingular trade between Britain, Africa and the Caribbean that developed during the stage of mercantilism. Lack of a unified market, politics and monopoly all play a role in institutionalizing this system of unequal exchange. Or take Britain's trade of cotton textiles with India in the first half of the nineteenth century. Here the interesting phenomena is not unequal exchange, but the ruinous impact on Indian craft production of cheaper British cotton textiles. Consider the export of cotton from Uganda to Britain in the 1920s. Many small peasant producers of cotton face a monopolistic buyer who forces low prices on the peasants. Here we have a sort of unequal exchange, but not of Emmanuel's type. Finally if we consider OPEC and the Seven Sisters, we see yet another type of unequal exchange which must be explained at least partially in political terms. None of these examples fit Emmanuel's conception of unequal exchange.

In order to understand underdevelopment in a particular region of the world, we need to look both at the economic structures and resources present in the region when it began to be incorporated within the capitalist mode of production, and at how the stage of capitalist development with its particular mode of accumulation related to this new region. A purely economic or a purely external approach which only looks at trade is insufficient. If we consider examples like Japan, China, Uganda, South Africa, Mexico and Honduras, the diverse paths of development become obvious and the dangers of over-generalizing from one or a few causes or of trying to rely on purely economic explanations becomes readily apparent.

Palloix

In recent years the work of Christian Palloix has become influential amongst Marxists concerned with the theory of imperialism and the history of capitalist development. As much as his work may have contributed to our empirical knowledge of the current conjuncture, his overall theoretical framework has serious shortcomings.

Let me begin by looking at some of Palloix's basic assumptions. According to Palloix 'Gramsci demonstrated that Marxism cannot be considered as a "science of the base", but must be a complex articulation of theory and practice in the base–super-structure relation.'[46] Palloix interprets this to mean that economic categories are simply the reflection of class struggle. Thus 'it is only the state of the class struggle *at any given moment* which defines the tendency towards the equalization of the rates of profit'.[47] As a direct consequence of this approach Palloix completely undermines Marx's effort to construct a science of the laws of motion of capital, because if the law of value is from moment to moment dependent completely on the state of class struggle, then there can be no law of value. In this case all we can do is empirically study the particular state of class struggle in each country at each moment. Palloix fails adequately to grasp the reification that differentiates capitalism so radically from other modes of production, and instead focuses on class struggle which is what capitalism has in common with other modes of production.

Palloix's failure to grasp the inner essence of capitalism is demonstrated by his claim that it is only since World War II that capitalism has become fully developed and that the law of value has really come into full operation internationally. This is claimed for a period that I would argue is transitional and is rapidly moving away from capitalism and where the law of value appears to be largely inapplicable. Of course, if capitalism is simply large-scale production with wage-labour, then capitalism is more dominant in the world than ever before. But what Palloix completely overlooks in his one-sided conception of capitalism is the extent to which capitalism and the law of value require a competitive market and the commodification of economic life. The law of value can only display its workings without distortion in a purely capitalist society. Even at the level of stage theory the law of value translates largely into structural relations which only approximate the law of value. At the level of empirical history the law of value loses all quantitative precision and must be understood in terms of structural tendencies which may be distorted and deflected by many local particulars and contingencies. The law of value operated historically most fully in Britain from 1830 to 1870, but even here large parts of the economy were not fully capitalist and political policy interfered with the law of value in a myriad of ways. While it is true that production has become more international than ever before, it does not follow that now for the first time the international law of value operates, and this is because the international production that we have today is not very capitalist.

Palloix's theoretical framework detracts from his interesting and valid empirical investigations into changes in the international economic order. By directly politicizing economic theory, Palloix ultimately forces us to abandon the theory of the necessary inner connections of capital in favour of empirical studies of class struggle. Empirical studies of class struggle are important and the theory of a purely capitalist society can aid us in carrying out such studies only if we appreciate the necessary theoretical distance between levels of analysis. Even though the law of value does not directly apply in the phase of transition, still it serves as a reference-point for the historical movement away from itself. Palloix both applies the law of value directly to the current period and at the same time undermines its explanatory power by making it a mere reflection of class struggle.

This brief survey of both classical and modern writings on capitalism in the twentieth century is meant to indicate some of the ways that the approach of Uno and Sekine can aid us in improving our study of capitalist history. Marxists in the West have never clearly grasped the dialectical character of the theory of capital and have therefore run into great difficulties in trying to relate the theory of capital to history. The central orthodoxy has been the logical–historical method, which solves the problem of relating theory to history by seeing it as a non-problem. A direct consequene of the dominance of the logical–historical method has been a pervasive one-sided economism, or as in the case of Palloix and others a pervasive one-sided politicism.

7 'PERIODIZING' CAPITALISM

Instead of developing a stage theory as a distinct level of analysis out of the objective dialectic of capital, many Western Marxists simply 'periodize' capitalist history by demarcating stages of development according to their own criteria. For this reason there are as many periodizings of capitalism as there are theorists trying to periodize. In this section I want to discuss two works where some effort is made to treat periodization seriously. What is needed is not the drawing of somewhat arbitrary lines dividing different phases of capitalist history, but a distinct level of analysis which externalizes the dialectic of capital.

In *Class, Crisis, and the State*, E. O. Wright goes further than most Western Marxists in developing a theory of stages of capitalist development. Wright's periodization is based on the central constraints on accumulation and the structural solutions to those constraints. Accordingly he develops six stages of capitalist development which are as follows:[48]

1. Early period of primitive accumulation: transition from simple commodity production to expanded reproduction.
2. Transition from primitive accumulation to manufacture.
3. Transition from manufacture to machinefacture.
4. Rise and consolidation of monopoly-capital.
5. Advanced monopoly-capital.
6. State-directed monopoly capitalism.

What is interesting here is not so much the periodization itself since it appears to be somewhat impressionistic, but Wright's argument that crises and forms of expansionism take different forms in different stages, and therefore his implied emphasis on the importance of some kind of stage theory. Thus although Wright is not clear on how to go about systematically constructing stage theory, his recognition that some kind of stage theory is important is a forward step within the context of Western Marxism.

Another serious effort at periodizing capitalism can be found in *Rereading Capital* by Fine and Harris. 'The general method for periodizing modes of production – according to their own material development toward a new mode – is adopted.'[49] For capitalism the development is towards socialism. Thus their criterion for periodization must be the progressive socialization of the means of production under capitalism. 'Our basic principle for periodizing the capitalistic mode of production brings about distinct stages involving restructuring of the social relations of reproduction.'[50] Using this criterion, Fine and Harris arrive at three stages: *Laissez-faire* capitalism, monopoly capitalism and state-monopoly capitalism. Production becomes increasingly socialized as we move from one stage to the next. The problem with their criterion is that instead of being derived from the basic value/use-value contradiction of the dialectic of capital, it is derived externally to the dialectic of capital from a future mode of production that capitalism is supposedly moving towards. As a result their criterion lacks any objective grounding in the dialectic of capital. The important contribution of their book is not the particular periodization that they arrive at, but the extended effort to construct a theory of stages at all – the recognition of the importance of stage theory.

I would argue that the key to constructing stage theory is a clear and precise understanding of the law of value, and this is what the dialectic of capital provides. Without such a rigorous and objective dialectic, the tendency is to treat Marx's *Capital* as a 'grab-bag' for extracting whatever criteria seem most appealing to the particular theorist. Thus one theorist uses Marx's forms of the circuit, another uses an impressionistic understanding of accumulation and yet another uses socialization of production. No doubt many other criteria could be extracted from Marx's *Capital* or even more broadly from the corpus of Marx's writings so that we could end up drawing many lines through history or just one line, as in Baran and Sweezy's two-fold competitive versus monopoly capitalism. But the project is not one of extracting criteria for the purpose of drawing lines through history, rather it involves a distinct level of theory which accurately represents the types of accumulation that are dominant as the dialectic of capital externalizes itself in history.

8 CONCLUSION

This approach to stage theory based on the work of Uno and Sekine can help resolve or shed light on many debates and confusions in the history of Western Marxism surrounding the relation between the law of value and history. Stage theory can help sort out issues concerning crisis theory, class and the state, to mention a few issues that have recently received a lot of attention. Also stage theory problematizes the relation between the law of value and history in a way that forces us to think clearly and precisely about this relationship.

My presentation here is only a beginning, and there is a great deal to be worked out. Not only does stage theory itself need to be developed so that it can better serve as a guide to more concrete historical studies, but also and even more pressing we need to develop the theory of the phase of transition in order to understand more clearly the main dynamics of the current conjuncture. This knowledge is essential in guiding the Left in developing effective strategies of change.

5 The Historical Analysis of Capitalism

Unfortunately there are no extended historical studies by the Uno School available in English.[1] I shall not try to fill this void by carrying out such a study in this chapter. Instead my focus will be on indicating some of the ways pure theory and stage theory can guide historical analysis, on the character of historical analysis as a distinct level of theory and on a number of recent debates that have a bearing on historiography. In particular I shall look at a number of reactions against economism and shall argue that in reacting against economism many thinkers have fallen into politicism. I shall argue that we can avoid both economism and politicism by rejecting the logical–historical method which gives rise to them. Another debate that will be briefly examined is the one that centres on structure versus agency that has so engaged English Marxism in recent years. Finally I shall look at some of the controversies that surround the use of the concepts 'class' and 'class struggle' in the historical analysis of capitalism.

This part of the book is entitled 'Political Economy', and I have made it clear that I am interpreting this term in the narrow sense to refer to the scientific study of capitalism as opposed to some broader meaning that might refer to Marxian social science as a whole. This chapter, then, is not on the Marxian approach to the study of history as a whole, but instead focuses more narrowly on the Marxian approach to *capitalist* history. The importance of this delimitation of our subject-matter will become clear later in the book when I discuss historical materialism. Suffice it to say at this point that only with capitalism is it possible to have a dialectical theory with three levels of analysis.

1 LEVELS OF ANALYSIS

I return once more to the topic of levels of analysis in order to explore the sense in which each level is distinct, to show how pure theory and stage theory can guide our historical/empirical studies and to indicate some of the dimensions of historical analysis.

The theory of a purely capitalist society is distinct in the sense that it achieves closure by allowing the motion of value completely to encompass the production of use-value. A purely capitalist society is self-contained because it is completely regulated by the self-expansion of value. The self-containedness of the law of value at the level of pure theory sharply distinguishes the law of value at this level from the level of stage theory where it is externalized in a concrete stage of capitalist development.

Stage theory represents a controlled reactivation of use-values in arriving at historically dominant types of capital accumulation. The law of value at the level of stage theory translates largely into structural relations in which the law of value may only be manifested in certain minimal or systematically distorted ways. Yet when we look at the stages of mercantilism, liberalism and imperialism, we find in each case a dominant way in which the motion of value subsumes the labour and production process in order to accumulate and expand. So stage theory does not represent so much the law of value as a whole, but an abstract-type that represents the purchase that the law of value has on history at different stages of capitalist development.

The distinction between stage theory and historical analysis is not so sharp as the one between pure theory and stage theory. To a certain extent stage theory and historical analysis interpenetrate. Historical analysis is needed in combination with pure theory to contruct the material-type of stage theory, and stage theory is needed to orient and guide historical analysis. The difference is one of focus. Stage theory does not focus on actual historical change but rather on constructing a dominant material-type that presides over historical change in a particular stage of capitalist development. Stage theory is basically static and structural whereas historical analysis can fully study the specificities and particulars of historical change, contingency and agency. But if historical analysis also makes abstractions, how do we differentiate historical abstractions from the abstractions of stage theory? Abstractions from history are constructed with the guidance of pure theory and stage theory, in contrast to the abstractions of stage theory which are concretizations of the law of value expressed in material-types. The distinction between stage theory and historical analysis is not a sharp one, but I hope that it will become clearer as the chapter progresses. Next let me turn to historical analysis. First, I want to discuss the contributions of pure theory and stage theory, and then I want to consider some of the principal aspects of historical analysis.

The primary controversy in the writing of capitalist history arises from lack of agreement over the meaning of 'capitalist'. Is capitalism primarily generalized commodity exchange, private control over the means of production, the exploitation of wage-labour, a market-governed society, a society dominated by industrial-capital or the predominance of relative surplus value extraction? Sometimes it seems as though there are as many meanings to 'capitalism' as there are theorists. Each theorist seems to make an aspect of capitalism primary, but this can produce a one-sided emphasis on the realm of circulation in defining capitalism (e.g. Wallerstein) or the realm of production (e.g. Brenner).[2] What is needed is a rigorous conception of capitalism in its totality and in its inner essence, and that is precisely what the theory of a purely capitalist society provides. As we shall see later, having a clear and precise concept of capitalism is especially important for theorizing the transitions to and away from capitalism.

The theory of a purely capitalist society not only provides an adequate synthetic definition of 'capitalism', but also it exposes the laws of motion of capitalism or its necessary inner dynamics. It shows how the 'fictitious commodities' (i.e. not capitalistically produced), labour-power, land and money, are subsumed to the commodity-form.[3] It brings out the fundamental importance of the commodification of labour-power to captialism and articulates the objective and necessary connections between capital and labour. It demonstrates the necessity for expansion, for periodic crisis and for an industrial reserve army. This can serve to guide our study of both structure and struggle at a historical level.

Stage theory not only aids historical analysis within each stage of capitalist development, but also the theory of the mercantilist stage contributes to the analysis of the transition from feudalism towards capitalism, and the theory of the imperialist stage helps the understanding of the phase of transition away from capitalism (and it is hoped towards socialism). It is obvious that the theory of imperialism will aid the study of British economic history from 1875 to 1914, but perhaps it is not so apparent how the theory of imperialism contributes to understanding the post-1917 phase of transition. The period between the wars was marked by the effort to reinstate the pre-World War I mode of accumulation. In order to understand the general failure of these efforts we need to grasp both the mode of accumulation of finance-capital and why because of changed historical circumstances it could not be successfully reinstituted between the world wars.

If stage theory is based on a dominant material-type, that type must always be located in a particular nation-state even if capital accumulation always has an international dimension. At the level of historical analysis, we look at how the dominant material-type actually operates in the core nation and on a global scale. This analysis must be both economic and political and should explore the intersection between capital accumulation and class struggle. The history of global capitalism from 1875 to 1917 is not the same thing as the stage theory of imperialism. Finance-capital operates somewhat differently in Germany, the United States, France and Britain and this must be studied at the level of historical analysis. In order to understand the development of finance-capital in France, it is necessary to study both the internal dynamics of the French economy and how it is situated in the global economy. I do not assume as Wallerstein does that the primary unit of analysis of capitalist history is the world system and that the secondary units are sub-systems. The extent to which capital develops within a national economy as opposed to between national economies is an open question, though in general I would contend that determinant modes of accumulation develop primarily within specific nation-states even though they may have an important international dimension. In so far as parts of the globe are pre-capitalist or post-capitalist they need to be studied in their autonomy from capitalist history as well as in their connectedness.

In so far as the history that we are concerned with is capitalist history, we would expect economic structures and processes to be predominant, but at the level of historical analysis where capitalism has a partial hold, it is often not so easy to separate the economic from the political and ideological. Very often the political and ideological, including class struggle, become important determinants of historical change especially as they intersect with the economic. At the level of historical analysis the political and ideological cannot be considered as passive epiphenomena of the economic base. On the contrary, they play decisive roles in certain kinds of historical change, and in the phase of transition, when the inner logic of the economic is severely weakened, the economic, political and ideological may be co-determinant.

Because stage theory is fundamentally structural, agency can only be fully studied at the level of historical analysis. Even though the Uno/Sekine approach analyses the economic policies at the level of stage theory, these policies are analysed as those required by the dominant type of capital accumulation – that is, in structural terms. At the level of historical analysis we are still interested in structural imperatives and structural constraints, but we are also interested in agency and the degree to which agency can change structures as opposed by being constrained by them. This means that we can deal with class struggle in all its complexity. Class struggle may play an important role in explaining some historical changes. Later in the chapter I shall argue for the importance of objectively grounding our concept of 'class' in the law of value in opposition to those who adopt a subjectivist approach that proclaims the primacy of class struggle in the determination of class.

2 LEVELS OF NECESSITY

In the previous chapter I gave some examples to illustrate the stronger necessity that exists at the level of pure theory and the weaker necessity at the level of stage theory. I wish to return to this topic here in order to complete the discussion of necessity in relation to the three levels of analysis. This is important because part of the reason for the distinctiveness of each level is that there is a different degree or kind of necessity asociated with each level. If we mix the levels of analysis we are likely to see a stronger necessity where a weaker necessity is appropriate or vice versa. The scientificity of our approach depends in part on grasping the degree of necessity that is possible at each level so that we achieve that level of necessity not less because this would produce a weaker theory and not more because this would produce dogmatism.

Marx sometimes refers to the law of value as 'the *necessary* inner connections of capital'. I have interpreted this to mean a theory of a purely capitalist society where total reification removes contingencies which would interfere with the strict necessity of the law of value. Since the totality of economic life is managed by the commodity-economic principle, we do not need to consider particular political laws such as tariffs or labour legislation that might interfere with the operation of necessity. The law of value in the context of the dialectic of pure capitalism is what we mean by 'necessity'. The dialectic of capital, for example, shows that the commodity-form necessarily generates the money-form which necessarily generates the capital-form, and though this cannot be demonstrated in detail here, the logic is of the sort: the commodity-form cannot fully be what it is without the money-form and the money-form cannot be fully what it is without the capital-form. Here the necessity involved is an inner logic which is inner precisely because capital is self-determining as opposed to other-determined. But as the law of value externalizes itself in the abstract-types of stage theory, the structural necessities at this level of analysis presuppose certain conditions which are in part contingent.

At the level of stage theory, we make statements like 'the capitalistic management of the sort of large and long-term fixed capital investment required by heavy industry requires finance-capital'. I cannot show according to the law of value that finance-capital would necessarily emerge in the core states in the late nineteenth century. But I can show that given heavy industry and perhaps certain other structural features of capitalism (these are contingent givens because they cannot be derived from the law of value), finance-capital must develop, though again not necessarily with the German steel industry representing its purest type. Thus at the level of stage theory, we are looking at structural necessities or in some cases tendencies which cannot be deduced from the law of value by itself but represent a reconsideration of the law of value in a concrete context which is in part a contingent given. To say that the context is a contingent given does not mean that there is no explanation for it, only that it is contingent relative to the law of value.

With stage theory contingency is reintroduced in a controlled and limited way in the material-type of a dominant form of use-value production which requires a corresponding concrete organization of value formation and augmentation. Necessity is modified by contingency in the form of historically specific concrete circumstances. In contrast, I would argue that with historical analysis contingency is modified by necessity. At the level of history, we are agents confronted by structural constraints. In so far as we are speaking of capitalist history, those structural constraints are predominantly economic, and for theorizing these, stage theory and pure theory are a direct aid. These constraints have to do with a further concretization and particularization of the law of value and of the necessities associated with it. But at the historical level there may also be economic or even political and ideological structural constraints that arise quite independently from the law of value. We can speak of the necessities arising from such structural constraints (those independent from the law of value) as contingent necessities since the structures are contingent, but because they have a power to persist, they give rise to certain necessities in relation to their persistence.

Because of their importance, let me summarize the points being made here. The levels of analysis of the Uno/Sekine approach are distinct in part because they reflect different degrees of necessity. Pure theory represents dialectical necessity unmodified by contingency. Stage theory represents necessity modified by historically specific types of contingency. Historical analysis represents agency modified by both necessity (concretization of the law of value) and by contingent necessity (persistent structures arising independently of the law of value though possibly influenced by the law of value). An example will help illustrate this. Let us say we want to understand a particular capitalist crisis in Britain in the 1880s. At the level of pure theory we can grasp the necessity and character of periodic capitalist crisis. Stage theory elucidates the type of crisis characteristic of a certain stage where necessity is modified by contingent historical circumstances. Historical analysis could look at the crisis from the perspective of agency operating within constraints resulting from political, ideological or economic structures which are more or less persistent. Thus the crisis may have been more or less inevitable given a speculation bubble which was bound to burst, and the speculation bubble may have been more or less inevitable given the configuration of constraints on capital investment. In theorizing these constraints, we would be guided by stage theory and pure theory. At the level of pure theory and stage theory, we analyse necessity by using the pair 'necessary/contingent', but with agency at the level of historical analysis the pair 'necessary/possible' must also be considered.

3   ILLUSTRATIONS OF HISTORICAL ANALYSIS

As an example, let us say that we want to know why the petty
commodity production of cotton came to prevail in Uganda in
the first quarter of the twentieth century. This example will be
useful because since stage theory theorizes the dominant type of
capital accumulation, it pertains in the first instance to the 'core'
or the 'centre' of global capitalism as opposed to the 'periphery'.
This example will show how stage theory can guide our study of
the history of the periphery.

Stage theory can help us to understand why the partition of
Africa took place when it did, and it can help us understand the
types of relations that existed between the centre and the
periphery, i.e. why finance-capital was expansive and the types of
expansiveness possible given the capabilities of finance-capital.
Stage theory, however, is too abstract to include why a territory
with particular boundaries came to be the British colony of
Uganda. Also stage theory is too abstract to answer the
questions, why cotton and why petty commodity production?
The answer to these questions requires knowledge of the historically specific use-value needs of Britain and the capabilities of
Uganda, in other words the realistic material possibilities that
existed for Britain to make a profit out of Uganda. What stage
theory tells us is that the 'centre' was increasingly protectionist
and nationalist, that the centre was interested in raw material
extraction from colonies at least cost, that the centre was opposed
to developing manufacturing in its colonies, that methods had to
be devised to control politically new, non-settler colonies with
minimum expenditure of manpower and minimum administrative costs, and that the existing mode of production in the
colony which generally lacked a labour-market posed serious
obstacles to any but 'primitive accumulation'. These structural
tendencies of the imperialist stage can help us to establish what
happened in Uganda and in other colonies, but the specifics of
why it was cotton and why petty commodity production require
investigations at the level of historical analysis and not stage
theory.[4] In this case stage theory provides guidelines and
structural constraints for the historical analysis that is necessary
to answer the question.

As a second example, let me briefly consider the much-disputed
issue of the transition from feudalism to capitalism. Here the

theory of pure capitalism is helpful in distinguishing the capitalist from the non-capitalist, and the stage theory of mercantilism is useful as the theory of the first stage of capitalist development to emerge out of the phase of transition.

The theory of a purely capitalist society makes it clear that the commodifiction of labour-power is central to the transition from feudalism to capitalism. At the same time it makes it clear that the realm of production and class struggle should not receive one-sided emphasis at the expense of the realm of circulation. These guidelines clearly indicate the superiority of Brenner's approach in the debate with Wallerstein since Wallerstein's position is based on a one-sided emphasis on circulation and trade almost to the exclusion of production and class struggle.[5] In reacting against Wallerstein, Brenner may go too far in a productivist direction in his strong emphasis on class struggle though he does accord some importance to the development of a world market.[6] Also Brenner has done important work on changes in the agrarian sector that fostered the development of capitalism in Britain. However, he mistakenly refers to these changes as 'agrarian capitalism'.[7] Here clarity about the precise meaning of 'capitalism' becomes important. In the previous chapter, I argued that because of its use-value character, agriculture is resistant to the law of value. It is one of the last spheres of production to be penetrated even partially by the law of value, and throughout the entire history of capitalism has been penetrated only to a small extent. Agrarian capitalism requires the full establishment of industrial capitalism as a prerequisite since even rent can only become a capitalist category to the extent that industrial-capital is fully established. Rent can then be conceived as a subdivision of the total surplus value which goes to landowners because of their ownership of limited and monopolizable natural resources.

The stage theory of mercantilism makes it clear that the central focus in the theory of transition should be on how it is that merchant capital comes increasingly to subsume production through the putting-out system. The rural domestic industry of the putting-out system was made possible by the separation of the direct producer from the land, and it also further facilitated this process. The putting-out system promoted both the com-modification of labour-power and the separation of manufacture from agriculture. While the putting-out system represented a first step in the subsumption of production to the motion of value, there were severe limitations placed on productivity by such a system. Growing international competitiveness and merchant-capital's hunger for increased profits eventually drove the system beyond its narrow productive base towards factory production. Brenner's discussion of the agrarian sector helps explain why the industrial revolution first occured in Britain. But he tends to place too much emphasis on 'agrarian capitalism' and class struggle and not enough on mercantilism as it intersects with the putting-out system in his explanation of the transition.

4 REACTIONS AGAINST ECONOMISM

I now want to turn to some recent debates in Marxian social science that profoundly effect the writing of capialist history. In recent years one of the strongest trends in Marxist theory has been a reaction againt economism. Economism has been blamed for nearly all the failures of Marxist theory and practice, and has been thoroughly rejected from ever more radically anti-economist perspectives. In some cases thinkers go so far in purging economism from their thought that they also purge most of what has been traditionally considered the core of Marxism. Economism has been a predominant trend in the history of Marxism, and it appears in nearly all approaches that emphasize the scientificity of Marxism. The different forms of scientific socialism as developed by both the Second and Third Internationals had a strong economistic bent. Marx's *Capital* was identified by Marx himself as well as by his followers as the basis for Marxist theory as science. But the effort to apply the laws of motion of capital or the law of value to the complex world of capitalist history and capitalist social life often resulted in a Marxian social science and a Marxian strategic thinking that were reductionist and dogmatic. These tendencies became most exaggerated with Stalinism, but even in its milder forms, economism is judged to have lead to very serious strategic errors in the history of Marxist practice.

In my view the source of error was not economism *per se* but the logical–historical method. Most of those who have reacted against economism remain within some form of the problematic of the logical–historical method. Instead of overcoming economism in a positive dialectical way that preserves its contributions while shedding its errors, we get reactions that tend towards equally one-sided and error-prone forms of politicism and culturalism. The result is that we get rid of all the bad aspects of economic determinism, but we also get rid of the law of value or we undermine it to the point where its explanatory power is severely weakened, and this, of course, weakens the objective basis of Marxian social science.

Althusserian Structuralism

Althusser's conceptualization of the capitalist mode of production as being an articulation of the relative autonomous practices of economics, politics and ideology struck an important blow against economism.[8] He argued that the political and ideological are not simply the superstructure, but are independent practices in their own right with their own causal efficacy. The problem with this approach was that the relationship between the logical and the historical or between the 'mode of production' and 'social formation' was never clearly specified. Nor were the relationships between the economic, the political and the ideological specified in a determinant fashion for the capitalist mode of production much less any other mode of production. As a result Poulantzas (one of Althusser's students) developed a tendency to study the political independently from the economic and ideological. In his later works, responding to critics who pointed this out to him, he moved from emphasizing the autonomy of the political to emphasizing its interdependence. Thus the economic, the political and the ideological all come to be inscribed within each other so that he turns full circle back to the kind of 'expressive problematic' that Althusser was origianlly attacking. In an expressive problematic everything is internal to everything else; there is no real externality and no substantial differentiation, with the result that all separateness is always on the verge of collapsing together into a simple unity. Especially in his last work, *State, Power and Socialism*, Poultanzas moves back towards the expressive type of problematic that Althusser tried so hard to break with. The structuralists never rigorously theorized the economic, much less the determinant relations between the economic, the political and the ideological. Althusser put forward the vague claim that the economic is determinant in the last

instance. But the theory of a purely capitalist society demonstrates that the economic is the base.

The lack of theoretical determinateness within the Althusserian
problematic has led to its disintegration. Lack of theoretical
clarity on the relation between the logical and historical left the
Althusserians open to attack from the British Historical School.[9]
A corollate to this was lack of clarity on the relation between
'mode of production' and 'social formation'. Confusion on this
issue generated a 'modes of production debate' which culminated
in largely rejecting 'mode of production' and returning to more
historical and concrete investigations at the level of social
formations.[10] Althusserians also failed to specify with any
theoretical rigour the relations between the economic, political
and ideological as is evidenced by their frequent use of the vague
term 'articulation' to specify these interrelations. A number of
problems flow from this lack of theoretical determinateness.
First, the relative autonomous practices are at times treated too
separately.[11] Second, at other times the practices are made so
interpenetrating that they tend to collapse into an undifferentiated cultural whole.[12] Third, political or ideological practice are
singled out and made predominant so that Marxism is converted
into idealism.[13] In some cases we see once-committed Althusserians, disappointed by the failure of 'high theory', turn on all
theory except for a skepticist minimum that limits social science
to the study of the interarticulation of discourses embedded in the
logic of particular concrete situations.[14]

Laclau and Mouffe

Recent work by Laclau and Mouffe represents a marriage of the
sort of discourse analysis that emerged from the deterioration of
the Althusserian paradigm and Neo-Gramscian politicism and
culturalism. They have made important contributions to the
analysis of ideology and to the critique of economism but their
overall approach to Marxist theory is inadequate. They argue
that there are two forms of economism, epiphenomenalism and
class reductionism, and that economism is the single most
important source of both theoretical and strategic errors in the
history of Marxist theory and practice. 'Epiphenomenalism' that
takes the base/superstructure metaphor seriously and therefore

sees the superstructure as a passive reflection of the base has, according to Laclau and Mouffe, largely been discredited and rejected. But 'class reductionism' still remains as the manifestation of economism that most bedevils Marxism and the Left generally:

> The prevailing conception – which manifests the general problematic of class reductionism – has been that all subjects are class subjects; that each class has a paradigmatic class ideology; and that each ideological element has a necessary class belonging. This conception necessarily leads to seeing ideological struggle as a confrontation between two closed ideological systems completely opposed one to the other, in which victory consists in the total destruction of bourgeois ideology. There is no space here for a process of transformation of ideological elements, of differential articulation through which new political subjects are created. Nor is there any space to understand the importance of determinants of consciousness which are not reducible to class position.[15]

I entirely agree with this quotation which summarizes what in my view is the most important contribution of Laclau and Mouffe. Where I disagree is with their analysis of the source of the problem of class reductionism and its solution. The problem is not caused by economism so much as by the logical–historical method that gives rise to economism by applying the law of value with its two-class dynamic directly to history.

In reacting strongly against economism, Laclau and Mouffe reject altogether the objective ground that Marx was trying to lay for social science with his *Capital*, and as a result fall back into the subjective idealism of discourse analysis. Their attack on economism leads them to the extreme position of not only attacking the primacy of the economic, but of undermining the notion of the economic as a relatively autonomous realm even in theory and finally asserting the primacy of the political defined by the vague and ubiquitous 'power'. In the process 'class' not only loses all privileged status in their explanatory framework by being reduced to simply one interest-group amongst others, but also 'hegemony' as the political/ideological articulation of subjects becomes the key concept of their entire explanatory framework. The result is a modern version of Weberian interpretive sociology complete with its 'internal point of view', 'meaningful action', its politicism and idealism, only now posed in the latest language of discourse analysis.

While I reject the epistemology of this position, I agree that class reductionism has been and still is a problem within Marxism. In the next chapter I shall argue that the 'legal subject' is the basic superstructural form of capitalism from which I derive the basic ideological and political forms. Also I shall argue for the importance of the ideological and for the importance of developing clear and determinate theoretical conceptions of the relations between the ideological, political and economic. Finally I agree with Laclau and Mouffe in their emphasis on the need for a 'war of position' in articulating ideological forms that will aid in the transformation of subjectivities. But I take the strongest exception to their general epistemology, and we disagree in my view because although we see some of the same symptoms, our diagnosis of the underlying disease and our prescriptions for cure are completely different.

Class Struggle Politicism

There are numerous thinkers who believe that the law of value is either a reflection of class struggle or is so altered by class struggle that it is no longer a law. In the previous chapter I discussed Palloix who claims that 'economic categories simply reflect class struggle'[16] and that 'The law of value depends upon a determinant force, which is class struggle.'[17] But if the law of value simply reflects class struggle, then it must continually change with the ever-shifting changes in the balance of force between classes. The law of value is therefore no longer a law, and cannot really add anything to the concrete class struggle. Palloix does not draw out these implications of his politicism, for if he did, he would drop value categories from his analysis and see that they add nothing to his explanation except a wrapping of Marxist orthodoxy.

E. P. Thompson takes this next logical step in *The Poverty of Theory* where he not only rejects the law of value, but actually claims that it represents a penetration of bourgeois ideology into Marxism.[18] In a *New Left Review* article on 'The Theory of the Falling Rate of Profit', Hodgson argues that the law of value is wrong and produces mechanical (economistic?) Marxism.[19] According to him, what matters is class struggle and the overthrow of capitalism – the law of value is a deterministic and mechanistic diversion from the task at hand. Even though it contravenes his structuralism, Poulantzas increasingly declares the primacy of class struggle in his later works. Writers from otherwise diverse perspectives agree in rejecting the primacy of the law of value in Marxian social science and substitute the primacy of class struggle.

In some cases the focus on class struggle has led to the view that the basic problematic of historical explanation is one of oppression and resistance, or of power and domination and the resistance to power and domination. It is no doubt true that power relations permeate all of capitalist society as they do of every other society; and it is important to study power relations and especially to demystify or to 'deconstruct' them when they are oppressive. But placing 'power' at the centre of social science and equating it with politics creates an expressive problematic which sees politics everywhere but which cannot make the clear distinctions necessary to understand the historical specificity of capitalism. Within a power problematic we can discuss the politics of the family, the politics of production, the politics of art and so on indefinitely; and though all these studies may be of interest they must be partial studies without objective grounding unless they are developed in a determinate relation to the dialectic of capital. By equating politics with power or coercion, we can indeed create an expressive problematic that places politics at the centre and finds that politics is ubiquitous in all forms of social life and in all societies, but this will not help us to understand the precise character of the economic and the political under capitalism and how they relate to each other. In the next chapter I shall argue that in order to understand politics in the capitalist mode of production we must first and foremost focus on the historically specific and *capitalist* character of the capitalist state and ideology. By focusing on the state, we can grasp capitalist politics as determinant structures and determinant policies flowing from those structures. Once we are clear about the dominant forms, functions and policies of the capitalist state, we can then develop determinant concepts to understand power relations which become especially important in historical analysis with the concern about agency. If we start by equating politics with power, then it is difficult to get beyond a vague and diffuse understanding of the political to any sort of understanding of the historical specificity of capitalist politics.

We have seen that many schools of Marxism – diverse in other respects – converge in their politicist abandoning of the law of value and in their insistence on the primacy of class struggle. This convergence makes the politicist perspective extremely strong in the current intellectual conjecture – so strong in fact that we can say it is the current orthodoxy. And yet, I want to argue, that in its own way it is just as wrong as the economism that it has reacted against. Politicism may seem to break with dogmatism and reductionism, it may seem more revolutionary and more activist, and it may even seem more creative as it breathes the heady 'let-a-hundred-flowers-blossom' air; nevertheless we must at this point emphasize the close relation between politicism and subjectivism and insist that Marxism has always been more than subjectivism and empiricism in theory and spontaneism in practice. And it is not just a question of re-emphasizing the objectivist side of the dualism – we must break from the logical–historical method altogether.

5   STRUCTURE AND AGENCY

Althusser's famous claim that 'history is a process without a subject' has given rise to vigorous counter-attacks from E. P. Thompson and his followers, who claim that Althusser's structuralism is a new formalism that denies the role of agency in history. In this section I shall briefly consider the issue of structure and agency by examining the debate between Althusser and Thompson.

Althusser takes Marx's *Capital* as the basis for a universal structuralist epistemology which achieves objectivity by suppressing the subject. But according to Marx subjects are converted into bearers of economic structures only by the reifying force of capitalism, where 'production relations are converted into entities and rendered independent in relation to the agents of production'.[20] Even with capitalism, I have argued that this reification is only total at the level of pure theory, so that as we move to more concrete levels, agency re-emerges. But with the structuralist approach of Althusser, the subject is epistemologically suppressed so that there is no way for it to re-emerge, and what is really only appropriate for the theory of a purely capitalist society is converted into a universal suppression of subjectivity for the sake of objectivity. Such objectivity is bought at too high a cost since it rests upon an artificial suppression of subjectivity and creates an unbridgeable gap between theoretical structures and agency at the level of the historical concrete. Contrary to this, the dialectical approach of Uno and Sekine does not assume away the subject, rather it lets the reifying force of the motion of value deactivate the subject. Objectivity then is attained not by a theoretical suppression of the subject but by allowing the objectification of social relations that develops with the commodification of economic life to complete itself.

Thompson's critique of Althusser in *The Poverty of Theory* is quite extensive and at times stoops to venomous polemics. The critique does not stop with Althusser's interpretation of Marx, but extends to Marx himself. According to Thompson, Marx's *Capital* represents the penetration of the formalism of bourgeois political economy into Marxian social science.[21] It is:

a mountainous inconsistency – its laws cannot be verified, and its predictions were wrong. As 'history' or as 'sociology' it is abstracted to a 'model' which has heuristic value, but which follows too obsequiously ahistorical economic laws.[22]

It is not surprising that Marx's *Capital* as the founding work of a new science should contain many imperfections and inconsistencies, but what is surprising is that so many 'Marxist' theorists should so easily abandon a work of monumental brillance instead of making extended efforts to enlarge and refine it.

Thompson fails to grasp Marx's distinction between the mode of inquiry and the mode of presentation. I have argued that the mode of presentation of the theory of capital is a dialectic that moves from the abstract to the concrete and therefore *appears* to be an *a priori* construction, or as Thompson puts it, capital appears 'as the unfolding of its own idea',[23] it 'has become an idea which unfolds itself in history'.[24] The mode of inquiry carefully sifts through classical political economy and the history of capitalism in order to arrive at a clear comprehension of the necessary inner connections of this mode of production. The self-purifying and reifying tendencies of capitalism enable thought to be guided by these tendencies in the construction of the theory of a purely capitalist society. It is not a question of the idea and thought being self-generating, but of grasping how material reality itself becomes self-generating and can therefore guide thought. In other words, it is capitalism itself which is the 'idealist' and not Marx the writer of *Capital* because it is quite true that under the total reification of pure capitalism men and women are mere bearers of economic relations, or personifications of economic categories. The problem is not idealism; the danger is in confusing pure theory where reification is total with actual history where it is ever only partial. Since Thompson sees no way of reconciling economic determinism at the level of pure theory with agency at the level of history, he rejects the law of value altogether. From the point of view of agency and class struggle, the law of value appears to be formalist, idealist, economist and determinist; so that it must be rejected except for a certain minimal heuristic value.

For Thompson there seems to be an irreconcilable contradiction between agency and the law of value. Thompson poses this contradiction most sharply when he points out that according to Marx the law of value consists of 'tendencies working with iron necessity towards inevitable results'.[25] But in opposition to this:

> no worker known to historians ever had surplus value taken out of his hide without finding some way of fighting back . . . and . . . by his fighting back the tendencies were diverted and the 'forms of development' were themselves developed in unexpected ways.[26]

> It is not only that gross historical materiality stubbornly refused to 'correspond' to the purity of its concept . . . for in every historical now the circuit of capital is being obstructed and resisted at every point – as men and women refuse to be reduced to its *träger* . . . so that the 'forms' are 'developed' and diverted in theoretically improper ways by the class struggle itself.[27]

The conclusion that Thompson draws is that the so-called 'laws of motion of capital' are not laws at all and that the history of capitalism must be understood as a process involving the exerting of pressures and counter-pressures.[28] But as I have shown in this chapter, this seeming contradiction does not compel us to either abandon the law of value or force history into the Procrustean bed of the law of value.

6 CLASS AND CLASS STRUGGLE

Historical analysis must concern itself with class and class struggle, but the recent politicist orthodoxy has tended at times to make class struggle the basis of all inquiry. It is therefore important for me to show why the Uno/Sekine approach opposes this position while maintaining that class struggle is an important factor in historical change. I shall in particular argue against the subjectivist position that claims the priority of class struggle over class in the sense that a class only exists in so far as it is created by class struggle.

In a purely capitalist society classes are simply 'personifications of economic categories' because reification is presumed to be complete. The capital–labour relation is thus objectively defined by the law of value, and by understanding the dynamic between capital and labour at this level of analysis, it is possible to understand the objective ground of class struggle even though there is no class struggle. Further, I want to emphasize that this objective determination of class is purely economic since at this level the political and ideological are simply passive superstructural forms that cannot convert commodified social categories into social agents or social actors capable of defying the law of value. At the level of pure theory classes are conceptualized as objective economic categories. As a result of the law of value, we understand some important things about capital and labour. First, we understand the fundamental antagonistism between the classes of capitalism with the one producing all surplus value and the other appropriating all surplus value. The consequence of labour-power being a commodity treated like any other commodity input into the production process is clarified. The necessity and function of an industrial reserve army and the impact this has on the working-class is brought out. We understand the nature of machine production and the necessary revolution in the means of production and how both impact on the capital–labour relation. We can see the mechanism of concentration and centralization as well as the mechanisms of periodic crisis, and as a result understand the impact of these dynamics on the class relation. Finally we can grasp the expansive nature of capitalism and its consequences for class. We understand all of this directly from the law of value and not from class struggle. In fact the law of value gives us a good understanding of why class struggle is likely to occur and at what points, and it achieves this only by the suspension of class struggle that follows from allowing reification to complete itself.

At the level of stage theory we can begin to analyse the state and ideology with interventionist capabilities in connection with stage-specific dominant types of capital accumulation. This demonstrates that class structure varies between different stages, and that there is only a general capitalist tendency towards a two-class polarization through the stage of liberalism. The 'working-class' is not some sort of constant given, but varies considerably even at the level of stage theory which only looks at dominant abstract-types. In the stage of mercantilism the 'working-class' is the rural domestic workers of the putting-out system. In the liberal stage, the 'working-class' is the industrial proletariat, and in the imperialist stage, the 'working-class' becomes a stratified complex structure which spans the monopoly and competitive sectors, and might be seen to include parts of a fledgling service sector. At the level of stage theory our analysis of class is still structural, but by bringing in the dominant political and ideological forms, we are setting the stage for a much more complex analysis at the level of history where we may want to analyze classes mainly as historical actors. In saying that the industrial proletariat is the dominant form of the working-class in the liberal stage, we are only saying that this is the structural form necessitated by the dominant type of capital accumulation, and we are not saying that the majority of all working people are in the industrial proletariat even as when the stage of liberalism reached its purest expression in Britain in the 1860s. Thus it is perfectly consistent with our approach for the dominant type of working-class to be the industrial proletariat, but for this type actually to contain a minority of the population. This only goes to show that the dominant type of capital accumulation is not ubiquitous, but is, in the words of Bukharin quoted earlier, 'the conductor in the concerto of economic forms'.

The analysis of class structure at the levels of pure theory and stage theory sets the structural constraints for understanding class as agency, but tells us nothing about which groups actually get organized and assert power in the political arena. We need to study actual class struggles in particular places at particular times as class structures struggling to be born as classes with real power. Sometimes classes will not succeed in organizing themselves as historical actors or will be only weak actors; at other times they will play a decisive historical role.

The objective meaning of 'class' is derived from pure theory and the only pure classes in capitalism are capital, labour and landlords in the context of a purely capitalist society. Capital and labour conceived at this level of analysis serve as an objective referent for clarifying issues concerning class and class struggle at more concrete levels of analysis. I categorically oppose the subjectivist claim that class struggle is prior to class. If we start with class struggle, then we are really starting with collectivities in struggle since we do not yet know what a class is. Now collectivities in struggle are of many types, so how do we know which collectivities succeed in constituting themselves as a class except in so far as they call themselves a class? Then any collectivity that calls itself a class is a class, and 'class' has no meaning except as a name that a group gives to itself. In my view the Marxist conception of class should be objectively defined by the economic structure of pure capitalism, otherwise a class is any economic power-group that calls itself a class while managing to assert its interest in the political arena; and any group that does not get itself organized and does not call itself a class is therefore not a class. But this seems a very inadequate and subjectivist approach to class analysis.

The approach to class analysis that I am advocating starts with an objective economic definition of class and then by developing determinant relations between the economic, political and ideological and between levels of analysis, enables us to re-integrate the political and ideological in a controlled fashion as we move towards the concrete, so that we can at the same time integrate structure and agency. In my view it is inadequate to claim that 'the structured totality of economic, ideological, and political relations constitutes at each moment of history the conjuncture of class struggles, these struggles in turn have the effect of transforming or preserving these relations'.[29] This is like saying everything is related to everything else, and in changing it determines everything else. This quote from Przeworski is vacuous, and does not help much in establishing determinant relations in the real world. The problem with Przeworski's approach is that he so emphasizes process as opposed to structure that class disappears in the protean flux of pure struggle and pure process.

The study of working-class history is a very important part of the study of capitalist history especially in the face of the silence of so much bourgeois history when it comes to class or the struggles of oppressed groups. It is important to understand that workers have not simply been passive victims of exploitation and oppression, but have actively fought back. But it is also important not to romanticize about the great victories of the popular forces. Wishful thinking would like to see the working-class victorious and therefore reads into capitalist history a degree of working-class triumph that makes it difficult to understand why socialism was not realized long ago. As long as capitalism lasts, the working-class may win some concessions from capitalism, but if it wins major concessions, we are talking about the transition to socialism. It would be wishful thinking in the extreme to see the working-class determining the course of history in advance of socialism. Class struggle is more important in explaining the advent of the ten-hour day than in explaining the advent of World War I. Instead of simply assuming the primacy of class struggle, we need to determine the actual role of class struggle in determining various historical events whether it is primary, secondary, tertiary or negligible.

On the surface, the major problems with a good deal of Marxian class analysis are economism and workerism. But in my view these are the surface manifestations of the deeper-lying logical–historical method. The problem is that by applying the laws of motion of capital too directly to history, researchers expect something too close to the two-class polarization of a purely capitalist society. Marxists too often look for homogeneous class-conscious entities where there are none, and make the mistake of speaking about *the* capitalist class or *the* working-class. We trace all major political and ideological phenomena back to determinant classes as though they were homogeneous self-conscious entities, instead of what they usually are, which is heterogeneous and groping conglomerates. Laclau and Mouffe have correctly called this 'class reductionism' and have traced many strategic errors to such ways of thinking.

The theory of a purely capitalist society shows that we should understand class in relation to the production and appropriation of surplus. Class is one basis upon which people unite to assert their common interests and the clearest case of class is the capital–labour relation in pure capitalism. At the level of history there is only a tendency towards this two-class polarization to the extent that history approaches pure capitalism and the law of value achieves total hegemony. Though there is a tendency towards self-purification in capitalist history, the further advance of this tendency is blocked once we reach the stage of imperialism. From this stage on, we should expect classes to become less homogeneous and more complex. In the phase of transition with the further undermining of capitalism's inner logic, there would be no further world-historic tendency for the capital–labour relation to become more polarized or for capital and labour to become more homogeneous.

7   CONCLUSIONS

Historical analysis is especially important to Marxists because future-oriented historical analysis is the basis of strategic thinking. If our historical analysis has problems, in all likelihood so will our strategy. In my view serious strategic errors have been made by Marxists throughout the history of the Marxist movement primarily because of the logical–historical method or an unconscious and simplistic view of the relation between the logical and the historical in the theory of capitalism. The effort to grasp history as a direct function of the law of value produces crude economic determinism. The reaction against such determinism generally produces a voluntarism which posits the primacy of action and struggle. The tendency to see a degree of necessity at the level of historical analysis that is only possible at the level of pure theory produces dogmatism. The tendency to see the two-class dynamic of pure capitalism at the level of historical analysis produces class reductionism. Closely connected to class reductionism is workerism which fetishizes the working-class as *the* agent of change and sees working-class power everywhere far in advance of actual socialism. The failure to understand the determinant relations between the economic, the political and the ideological and between levels of analysis can produce tendencies to collapse them all together into a vague culturalism or to treat either the political or ideological as dominant as in politicism and ideologism. All of these errors stem ultimately from the logical–historical method and they all lead ultimately to bad strategy.

For socialists the goal must be the most effective mass

mobilization of people possible with the aim of achieving democratic socialism. Theory can be a great aid in clearly understanding the historical context, the realistic possibilities for change and the weak points of the system. Of course when dealing with concrete conjunctures, experiential or practical wisdom is important. But strategy is bound to be weakened by any of the errors that I have mentioned because they all lead to approaches that are in some sense one-sided and incomplete. If we combine economism, dogmatism and class reductionism we get the sort of errors that were typical of both the Second and Third Internationals and in the extreme we get Stalinism. If we adopt any of the varieties of voluntarism, we give up the guidance of the law of value and place our faith in the spontaneity of the people or the working-class to bring about socialism. In its extreme form this is anarchism. Of course, the subjective factor is extremely important in the transition to socialism, but to give up the guidance of an objectively grounded social science could have disastrous results.

Throughout this chapter I have referred to the 'determinant relation between the economic, political and ideological', but so far I have not really expanded on this problem. So in the next chapter I shall discuss the nature of capitalist superstructural forms and how they are concretized in a levels of analysis approach.

6   The Theory of the Capitalist Superstructure

The analysis of the capitalist superstructure should start with achieving clarity on the precise sense in which the capitalist state and ideology are capitalist. This, of course, requires that I have already clarified the meaning of 'capitalism'. Since this was the primary aim of the previous five chapters, I now proceed from this foundation to analyse the capitalist superstructure. In order to do this it is necessary to clarify the relation between the economic, the political and the ideological at each of the three levels of analysis.

I believe that for many readers it will be especially this chapter that brings out most forcefully the important contributions of the Uno/Sekine approach. But it is also with this chapter that I develop the most significant innovations.

Besides the nearly ubiquitous logical–historical method, another reason why the economistic tendency was so strong in orthodox Marxism was because of the strong impact of Marx's *Capital*. In *Capital* Marx sets forth the law of value without developing a theory of politics or of ideology based on the law of value. This meant that the law of value (the economic) was very often directly applied to history resulting in economism. Or sometimes it has meant that the ideological and political have been tacked on to the economic in *ad hoc* ways. As we shall see later there are hints in *Capital* about the nature of the capitalist superstructure. But if we want to avoid economism, it is necessary to root the theory of the political and ideological in the law of value. This is because the law of value depends upon reification, upon the domination of objects in motion over the subject, the individuals of human society. But if total reification makes the object totally subsume the subject, that does not mean that the subject disappears. The subject is neutralized in a purely capitalist society, but it re-emerges as we move to more concrete levels of analysis. Now the economic in the form of the law of value represents the domination of the commodity or of the object, but to complete the picture we need a theory of the subject, even if in a purely capitalist society the subject is merely a bearer of economic structures. The subject is passive, but is still present, and it is this passive presence of the subject that provides the basis for deriving a theory of basic superstructural forms.

The approach of the Uno School does not preclude deriving a theory of the superstructure in a purely capitalist society, but the work of Uno, Sekine and Itoh tends to focus mainly on the law of value and Marxian economics. Sekine's *Dialectic of Capital* demonstrates that the objectification of social relations consequent on the completion of reification in a purely capitalist society makes it possible to theorize the inner logic of capitalism as a rigorous dialectic. But the objective economic categories require that subjects play the role of passive support. To be more concrete, the commodity implies commodity-owners. The commodity-owner first appears in the dialectic of capital as an active subject proposing an exchange. As the dialectic proceeds the subject is increasingly converted into a passive bearer of economic categories, but never disappears and always retains a freedom as consumer that makes assumptions such as 'fixed baskets of wage-goods' unrealistic. A purely capitalist society is one where socioeconomic life is governed in its totality by the self-regulating market. Socioeconomic life is therefore not governed by the political and ideological. And yet a purely capitalist society is made up of individual subjects, and based on the nature of subjecthood necessitated by pure capitalism, we can begin to grasp the most fundamental forms of the state and ideology. The dialectic of capital is not complete without a theory of superstructural forms because without such a theory it is only a theory of the objective side of social relations without the corresponding subjective side. And even though the subjective side consists of relatively passive forms at the level of pure theory, these forms must be precisely grasped if we are correctly to theorize the state and ideology as they become more active and concrete at the level of stage theory and historical analysis. Until this subjective side is adequately theorized from the level of pure theory where it is relatively passive, to the level of historical analysis where it is relatively active, the approach of the Uno School to political economy will tend to display economistic tendencies and tendencies to theorize the political and ideological in somewhat lose and *ad hoc* ways.[1] I hope that this chapter in attempting to ground the political and ideological at the level of pure theory will make a significant contribution to the Uno School and will serve as a corrective to the possible economistic tendencies in the present formulations of pure theory.

The 'base/superstructure' metaphor has been so strongly attacked and discredited in recent years, that in trying to resurrect it, I may be accused of waving a red flag at a bull. In what follows it will become clear that I consider the 'base/superstructure' metaphor an accurate concept only in the case of a purely capitalist society. But because in this case capitalism is most fully itself, the 'base/superstructure' concept yields important insights into the essential character of capitalism even though at the level of historical analysis we should remember its metaphorical character and hence use it only as a rough guideline.

Another reason for using the term 'superstructure' is that it refers to both the political and the ideological, and it is my view that at the most abstract level of a purely capitalist society the political and ideological overlap in basic superstructural forms. This is important because Marxists have very often constructed a theory of the state or of ideology too separate from each other, and this tendency can be countered by theorizing their common roots in the superstructural forms where the political and ideological are not yet clearly differentiated. Thus the theory of the superstructure analyses the political and ideological in their interconnectedness, paying attention to the differentitation from a common root.

1 THE SUPERSTRUCTURE IN A PURELY CAPITALIST SOCIETY

If a purely capitalist society is totally self-contained and is governed by the law of value working through the market, then how can we derive the basic superstructural forms? At this level of analysis the dialectic of capital shows us how the motion of value completely subsumes economic life without any outside help so that the political and the ideological can play no direct or active role in the dialectic of capital. In this sense the theory of a purely capitalist society is a theory of the economic base and at the same time is a theory of a social totality because in this instance the reproduction of social life is governed by the economic alone. But we know that any really existing society is in part governed by the state and ideology. The question, then, is: how can the theory of pure capitalism, which objectively reveals what capitalism must be, help us to undestand the specifically *capitalist* political and ideological forms?

Since with a purely capitalist society, capitalism has been allowed to become most fully itself, this must be our reference-point for understanding what capitalism is in its inner essence. It follows that those state and ideological forms which are implied by a purely capitalist society and are consistent with such a society must be the forms most characteristic of capitalism. At the level of stage theory we may analyse the ideological and political forms most characteristic of mercantilism, liberalism or imperialism. At the level of historical analysis we may analyse the political and ideological forms most characteristic of France in 1848 or Germany in 1937. But it is only at the level of pure theory that we can fix upon the basic character of capitalist, political and ideological forms in general. If, then, we are to speak of the 'capitalist state' and 'capitalist ideology', we must ground these concepts in the theory of a purely capitalist society. Otherwise 'capitalist' can have an indefinite number of possible meanings. I have argued throughout that 'capitalism' has one objective meaning and that is the meaning revealed by the law of value which so far has been most rigorously stated by Sekine in *The Dialectic of Capital*.

The analysis of the state and ideology at the level of pure theory can be referred to as 'form analysis'. Here I am using 'form' in contrast to 'content' or 'substance'. At the level of pure theory the state and ideology are not embodied in material institutions, which, as material institutions, would have an independent capability to intervene in the economic. Materiality is totally subsumed to the motion of value, so that the state and ideology can only be theorized as passive forms or background conditions, shadows implied by the objectified motions of social relations. These abstract forms only take on material institutional content with the re-emergence of the subjective element at more concrete levels of analysis. Thus, for example, at the level of pure theory the basic capitalist state form is the *rechtsstaat*.[2] At the level of stage theory this abstract-form takes on definite material content which differs between various stages of development. Further, the dominant material-types of political and ideological institutions at the level of stage theory serve as guides to the specifics of historical/empirical analysis. Thus from form analysis at the level of pure theory, it is necessary to develop the material content of the state and ideology as we move through levels of analysis to the concrete.

Often in the pair form/content, we think that the form is less important than the content. Not so in this case. What makes the state and ideology capitalist is not any specific content, but only a specific form. The capitalist state is primarily a form. Capitalist ideology is first and foremost a form. And these forms are absolutely crucial to understanding the state and ideology at more concrete levels of analysis. It is under the aegis of these abstract forms that the material institutional content develops and that we understand the capitalistic character of that content.

The Objective and Subjective in a Purely Capitalist Society

Marx points out that while capital may be conceived as the 'self-expansion of value' taking on an existence and motion of its own, the insurmountable fact remains that 'commodities cannot go to market and make exchanges on their own account'.[3] The commodity-form entails the category 'subject' because commodities do not exchange themselves but instead must be owned by a subject 'whose will resides in those objects' – commodities have no will of their own until they conspire collectively in the market place to form prices and rates of profit which in turn govern society. But in order to get to the market, they must first be produced and secondly appropriated as someone's private property. Thus the commodity connects autonomous subjects through exchange; indeed, more than just connecting, it actually regulates social relations so that from the point of view of the market, '. . . persons exist for one another merely as representatives of, and therefore, as owners of, commodities'.[4]

The self-regulation or objectivity of the market requires that the subject should be unable to intervene and alter the objective workings of the market. This means that the subject must be split off from the objective, and in this case the splitting off takes the form of isolated subjects that relate to each other only through commodity exchange in the market-place. Each subject is privatized to be a little sovereign over the private property that he or she owns. This means that inter-subjectivity can only be created through the commodity which connects one isolated subject with another. There is no socioeconomic inter-subjectivity based upon direct relations between persons in a community or society. What we end up with, in the succinct words of Marx, are 'material relations between persons and social relations between things'. This materialization, this naturalization, this objectification of social relations is achieved through a commodification of social relations that establishes objectivity by banishing the subject to the private realm where his powerlessness in the face of market forces is made up for by making each subject a little dictator within the realm of his own property. Thus the basic superstructural form of pure capitalism consists of isolated subjects confronting an objectivity which depends upon their remaining isolated subjects connected only by commodities.

With capitalism we have the following paradoxical situation. The subject (person) owns the object (commodity), but all the objects are exchanged and in the process a self-regulating market is created which governs the economic activity of the subject. As commodity-owner the subject has absolute dominion over the commodities owned, and yet the price of those commodities is totally dependent on a society-wide market over which the subject has no control. In relation to his commodities the subject is totally dominant, and in relation to the market the subject is totally subordinate. This domination of the circulation of commodities or the market over the subject is a principal aspect of 'reification'. It seems as though the market is sovereign and at the same time the individual is sovereign. When we emphasize the objective side, we adopt a deterministic or fatalistic view of society; and when we emphasize the subjective side, we tend towards a voluntarism that thinks any individual can be what he or she wills.

In a purely capitalist society the complete domination of the commodity (the object) over society makes the law of value seem to be eternal and natural so that the law of value seems to be like a natural law. Marx took great pains to analyse the fetishism of commodities which in his view was the material basis for most of the misconceptions of bourgeois economics. Because of the fetishism of commodities, bourgeois economists tend to view the reign of things over humans as natural and fail to see the social relations underlying the motion of things. As a result they do not see that capitalism is a historically limited mode of production, and they do not see the potential problems created when social life is governed by prices and profits. Fetishism of commodities is based on the truth that the market governs, but this perspective is a partial truth which fails to see the underlying sociohistorical limitations and contradictions of such a situation. Thus Marx's *Capital* develops the law of value out of a critique of classical political economy, which was prone to error because of its failure to see through the fetishism of commodities. The fetishism of commodities is dispelled theoretically once we see the exploitation of wage-labour that underlies the formation of profits and prices. But, of course, at the level of everyday life the fetishism of commodities continues to have ideological effects as long as capitalism lasts. These effects tend to hide class exploitation by focusing on the market with its seeming objective and impersonal fairness. The fetishism of commodities or of the object is one basic form of capitalist ideology.

The second basic form, and the more important for deriving the theory of the superstructure, is the fetishism of the subject. The fetishism of commodities that Marx analysed at such lengths in *Capital* has as its counterpart the fetishism of the subject. The fetishism of the commodity or of the object makes capitalism appear to be natural or eternal and therefore not alterable by human agency; whereas the fetishism of the subject fails to see the reification of capitalism and sees capitalism as therefore the product of sovereign individuals. The fetishism of commodities accepts the domination of things over human beings by accepting total reification as so natural that it becomes unnecessary to translate material–technical economic categories back into their underlying social relations. Social facts appear as natural facts. This is convenient to the bourgeoisie, who, as a result, do not have to take responsibility for the problems of society.

The extreme voluntarism generated by the fetishism of the subject is even harder to combat than the fatalism generated by the fetishism of the object, and this is because the commodity-form sharply accentuates the predisposition for individuals to experience themselves as the centre of power in their own lives. This form of fetishism sees the subject as sovereign over his or her property and therefore sovereign over his or her life. Each subject is a self-sufficient monad with a sovereign will. The superstructural forms deriving from this category 'subject' are more prevalent and harder to combat than those deriving from the category 'object', because they are so deeply embedded in everyday life and the very identity of individuals in a capitalist society.

If it is roughly accurate to say that capitalism is a historically delimited mode of production which tends towards reification, then the fetishism of the subject is even further removed from this actuality than the fetishism of the object. Object fetishism accurately sees the domination of things, but accepts this as natural and eternal; whereas the fetishism of the subject not only fails to see the domination of things over men, but tends to see whatever objectification that exists as the direct product of subjective and sovereign wills. This position of extreme voluntarism seems further removed from the reality of capitalism than its fatalistic objectivist counterpart. The peculiar nature of the fetishism of the subject under capitalism is crucial for our understanding of the basic superstructural forms.

The objective moment of a purely capitalist society is the economic, and I have argued that the economic, because of the fetishism of commodities, gives rise to one form of capitalist ideology. The second basic form of capitalist ideology derives from the fetishism of the subject, and it is this peculiarly capitalist category of subject that is the basis of the capitalist political form. It is with this fetishized category of subject that we come to see the common root of that capitalist ideology which arises from the subjective moment of a purely capitalist society and the basic capitalist political form. There are many excellent studies by Marxists on the fetishism of commodities as a basic capitalist ideological form, but few have explored the subjective side of the antinomy. Let me turn next to analyse the fetishism of the subject as a basic capitalist ideological form.

The Legal Subject and Capitalist Ideology

C. B. Macpherson's *Political Theory of Possessive Individualism* is an important contribution to the analysis of the subjective side of capitalist society, but by far the most important work to date is Pashukanis's *Law and Marxism: A General Theory*.[5] I believe Pashukanis was essentially correct in arguing that the most basic form of the fetishism of the subject is the 'legal subject'.

A legal subject is a person with rights on the basis of which he/ she actively makes claims.[6] Basing his argument on the following passage from Marx's *Capital*, Pashukanis claims that the commodity-owner in a capitalist society is the paradigm case of the legal subject:

> It is plain that commodities cannot go to market and make exchanges of their own account. We must, therefore, have recourse to their guardians, who are also their owners. Commodities are things, and therefore without power of resistance against man. If they are wanting in docility he can use force; in other words, he can take possession of them. In order that these objects may enter into relation with each other as commodities, their guardians must place themselves in relation to one another, as persons whose will resides in those objects, and must behave in such a way that each does not appropriate the commodity of the other, and part with his own except by means of an act done by mutual consent. They must, therefore, mutually recognize in each other the rights of private proprietors. This juridicial relation, which thus expresses itself in a contract, whether such contract be part of a developed legal system or not, is a relation between two wills, and is but the reflex of the real economic relation between the two.... The persons exist for one another merely as representatives of, and therefore, as owners of, commodities.[7]

This passage makes it clear that commodity exchange implies legal subjects 'whose will resides in those objects' (commodities) and who carry out exchange only by 'mutual consent'. If in a purely capitalist society 'persons exist for one another merely as representatives of, and therefore, as owners of, commodities', then it follows that in the first instance persons are defined as legal subjects. A legal subject is a property-owner with exclusive rights to the property owned, who therefore only parts with his or her property through consent.

The legal subject is an abstract and impersonal atom existing in a society of traders connected by the commodity and by the mutual recognition of abstract subjecthood with right. Each act of exchange implies as a 'passive reflex' a relation between subjects with property rights and at least an unspoken contract to exchange only through mutual consent. Since in a totally reified society there are no direct economic relations between persons, there can be no sharp distinction between law of property and law of contract. Law of contract is simply law between persons whose relation is mediated by property. Since society is totally governed by the market, law is simply a passive background condition. Legal regulation only comes to the fore in so far as disputes between property-owners arises due to some perceived breach of property right or contract. Commodity-owners buy and sell, and each transaction is also a legal relation involving a contract between subjects with rights. In the normal course of trade the legal relation remains a passive background condition, but if a perceived breach of contract occurs, the legal relation comes to the fore in the form of litigation between legal subjects claiming their rights.[8] According to Pashukanis:

> The legal system differs from every other form of social system precisely in that it deals with private, isolated subjects. The legal norm acquires its *differentia specifica*, marking it out from the general mass of ethical, aesthetic, utilitarian, and other such regulations, precisely because it presupposes a person endowed with rights on the basis of which he actively makes claims.[9]

It is the legal subject that is prior to the moral subject and even to the egotistical subject or 'possessive individual'. Individuals in a purely capitalist society are first and foremost proprietors whose wills reside in their commodities which connect them in the market-place and regulate them through prices and profits. This means that an individual's very sense of selfhood and identity develops within the form of the legal subject. According to Pashukanis, 'The egoistic subject, the legal subject and the moral personality are the three most important character masks assumed by people in commodity-producing society.'[10] I would add to this that the legal subject is the fundamental 'character mask' of these three, and indeed it is a good deal more than a character mask since it is the basic form within which the individual's character and identity develop. And this is because in a purely capitalist society, individuals are first and foremost legal subjects – their essential being is defined by their legal subject-hood. In the language of structuralism, individuals are 'inter-pellated' as legal subjects.

It is now apparent that the commodity-form is the basis of both objectivist and subjectivist capitalist ideological forms. The reified relation between object and subject creates both the fetishism of commodities and the fetishism of the subject. The basic form taken by fetishized subjectivity is the legal subject. The legal subject capable of property-ownership and commodity exchange is the most important superstructural form of capitalism, or in the words of Pashukanis: 'in capitalist society . . . legal ideology becomes the ideology *par excellence*'.[11] According to Marx the economic cell-form of capitalism is the commodity-form, and according to Pashukanis the superstructural cell-form of capitalism is the legal form. Later I shall show the sense in which it is a hybrid, serving as both the embryonic political form and the most important embryonic ideological form.

Though grounded in the commodity exchange between subjects, legal ideology spreads widely throughout capitalist society because 'the most diverse relations approximate the prototype commercial relation and hence assume legal form.'[12] Thus, for example, even one's reputation can be considered a commodity, and those who trespass against it can in some circumstances be charged with libel or slander. Thus 'if all economic life is to be built on the principle of agreement between autonomous wills, every social function, in reflecting this, assumes a legal character'.[13]

The reification of social relations gives rise to fetishism of commodities and at the same time to legal fetishism.

The social relation which is rooted in production presents itself simultaneously in two absurd forms: as the value of commodities, and as man's capacity to be the subject of rights.[14]

The abstract capacity of everyone to be a bearer of property rights makes it difficult for bourgeois thought to see anything else than subjects with rights: legal fetishism complements commodity fetishism.[15]

Both forms of fetishism can be overcome by the de-reification of economic life in which society takes full responsibility for economic life so that the relation between subject and object that counterposes isolated and formally free subjects to the iron necessity of the laws of motion of capital begins to break down.[16]

The reader may wonder why in all this analysis of the fundamental ideological forms of capitalism, there has been no

mention of class and class struggle. The reason is that the basic
ideological forms of capitalism do not recognize the existence of
class. Like any dominant ideology, capitalist ideology in its basic
forms must present itself as universal. Indeed the very legitimacy
and rationality of capitalist society depends heavily on the non-
recognition of class. In a purely capitalist society, where the
commodification of labour-power is completely secured, capital
treats labour-power the way it treats any other commodity.
Capitalist ideology does not distinguish between those commodity-owners who own capital and those who only own their
labour-power. All individuals in a purely capitalist society are
commodity-owners, and as such they are all equally legal
subjects.

Capitalist ideology derives from the realm of circulation and
not from the realm of production, because even in a purely
capitalist society, when we look closely at the realm of production, we see class and we see the potential for class struggle. But
capitalist ideology sees capitalist society made up of legal subjects
and not of antagonistic classes. It does so by basing itself on the
universalization of the commodity-form. Marx seemed to recognize the importance of the realm of circulation to capitalist
ideology when he referred to the realm of circulation as 'a very
Eden of the innate rights of man. There alone rule Freedom,
Equality, Property and Bentham'.[17]

Of course, as Marxists we can argue that viewing the world in
non-class terms is in the interest of the capitalist class. But saying
this does not get rid of the commodity-form and the legal subject.
And it is their continual reproduction that provides a realistic
basis for capitalist ideology. Unless we fully understand this, we
will not understand the real strength and appeal of capitalist
ideology. Such understanding is essential to combating the
powerful hegemony of capitalist ideology. In a purely capitalist
society subjectivities are not interpellated as class subjectives at
all. Capitalism in general primarily creates legal subjects as
possessive individuals so that class-consciousness is secondary
and must always struggle against the primary ideological forms.
Furthermore, at the level of stage theory and historical analysis it
is apparent that the class composition of capitalist society is
always complex, that groupings other than class must be taken
into account and finally that ideological forms do not necessarily
have a 'class belonging'.[18] These conclusions can have important

strategic implications. For example, in most cases it is likely to be futile simply to assert class solidarity or community in opposition to individualism. If individualist ideologies are hegemonic, then the Left is likely to have more success if it demonstrates how capitalism cripples the development of the individual.

Let me briefly summarize this section. The universal hegemony of the commodity-form in a purely capitalist society gives rise to two basic ideological forms: the fetishism of commodities and a corresponding fetishism of the legal subject. While these two fetishisms represent the two sides of an object/subject antinomy and therefore mutually support one another, it is especially the legal subject that is important and that has not been adequately studied in the past by Marxists. I have claimed that the legal subject is the most important of the two basic capitalist ideological forms. The next section will support this claim by showing that the legal subject is the basis for deriving the capitalist state form.

The Legal Subject and the Capitalist State

It is the superstructural form legal subject that is fundamental to the derivation of the basic form of the state at the level of pure theory. In its embryonic form the state form is a legal subject raised about the rest or in other words the legal subject writ large.[19] If a purely capitalist society is made up of legal subjects, then the state form must be a form that legal subjects can create. It would be contradictory for the state to have the right to invade the property of its subjects. All legal subjects can do is create through the mutual consent of a social contract, a special legal subjectivity capable of resolving disputes between legal subjects and of protecting their property. Such a neutral judge is one legal subjectivity raised above the rest with the right to settle disputes and protect property. If each legal subject must protect his own property with his own weapons, there is always a threat of a Hobbesian war of all against all. Such a Hobbesian state of nature would destroy the category 'legal subject' because legal subjects must only relate to each other through consent. To ensure exchange according to universal consent and the universal arbitration of claims, each legal subject gives up the right to use force to protect his property so that the state is given a monopoly of force to enforce the law. The state as legal subject writ large may also find it necessary to interpret the law from time to time, and this we may call 'law-making'. The basic state form is an abstract Legal subject realised above other legal subjects by a contract which gives the state the right to adjudicate disputes, to make or interpret laws only for the protection of property and to monopolize the legitimate use of force to enforce the law. Though having the definite form of legal subject, made *primus inter pares* (first among equals) by mutual consent, the state becomes a peculiar type of legal subject. Legal subjects have more or less absolute control over their property to sell, to hoard or to destroy; but of course the legal subject as state does not have property rights over its subjects since that would mean that it could use force at any time to invade their property and this would destroy the entire *raison d'être* of the sovereign state. In a purely capitalist society, the sovereign state must therefore be completely divorced from property-ownership and from the economic and must instead be simply the passive regulator of the relations between legal subjects. In its embryonic form the state must not have the capacity to intervene into the economic arena, and this is ensured by the state's use of force being entirely extra-economic and therefore extending only to the enforcement of property law. Since force is removed from the economic, the state becomes a kind of repository of extra-economic force.

Let me summarize the argument to this point and take note of the basic characteristics of the political or the basic state form in pure capitalism. The commodity-form posits legal subjects as the passive reflex in the circulation of commodities. But the category 'legal subject' is very tenuous in a situation where each must defend property against all others. A sovereign state is therefore necessary really to secure individuals in the status of legal subjects. Without a state the category 'legal subject' can easily dissolve for it depends only on mutual recognition. But the state cannot be so powerful that it can infringe on the economic; it cannot represent any collective or communal will. Legal subjects, whose only connection in the first instance is commodity exchange, cannot produce a 'general will'; they are only capable of creating a legal subjectivity which by mutual consent stands above other legal subjects in being able to mediate disputes between them to ensure that the peace of mutual consent does not degenerate into a war of all against all. In the first instance the state is therefore the passive reflex of legal subjects needing to maintain their status as legal subjects. It is a superstructural form that is derived as a passive reflex from the economic base. The state is also entirely separate from the economic base in the sense that it represents a legal subjectivity entirely divorced from property-ownership.

In a society of legal atoms, the unifying element is in the first instance the market, for it is primarily the commodity that connects legal subjects into a cosmos as opposed to a chaos. Three is no community based upon direct human relations; the only connectedness is based on the commodity and the market. But this also means that the basic state form cannot arise out of any sort of political collectivity or community; indeed, if it did, it would threaten the sovereignty of the market. There cannot be a real public realm arising from a political community. The 'public' as opposed to the 'private' is created by raising a legal subject above the rest and abstracting it from direct property-ownership so that it can play the role of mediator between legal subjects. The public realm is essentially a legal fiction for the sake of smoothing the intercourse in the private realm. The sole purpose of the public realm is to protect the private property and inwardness of the legal subject; the public realm is therefore artificial and parasitic off the private realm. When considered more concretely, such a state of affairs can lead to a vicious circle in which the less there is any real political community to deal with collective needs and to provide security, the greater the need for privacy and the only way of securing needs available – private property.

In a society of legal subjects, all conflict is privatized and treated as a problem of law. Conflict between privatized entities is settled by a privatized entity made public through a legal fiction for the purpose of mediating conflicts between privatized entities. For this reason it is extremely important for the state to be neutral, and this is achieved by disconnecting the sovereign legal subject from property. In a purely capitalist society legal subjects do not have to learn the sort of creative conflict that is required by real political community since conflict is avoided by encouraging it to remain within the private realm where it can be resolved by a neutral judge.

This analysis has demonstrated that the basic form of the political in a purely capitalist society is the legal state or the *rechtsstaat*. The legal subject is a hybrid superstructural form in the sense that it is the common source of both the capitalist state form and the most important ideological form. It follows that the capitalist state form is very closely connected to the capitalist ideological form. The abstract citizen of the capitalist state is basically a legal subject, and as a *rechtsstaat*, the capitalist state is dependent on the legal subject and legal ideology for its legitimacy.

Just as with the basic ideological forms, the basic state form does not recognize the existence of classes. The capitalist state form must be derived from the legal subject posited by the circulation of commodities and not from the realm of production where class always lurks behind the factory walls. In a purely capitalist society the legal state is a passive background condition that serves only to resolve disputes between legal subjects in order to secure the legal subject status of commodity-owners. At more concrete levels of analysis with the re-emergence of the active subject and agency, it becomes apparent that the state usually does serve the interests of the dominant fraction of capital in so far as it is clear about what those interests are. But this class content of the capitalist state is always hidden behind the *rechtsstaat* form. The success that the capitalist state has had in appearing to be neutral and in appearing to serve the 'public interest' is rooted deeply in the reality of the basic superstructural form, the legal subject.

In order to understand the nature of the political in capitalist society, it is important to start with the state form and not with the vague and ubiquitous 'power'. In pure capitalism, society is completely governed by the market. The state does not exist as an institutional force capable of intervening in the market, instead it passively secures the legal subject as a background condition to commodity exchange. We do not conceptualize the basic state form in terms of power, rather we understand it as a legal form. The capitalist state appears as a power-wielding apparatus at the levels of stage theory and historical analysis, but in order to understand the capitalistic character of state power, we need to understand the basic form of the capitalist state. The capitalist state cannot be adequately understood as simply a repressive apparatus or as an instrument of the capitalist class. In order to understand the capitalist state we need to understand the basis of its legitimacy, and we need to understand the tension between its *rechtsstaatlich* form on the one hand and ways and means of serving the interests of the dominant fraction of capital on the other. Above all we need to understand that the continuing appeal of the capitalist state rests on the fact that in its basic form it is not a class state at all, but a neutral arbiter between abstract citizens. This tension between the non-class form of the capitalist state and its class content has sometimes been expressed in recent theory as 'the relative autonomy of the state'. It is true that the state is relatively autonomous from class struggle, but we can never adequately understand the nature of this autonomy if we start by equating the political with power. Politics then becomes completely diffuse and indeterminant. It is necessary first to grasp the capitalist state form and then to explore power relations in relation to this dominant form. Similarly, it is difficult to make much headway if our starting-point for understanding capitalist society is class struggle. Instead, by starting with the law of value, we can generate a theoretical framework which will enable us really to make sense out of the forms of class struggle that are characteristic of capitalism.

All societies have norms and rules, but the legal form is most characteristic of capitalism. Historically the legal form develops most fully where the commodity-form develops most fully. That is why prior to the rise of capitalism the legal form developed most fully in ancient Rome. Legal ideology only becomes really developed and hegemonic with the universalization of the commodity-form under capitalism. With the advent of demo-cratic socialism neither the market nor the legal form remain hegemonic, but instead are democratized and humanized. Up to now socialists have not sufficiently considered the forms of normative regulation appropriate to democratic socialism or what speaking loosely might be called socialist 'law'.

Conclusions

In this section I have tried to derive the basic superstructural forms from the economic relations of a purely capitalist society. Later in the chapter I shall discuss the development of capitalist ideology and politics at the levels of stage theory and historical analysis. But here I want to stress the importance of deriving the basic superstructural forms at the level of pure theory. If we cannot arrive at a clear conceptualization of the relation between the economic, political and ideological at the level of pure theory, then there is little chance of doing so at more concrete levels of analysis where capitalism is less pure. It is when capitalism is pure that we can clarify the types of superstructural forms that it generates. If we neglect these forms at the level of pure theory, our entire approach will incline towards economism, and instead of having a conception of determinant relations beween the economic, political and ideological, the tendency will be to add the political and ideological on to the economic in an *ad hoc* fashion.

My analysis has demonstrated that Marx's base/superstructure metaphor is very felicitous at the level of pure theory. Since a purely capitalist society is governed by the market, the economic is indeed the base, and politics and ideology are derived as the passive superstructure that backs up this base. Ideology is derived from both sides of the object/subject antinomy created by reification and politics is derived from the subject side of the antinomy. The superstructure conceived in this way does not refer to all ideas and institutions other than economic that might exist in a purely capitalist society. Rather the superstructure refers specifically and only to those ideological and political forms generated by the universal domination of the commodity-form over social life.

I have argued that capitalist ideology derives from both the fetishism of the object (commodity) and of the subject. The economistic ideological form which claims the law of the market to be a sovereign natural law not to be interfered with needs to be complemented by the voluntaristic legal form based on the premise that 'a person is juridicially dominant over things because, as an owner, he is posited as an abstract impersonal subject of rights in things'.[20] Thus in capitalism the individual is master of his property and the slave of the market – he is master of his little (or big) island of property, but he is slave to the all-powerful sea of value relations that engulf his island.

The logical derivations of the state form from the objective ground of the dialectic of capital tend to be confirmed by the fact that the stage of liberal capitalism which most closely approximates a purely capitalist society also strives towards the ideals of free-trade and *laissez-faire*. Of course at the level of pure theory we can only derive the abstract and embryonic state form which is bound to be very far removed from the materiality of any actually existing historical state. But the similarity between the logical derivation here and the political theory of such classical liberals as John Locke is no accident. For example, Locke argues that the principal task of political thought is to define the law-maker which is the same thing as government.[21] Further, according to Locke the primary purpose of all government is the protection of property, and civil laws are but 'guards and fences' to men's property.[22] Furthermore, for Locke the legitimacy of government is based on the legal fiction of a contract between legal subjects. Perhaps the most forceful logical derivation of the state form from legal subjects in the classical writings is Hobbes's *Leviathan* where it is clear that the main function of the sovereign is to secure possessive individuals in their status as legal subjects. The work of Max Weber which develops the legal–rational character of political authority under capitalism also lends support to the results arrived at here. Finally the legalism of liberal theory and practice is notorious.[23] Liberals have always as much as possible converted political problems into legal problems, and have feared any form of political collectivism or political mobilization that might interfere with the market or the property right of legal subjects.

The dialectic of capital demonstrates that a capitalist society can reproduce itself entirely according to commodity-economic principles without the intervention of extra-economic force. However, we can logically derive the basic state form from the dialectic of capital, even though the state plays no active role in the dialectic itself. We see clearly that the state and ideology must be separated from the self-expansion of capital as a passive reflex that secures the background conditions of the dialectic.

At the level of pure theory, I am trying to conceptualize the cell-forms of the superstructure as they must exist in a purely capitalist society. Though very abstract, formal and embryonic, these cell-forms are crucial for our entire understanding of the state and of ideology, their relation to each other and to the economic base. I have tried to show how the legal subject is the basic superstructural form that gives rise to the political, and how it is this form along with the fetishism of commodities that gives rise to the ideological. I have noted that at their root the political and ideological are not clearly differentiated, so that the basic form of the capitalist state is both ideological and political. I have argued that in its basic form the capitalist state is a *rechtsstaat* or a legal sovereign. Of course, this does not imply that the capitalist state does not in practice ever do anything illegal, since at this level of analysis we are only speaking of the cell-form and not the state as a material reality. Also it should be noted that in its basic form the capitalist state is a covenant of legal subjects or isolated and abstract citizens. As such it does not recognize the existence of classes, and indeed, I may even say that its basic form requires a total divorce from class. It is not, then, a form derived from the capital–labour production relation, but instead it is derived from the commodification of social life including crucially the commodification of labour-power.

Finally I should emphasize that the political in the perspective being developed here must first and foremost be conceptualized as a legal state form and not as 'power' or as 'class struggle'. These latter aspects of capitalist politics must be developed at more concrete levels of analysis and must be understood in relation to the basic form developed at the level of pure theory. Our whole understanding of the nature of the political in capitalist society will be misconceived if we do not grasp the peculiarly *capitalist* nature of the political. This we have argued is the *rechtasstaat* created by legal subjects as a passive reflex of the self-contained economic base. Later I shall argue that this conceptualization of the political is not only crucial for accurately grasping the nature of the political, but also plays an important role in grasping potential or actual contradictions between the economic, the political and the ideological. It can scarcely be overemphasized how much an accurate understanding of capitalism depends on firstly an accurate theory of the economic base and secondly an accurate understanding of the political and ideological and how they relate to the base.

2 THE STAGE THEORY OF THE CAPITALIST SUPERSTRUCTURE

Previously I argued that stage theory represents an externalization of the value/use-value contradiction in a concrete stage of capitalist development where the motion of value must manage a dominant type or types of use-value production. At the level of stage theory the motion of value needs the active support of the state and ideology, so that the superstructure is no longer conceived as passive forms. At this level of analysis, the state and ideology take on material institutional content and may play an active and interventionist role in supporting accumulation. The term 'superstructure' is therefore no longer accurate. Instead, it is necessary to look for types of ideology and types of state structure and state policy that most typically support the dominant mode of capital accumulation.

A purely capitalist society is conceived as a global society without external relations, but this is a high level of abstraction that can never exist in history. In history capitalism does not descend like a great flood that equally engulfs the entire globe at once. Rather it gains a foothold first in one region and then in another, and when one region is compared to another, we find that it grows very unevenly. At the level of stage theory, it is necessary to consider the issue of territory. The legal state discussed at the level of pure theory now becomes a territorial state with definite boundaries separating the domestic economy from the rest of the world. The territorial state exists as one state amongst many – as one legal subject writ large amongst many.

The category legal subject requires not only that there be clear boundaries separating my property from yours but also that any movement of property across boundaries only occurs through the mutual consent of the respective property-owners. Since the territorial state is internationally one legal subject amongst many, it must also guarantee that legal subjects from foreign territories do not use force to invade the property of its own legal subjects. Since there is no international state to guarantee the status of the state as legal subject, this status is from an international point of view somewhat tenuous and is only based on mutual recognition. For this reason there are strong pressures for the territorial state to develop a standing army.

At the level of pure theory the state is nothing but a passive background form securing the status of legal subjects. I have pointed out that such a state is not based on any kind of community since it is only the commodity that connects isolated legal subjects. But from the point of view of the territorial state, this is a severe defect since it needs to represent some kind of unified force in dealing aggressively with other states. It is here that the capitalist concept 'nation' comes into play and along with it the ideology of nationalism. The ideology of nationalism unites legal subjects into a nation. A nation is not based on any real political community but is a way of uniting legal subjects within a territory against the legal subjects of other territories. The nation is not based on a political community that would enable the people to control the state and organize their joint economic life, rather it is an adjunct of the territorial *rechtstaat* which must become a power in order to preserve itself. The nation may be based on anything that a people living within a territory have in common except positive political community because that would destroy the legal subject and undermine capitalism. Nationalism is basically a means of giving the commodity-traders in one territory a separate identity as against the commodity-traders in another territory. Ultimately it is a way of mobilizing legal subjects in one territory to fight against those of another territory. Since the nation is an adjunct of the territorial state the concept 'nation-state' is very appropriate.

Stage theory brings out the extreme importance of the nation-state and the ideology of nationalism to capitalism. Nationalism converts a passive shell of a state into a real power. A market-governed society is an atomized society, and a state based only on legal subjects can have no real power. Though the market orders society, it does not create community and indeed tends to dissolve traditional communities. Nationalism is a way of building a common identity in a market society without undermining the atomization required by the market. It creates a common identity that can be mobilized as a force, but it does not create real political community. Nationalism therefore picks up on any trait that the people in a territory have in common that differentiates them from the people in another territory, be it language, race, religion or culture. Nationalism then uses the couplet domestic/ alien to set the people of one territory against those of another.

At the level of stage theory, the *rechtsstaat* of pure theory is converted into a class state. Now the dominant ideologies and state policies clearly serve the interests of the dominant type of capital accumulation. But in order to maintain its fundamental legitimacy as a *rechtsstaat*, the capitalist state must not appear to be primarily a class state. Nationalism again plays a crucial role in mobilizing the populace behind the state, while it essentially carries out class policies. In this case, nationalism attempts to assert the primacy of the nation over whatever forms of dawning class-consciousness may be developing. In the stage of mercantilism the state basically serves the interests of merchant-capital, in the stage of liberalism industrial-capital and in the stage of imperialism finance-capital. At the same time its legitimacy depends upon its appearing to serve the 'national interest'.

Nationalism may of course at times become a popular and progressive anti-capitalist ideology, but here I am only interested in analysing the character of nationalism as a *capitalist* ideology. I have stressed the extreme importance of this ideology as a support for the capitalist state and as an ideology that suppresses class identifications. In short nationalism is central to capitalist ideology.

At the level of stage theory we see the basic *rechtsstaat* form embodied in dominant historical types. The *rechtsstaat* now takes the form of the nation-state which monopolizes the legitimate use of force within its territory for the sake of protecting life and property. The dominant type or organizational structure and policy of this state varies from stage to stage. Closely connected with the dominant type of nation-state is the dominant type of ideology since ideology always plays an important role in legitimizing the state, which with capitalism must take a legal form. We see again at this level that the state is in a basic sense both an ideological and political institution.

Capitalism develops in the first instance within nation-states and only secondarily internationally. In its infancy capitalism needs to be fostered and protected by a strong state, so that it develops first where the nation-state is most developed. Where there is no nation-state, the developent of an integrated 'home' market creates one, as in the cases of Italy and Germany. I want to turn next to examine the most typical state and ideological institutions of the stages of mercantilism, liberalism and imperialism.

During the stage of mercantilism where the dominant form of capital accumulation is the putting-out system, the motion of value has not yet completely subsumed the production process. Being internally weak, capitalism is heavily reliant on external relations and thus on a strong state. During this stage we see absolute monarchy begin to be transformed into constitutional monarchy which is a move in the direction of the state form as abstract legal subject. The dominant form of the state in this stage is the absolute/constitutional monarchy, and the dominant type of state policies are those generally referred to as mercantilist and most typically represented by chartered trading companies and the Navigation Acts and Corn Laws in England. So in concretizing our theory of the state we locate the dominant form of capital accumulation for the stage, in this case British wool production organized as a putting-out system by merchant-capital, and we then study the state and ideological forms and state policies required to support this type of accumulation.

The stage of mercantilism is still a stage of primitive accumulation in which capital has only partially subsumed the labour and production process as typified by the putting-out system. Thus profits are not so much based on surplus value as on unequal exchange maintained by monopoly and extra-economic force. The state supports enclosures because it supports the putting-out system of wool production and thereby unwittingly lays the foundation for the next stage which rests on the commodification of labour-power. State policy is necessarily very protective of the emerging home market and infant industry. State policy is also aggressive and war-like in plundering the rest of the world and in supporting slavery and other forms of forced labour in foreign lands where there is no significant labour-market. At home the state resorts to various forms of forced labour to support infant industry and the merchant marine through such institutions as workhouses and impressment.

In the stage of mercantilism we not only see the territorial state emerge as a sovereign legal subject serving to protect and nurture infant capitalism, but also we see the creation of the nation as the ideological complement of the territorial state. Thus the ideology of 'possessive individualism' which flows from the sovereignty of the legal subject needs to be complemented by nationalism that can wield legal subjects together into an effective fighting force. The more aggressive the state wishes to be, the more it must foster nationalism. Though nationalism is important in all stages of capitalism, it is most important in the stages of infancy and decline when capitalism needs the support of a strong state. In the mature stage of liberalism, nationalism does not wither away, but it is somewhat tempered by free-trade policies. It would be incorrect to see a strong internationalist thrust attached to free-trade; the capitalist state can never afford to be truly internationalist given the importance of nationalism to its legitimation and strength.

In a historical sense the state, of course, is not a capitalist institution. In looking at the historical development of the capitalist state we are looking at the gradual 'domestication' of an alien institution. In the stage of mercantilism the feudal absolutist state is transformed gradually or by fits and starts into a state which is conducive to the development of merchant-capital. Trade wars require a strong state with a strong currency, and economic growth in this period rests mainly on trade. It is necessary to create a standing army and navy independent of the feudal aristocracy to carry out successfully such mercantilist policies, and this depends upon a system of orderly taxation and the development of a domestic market. This development of the state as a centralized administrative and repressive apparatus requires a process of gradually breaking with dependency on the feudal aristocracy – a process the aristocracy naturally resisted. But already in the mercantilist stage in Britain we see the emergence of more legal forms of domination, and indeed the most important political theory written in this period advocates legal domination and constitutional as opposed to absolute monarchy.

With the development of industrial capitalism and the stage of liberalism, we see the state increasingly adopt *laissez-faire* and free-trade policies. This stage reached its purest expression in Britain in the 1860s with the general abandonment of protectionism in favour of free-trade. The movement away from protectionism meant revoking the Corn Laws, which symbolized the fact that the divorce of the direct producer from the land was sufficiently complete that the commodification of land and of labour-power could be maintained without the extreme protectionism and state support that was needed in the previous stage when the commodification of land and labour-power was still in its infancy. The Factory Acts became necessary in order to secure the reproduction of labour-power and quell the growing rebellion of workers. They represented the recognition that the continued securing of the commodity labour-power requires some protection of the human substance.

The stage in which liberal ideology and liberal policy becomes most dominant is one where the mode of accumulation of capital is typified by cotton manufacturing in Britain or in other words by the light manufacturing of consumer goods where competition is fostered by the ease of entry into an industry. It is in this stage that the idea of legal subject becomes most manifest in the dominant form of government which is 'representative democracy' (in practice not very representative or democratic).[24]

Just as the liberal stage is closest to pure capitalism so is the ideal of representative democracy closest to the state as sovereign legal subject. In theory, representative democracy does not require any sort of political community since it can be created entirely by isolated legal subjects who cast their ballots just as they spend their money in commodity exchange. In this case the impersonality of the market is transferred to the government which presumably reflects the interests of legal subjects as expressed by voting. Also representative government combined with checks and balances assures a relatively weak government and a truly impersonal rule of law.

The development of heavy industry results in the stage of imperialism in which the dominant form of capital accumulation is finance-capital. Finance-capital requires a strong state with protective policies both at home and abroad. Protective tariffs give cartels a home base safe from foreign competition. But the state is also needed to protect finance-capital in its aggressive expansionism so that the resulting national chauvinism and militarism culminate in an array of policies that we may label 'imperialist'. The development of heavy industry and monopoly also fosters the rapid socialization of the labour process with very large numbers of workers being controlled by one corporation or one cartel, and this in turn fuels the class struggle which concretely takes the form of a trade union movement and a socialist movement. Capitalism is now sufficiently developed that it can through taxation support a growing state apparatus with a growing standing army and an embryonic welfare state. These institutions are needed to buy off, or failing that, threaten the growing workers' movement. An enlarged standing army is also needed to back up the aggressive expansionism abroad. Finance-capital requires increased state intervention both to support its mechanisms of accumulation and to maintain the commodification of a working-class which is becoming more powerful and more political.

As Weber argues, the legal–rational authority of the capitalist state tends to foster bureaucratic forms of social organization. This is also fostered by military developments, especially the Napoleonic army. But far and away the most important source of bureaucratic organization is the capitalist enterprise based on the commodification of labour-power. No historic event so fostered the spread of bureaucratic forms in society as the merger movement of the late nineteenth century. The development of giant monopolistic corporations provided a model that government was soon to imitate as the needs of finance-capital required a large, powerful and interventionist state. The state began to imitate scientific management's creation of artificial hierarchies which served to control and undermine the growing worker solidarity and militancy.

Since Germany represents the purest expression of finance-capital, I turn to Germany in arriving at the most typical political and ideological institutions of the stage of imperialism. Just as monopoly and political intervention begin to undermine the law of value in this stage, so the development of a bureaucratic state as opposed to representative democracy begins to undermine the rule of law. In so far as the interventions of the state begin to move economic resources around, the universal and impersonal character of the law, which accords so well with the impersonal rule of the market, begins to break down in favour of particularistic bureaucratic decrees. Therefore, although the bureaucratic state is still in basic form a *rechtsstaat* and the type of legitimacy is still legal–rational, the rule of law *per se* is to some extent undermined by the rule of bureaucratic expertise.

The economic policies of imperialism include: protectionism and dumping, support for the export of capital, the creation of colonies and spheres of economic influence, and the pacification of the working-class and socialist movements. These policies are supported by ideologies which are: national chauvinist, racist, militarist, anti-democratic and anti-socialist. In this stage both the working-class and the capitalist class become more complex and stratified.

A great deal of work needs to be done to develop our understanding of the capitalist superstructure at the level of stage theory. It is at this level that the relation between territory, nation and class needs to be explored. At this level the capitalist state is no longer simply a legal form, but begins to emerge as a class state with a repressive apparatus encased in a legal form. To a certain extent politics and law become differentiated and each one becomes internally complex as it is embodied in material institutions. At this level the legal form of capital itself must be studied whether the dominant form is the chartered trading company, the industrial entrepreneur or the limited-liability joint-stock company.

At the level of stage theory I have adopted the approach of conceptualizing the dominant political and ideological forms as required by the dominant form of capital accumulation in the nation-state where this dominant form is located. Thus I look to Britain to find the material-types of policies and ideologies that are most conducive to the operaton of merchant-capital; I look to Britain again for the types of policies and ideologies that accord with the material-type of industrial-capital; and I look to Germany for the dominant material-types that accord with finance-capital. At the level of pure theory I derive the cell-forms of the superstructure, at the level of stage theory the superstructural forms begin to take on a material content as they take on a historical and geographical specific location, but they still only represent dominant abstract-types. To a very large extent the concrete material content to the theory of the capitalist state and ideology must be developed at the level of historical analysis. It is to this level that I turn next.

3   HISTORICAL ANALYSIS AND THE CAPITALIST SUPERSTRUCTURE

Both pure theory and stage theory are useful in guiding the historical analysis of the capitalist state and ideology. At the level of pure theory, besides deriving the basic ideological and political forms, we can begin to consider likely functions of the state at more concrete levels of analysis, where it must become more active. By looking at those points of the dialectic where the value-form has most difficulty in subsuming use-values, it is possible to see where, as a result, the domination of the commodity-form is going to need the most support as we move away from total reification. Where state intervention and regulation is most likely to occur is in connection with the 'fictitious' commodities, money, labour-power and land.[25] Though these three commodities come to be regulated by the commodity-economic principle, they are not the direct product of a capitalist production process. In this sense they are fictitious commodities – not products of a labour process but in capitalism subsumed to the commodity-form.

Money as gold is of course a real commodity. But even in the dialectic of capital the minting of coins and issuing of paper money requires some sort of institutionalized agreement among traders; and though this is not necessarily a state, it is a step in the direction of a public institution that acts to manage the affairs of the capitalist class that it cannot manage privately. When we analyse the territorial state at the level of stage theory, it becomes even more evident that the state must play a role in regulating the relation between internal money and external money. In order to help maintain a stable domestic currency, the state establishes a central bank. The state may also try to maintain a positive balance of payments. Further, the state may supplement the development of commodity-money and credit-money by issuing inconvertible paper money or what is essentially state-made fiat-money. This, of course, always runs the danger of creating inflation. In recent years, a favourite way of the state to regulate the economy has been through manipulation of the money supply. This manipulation becomes all the more possible and necessary once money has become disconnected from its commodity-form as gold. In recent years, the partial decommodification of money has created an international monetary system of freely fluctuating currencies, which means that state economic policy must ensure a strong currency in order to maintain any status in the international economic order.

Land as a fictitious commodity invites state regulation because initially the land-owning class is separate from the capitalist class. Agriculture and food production, as has already been pointed out, does not easily lend itself to capitalist production and to industrialization, and yet food is a basic need in any community. Also the continued separation of the working-class from the land is crucial to maintaining the commodification of labour-power. Finally land is the basis of all production and is in some ways a non-renewable resource that can be polluted, turned into wasteland or converted from agricultural uses to other uses.

In connection with land we may also mention fixed capital. Sekine points out that fixed capital has two aspects: it is a reproducible means of production and it is a temporarily irreproducible means of production comparable to land.[26] This land-like aspect of fixed capital is the material basis for the alternation between the deepening and widening phases of capital accumulation that we discussed earlier. In other words it is the material basis for periodic crisis along with the commodity labour-power. In so far as large-scale technical innovation or fixed capital investments are tied in with periodic crisis, this is an area that is bound to call forth state economic policy. This is because crises bring out the fundamental contradiction of capitalism between value and use-value and underscore its mortality, so that state policies are often called for to help alleviate the severe social dislocations that accompany periodic crises.

The most problematic fictitious commodity for capital and the one that therefore invites the greatest amount of state intervention is of course the commodity labour-power. This is so for the obvious reason that human beings resist being treated as things and therefore organize to resist the exploitation and oppression that exists in capitalist society. Furthemore, the mere continuation of the commodification of labour-power in a purely capitalist society requires periodic crisis, and each crisis exposes capitalism itself to dangerous disruption. It is especially in a crisis situation that the state is likely to expand its regulation of the economy and particularly the reproduction of labour-power as a commodity; for any substantial decommodification of labour-power must spell the end of capitalism.

Though in a purely capitalist society, capital simply leaves the reproduction of labour-power up to the worker's instinct of self-preservation, at the level of concrete history this proves to be disastrous, so that the state is forced to step in with policies that guarantee the continued reproduction of labour-power in a commodity-form suitable for needs of capital. Thus it is the continued commodification of labour-power that is most difficult for capital to achieve and that therefore calls for state policy that intervenes and that regulates the reproduction of this most crucial and vital of all commodities.

Class struggle emerges primarily around this issue of the commodification of labour-power. When we move away from the total reification of pure capitalism, capital requires the support of the state to maintain this commodification while the working-class resists and attempts to protect itself from the insecurities and ravages of being reduced to a mere commodity in the capitalist market. In particular the working-class must be concerned with improving working conditions, job security, and level and security of income. In moving away from the total reification of pure capitalism, the objective positions of capital and labour in the inner organization of capital give rise to class struggle and to state intervention to keep it within bounds.

These considerations of the fictitious commodities, money, land and labour-power can serve to guide our analysis of the state at the level of historical analysis where we need guidance through particularity and contingency. We would expect, then, to see state regulation of the economy develop most strongly in these areas of the economy where the commodity-form must secure more or less alien use-values, and where, therefore, in a less than totally reified society, we would expect difficulties to occur.

Stage theory offers a framework for theorizing the actual history of particular states and ideologies as well as state and ideological systems. Thus, for example, British mercantilism is the material-type for the stage of mercantilism, but specific mercantilist policies in their detailed development and evolution must be studied at a historical level. Further, the mercantilist policies of France or Spain or Holland were not necessarily the same as the British. We need to see also how mercantilist policies affected the periphery and semi-periphery of capitalism. Finally we need to analyse the type of international political system spawned by the dominant type of capital accumulation, whether it is hegemoney by a single state, or an international system where hegemony is established by two or more states in some sort of balance or stalemate, or an international system involving a real international state as in the world-state. This last possibility is, however, unrealistic because capitalism is so rooted in the nation-state historically, that world government would only be a realistic possibility in a transition phase away from capitalism.

The historical analysis of the superstructure of a particular nation-state involves an analysis of the history of the nation-state's involvement with the international dimension of capitalism. At this level we look concretely at how the political and ideological institutions promote or maintain the commodification of the fictitious commodities, labour-power, land and money. Struggles may develop around any or all of these commodities and the state policies regulating them, but the most important are the class struggles that develop around the commodification of labour-power. These struggles may become particularly intense during periodic crisis when capitalist production is temporarily disrupted by the need to replenish the industrial reserve army and revolutionize fixed capital.

The dominant state and ideology always try to appear to serve the interests of the abstract citizen and this appearance is confirmed in their basic legal form. But in fact that state generally serves the interest of the dominant fraction of capital if there is one. The capitalist class is not usually homogeneous or very clear about its best short-term or long-term interests, so we cannot say without qualification that the state always serves the interests of the capitalist class. Instead we may say that the state cannot go against the fundamental interests of capital except in a phase of transition or extreme crisis. In other times there is a groping relationship, with the capitalist class trying to gain clarity about its interests, and the state trying to find policies that best serve these seldom unambiguous class interests. Also because there is a tension between the legal form of the state and its class content, the state may at specific junctures not respond to the interests of the dominant fraction of capital. In situations of extreme crisis the capitalist state may temporarily lose its constitutional form and become dictatorial but this is always by way of exception. (I agree with Poulantzas's classifying these states as 'exceptional states'.)

Sometimes the capitalist state is forced to give in to the demands of the working-class or socialist movements. But these concessions cannot fundamentally undermine the accumulation of capital or we are talking about a transition away from capitalism. Whatever concessions are made are generally subverted in the long run or are implemented in such a way that they become another growth industry for capitalism. Real and lasting gains will be made by the working-class only in a transition towards socialism.

One of the unique features of this approach to the capitalist superstructure is the emphasis placed on the fundamental non-class character of the superstructure and therefore on the importance for the legitimacy of the capitalist state that it appears to be neutral, disinterested and above class. Gramsci is one of the few Marxist theorists to begin to realize the power of the capitalist superstructure to mobilize support by appearing to further the best interests of the majority, if not of all. This hegemony is not simply a power to manipulate and control culture, but is embedded deeply in the very basic superstructural forms which always address individuals as legal subjects, abstract citizens and property-owners. It is this basic way of 'interpellating' subjects that makes the ideology of the nation so strong as a unifying alternative to class interpellations. Understanding all of this is extremely important strategically in order for the socialist movement successfuly to organize a counter-hegemonic force. In this I agree most strongly with Laclau and Mouffe who point out the sectarian damage that has been done historically by class reductionist approaches to political and ideological struggle. This becomes especially important in the present transitional period, where in advanced industrial countries the industrial proletariat is a minority of the population and in some cases much better off than many other working people. The socialist movement must be seen to represent the interests of humanity as a whole in a most forceful way in opposition to the narrow sectarian interests of the capitalist class and the capitalist superstructure. Socialists must hold up the possibility of real community and real democracy in a de-reified society as a realistic possibility in opposition to the pseudocommunity held together by the market and pseudodemocracy which is based on the abstract legal subject instead of any substantial equality. In fighting to overcome the divide-and-rule nature of capitalism, socialists must understand how much the basic superstructural reflexes are also the reflexes of each subjectivity and we must learn to communicate with people so that their subjectivity can be 'interpellated' to the socialist movement. We must take notions like 'individual', 'freedom' and 'democracy' and then turn them against capitalist hegemony.

The capitalist superstructure becomes less of a superstructure and more interventionist as we move away from a purely capitalist society whether it is to more concrete levels of analysis or back in history towards pre-capitalism or forwards towards post-capitalism. In the world-historic transitional phase away from capitalism the law of value can less and less manage the more complex and social use-values that are produced, and the remaining commodified sector increasingly depends on a decommodified state and service sector. As more and more of economic life escapes effective market regulation, the state steps in to regulate economic life. But if the legitimacy of the capitalist state depends largely on its seeming disinterestedness, then involvement in the economy is bound to undermine its legitimacy. The state is caught in a double bind for it must increasingly manage the economy, but in doing so, it undermines its own legitimacy. At the very time that the state must expand spending to bolster its fading legitimacy, it is also faced with a fiscal crisis.

In this situation the need for a socialist state based on real community and democracy becomes a necessity. Such a state could produce policies which really represent the general interest rather than representing the dominant class or fraction while hiding behind a legal–rational facade. Therefore the legitimacy of such a state would be grounded in an egalitarian community and not in a split-off formal legality. Private life would no longer be grounded in an objectified economic order in contraposition to a subjectified and formalized public order. In a socialist society economic life would be de-reified and as a result would become public so the equating of the economic with the private (as in 'private enterprise') and the political with the public would come to an end. With the end of the reification the divorce between object and subject which gives rise to the basic character of the capitalist superstructure would come to an end. The state would no longer be a split off formal object based on the legal subject or abstract citizen but would be based on real citizens as they participate in the democratic organization of all social institutions from the workplace to the neighbourhood to governmental institutions. The passive legal subject of the purely capitalist society would be replaced by the politically involved and informed member of a political community. The contradictions of decaying capitalism make advanced industrial countries less and less governable by the old capitalist state forms. The decline of legitimacy will lead to more and more authoritarian political forms and reliance on force. The only realistic option to this drift is a thorough democratization of the economy and society or in other words socialism.

4 CONCLUSION

The dialectic of capital combined with a levels of analysis approach produces a theory of the capitalist state and ideology which clearly and precisely sets forth the relation between the economic, the political and the ideological at the level of pure capitalism. My theory of the capitalist superstructure is grounded at the level of pure theory because it is at this level that the meaning of 'capitalist' is objectively grounded. At this level of analysis I explore the cell-forms of the superstructure while holding its substantive content implicit. At the level of stage theory I begin to develop the substantive content of the capitalist superstructure as material-types of institutions and policies dominant in different stages of capitalist development. At the level of historical analysis, pure theory and stage theory can serve to aid in studying the relations between the economic, the political and the ideological in concrete historical environments. In the transitional phase away from capitalism state intervention reaches such proportions that it is difficult to distinguish the economic and the political since the economic becomes politicized and the political becomes economicized. To some extent the distinction between the economic and the political can still be made analytically using as a reference-point pure capitalism and stage theory where the economic and political are more clear and distinct.

Part II
Dialectical Materialism

7 The Uno/Sekine Approach to Dialectical Materialism

Part I dealt with Marxian political economy or the theory of capitalist society. In Part I I showed the sense in which the theory of a purely capitalist society serves as the foundation for Marxian political economy as a whole. It was necessary that this discussion of substantive content precede a more extended discussion of ontology, epistemology or methodology, because such philosophical discussions tend to be formal and empty unless they are based on a theory or an approach that achieves substantive knowledge. In Part II I shall briefly explore the implications for dialectical materialism of the fact that Uno and Sekine have brought to light the dialectical logic embedded in the theory of capital. I shall argue that the best way to clarify 'dialectical materialism' is not to start with some sort of general philosophy of materialism or general philosophy of dialectics, but rather to derive our understanding of dialectical materialism from the one completely worked out and rigorous dialectical theory, namely the dialectic of capital. Our understanding of dialectical materialism should be based on reconstructing the logic embedded in the theory of a purely capitalist society, and on drawing out the implications of such a logic. Without a reference-point in substantive knowledge 'dialectic materialism' becomes another philosophical concept set adrift without rudder, keel or anchor to be blown by every philosophical wind.

The history of debate over dialectical materialism and over the usages of the concepts 'dialectical' and 'materialism' has produced little agreement, or even a common point of reference. Sometimes 'dialectics' is used as a term meaning roughly 'interaction' as in 'dialectic between base and superstructure' or 'dialectic between theory and practice'. A somewhat less loose usage is to think of dialectical materialism as a set of maxims for good thinking such as: 'think about things in their interaction, in their motion, and in their relation to the whole'. An even more definite approach is to base dialectical materialism on Engels's three 'laws': quantity into quality, negation of the negation and interpenetration of opposites. The problem with all these approaches is that they do not derive their understanding of dialectical materialism from a theory which achieves substantive knowledge and is at the same time both dialectical and materialist. To say that there is a dialectic of nature or a dialectic of history is merely a hypothesis until someone actually produces a complete dialectical theory of nature or of history. But a dialectical theory of capital exists, and therefore one clear exemplar of dialectical materialism. This paradigm case clarifies our understanding of what dialectical materialism is and therefore what it would take for there to be a dialectical theory of nature or history.

In his manuscript *The Dialectic Capital* Sekine has not only developed a logically rigorous dialectical theory of pure capitalism, but also has shown that there is a close parallel between this dialectic and Hegel's *Logic*. Those who have not read Sekine's work will probably not be convinced by this chapter that the dialectic of a purely capitalist society is rigorous in the sense that it has a necessary beginning, unfolding and closure, and that this logic is parallel to that in Hegel's *Logic*. In this book I expand on these points a little, but there is no substitute for actually reading Sekine's *The Dialectic of Capital* as a whole. The existence of such a work is a momentous event for the debate over dialecticial materialism because it provides a much firmer foundation than heretofore upon which to build a common understanding.

1 HEGEL'S DIALECTIC

There has been considerable debate in recent years over the relation between Hegel and Marx: does Marx invert Hegel, extract the rational kernel or break with him entirely? Clearly Hegel had a very large impact on Marx, particularly in Hegel's claim that dialectics was a method of achieving objective knowledge. Marx's *Capital* has a dialectical logic embedded in it, although it is not made explicit by Marx. Uno's refinement of Marx's law of value brings out its dialectical structure, and although Uno was familiar with Hegel's *Logic* he did not make explicit the close structural parallel between Marx's law of value and Hegel's 'law of "Being" '. It is only with Sekine's *Dialectic of Capital* that the dialectical logic of the law of value is made fully explicit, and the parallels between it and Hegel's *Logic* are drawn. The logic is basically the same in both cases, only the ontology and theoretical object differ. For Hegel the dialectic involves the unfolding of the Absolute Idea in the Universe, and for Marxian political economy the dialectic involves the unfolding of capital in the capitalist mode of production (or in a purely capitalist society). According to Sekine, Hegel developed the logical form of the dialectic despite an idealist ontology that prevented the dialectic from serving as a basis for social science.

Later I shall argue that there are in fact some important differences in the dialectical logic of Hegel and Marx stemming from their different ontologies, but these differences occur within an overall parallel. In fact one would expect that the radical difference in their ontology would be reflected in a radical difference in their logics. That this is not the case stems mainly from the fact that the reification of capitalism purifies economic categories much as philosophical universalization purifies metaphysical categories. The general close parallel in dialectical logic between the two makes it desirable to start with Hegel, then to develop the dialectic of capital and finally to explain dialectical materialism by contrasting the dialectic of capital with Hegel's dialectic of the Absolute Idea.

Hegel believed that concepts arising from sensation present the world of outward appearance and not the inner reality of things, because imagistic concepts are permeated with contingency and particularity. Being based on sensation, most everyday discourse clings to appearances and is therefore not suitable for achieving knowledge. In contrast, according to Hegel the history of philosophy generates abstract universals. Though at first relatively empty or one-sided, these philosophic concepts become purified of contingency and taken together become ever more adequate to grasping the inner structure of reality. This inner structure is rational necessity in the sense that the philosophical universals hang together in a totality in which the inner connections are necessary connections freed from contingency through the universalization of reason. But this means that the inner reality of the universe is rational necessity which governs the universe in the sense that reason is self-synthesizing (it necessarily unfolds into this and only this totality).

Hegel's philosophic system consists of three levels: *The Logic* which traces the necessary inner connections of pure reason, the philosophy of spirit which traces the unfolding of reason in the human spirit and the philosophy of nature which shows that even the material universe is ultimately a manifestation of Reason. To understand Hegel's dialectic, the primary focus should be on its purest and most logically rigorous manifestation in *The Logic*.

Hegel's *Logic* brings out the nature of an object capable of being theorized dialectically. It is divided into three main parts or moments of reason: the Doctrine of Being, the Doctrine of Essence and the Doctrine of the Notion. Each of these doctrines brings out an aspect of the dialectic. The Doctrine of Being brings to the fore the self-containedness of the dialectic, the Doctrine of Essence emphasizes that the dialectic is self-determined and the Doctrine of the Notion brings out that the dialectic is self-revealing. An object capable of being theorized dialectically must therefore be self-contained, self-determined and self-revealing. Let me expand on each of these dimensions of dialectics.

The Doctrine of Being starts with the most abstract and empty and universal category of 'Being'. But because 'Being' is both universal and empty it threatens to collapse into 'Nothing', but that would be absurd. The movement between 'Being' and 'Nothing' that does not collapse into one side or the other is 'Becoming'. In this way the Doctrine of Being proceeds to show that a category that initially is considered in its discrete immediacy cannot stand on its own, and indeed implies other categories that also cannot stand on their own. Taken together the categories of the Doctrine of Being necessarily imply one another and therefore hang together in a self-contained totality.

Where the Doctrine of Being looks at categories in their immediacy and traces necessary connections through a logic of transition that moves from one seeming discrete category (e.g. Being) to another (e.g. Nothing) and to a third (e.g. Becoming), the Doctrine of Essence analyses the underlying substance of this self-contained totality to show how it is self-determined or grounded within itself. Here the concepts are paired concepts such as 'positive' and 'negative' or 'ground' and 'appearance' – concepts that imply one another or mediate one another. The concepts of the Doctrine of Essence are mediated pairs as opposed to the immediate discrete categories in the Doctrine of Being. In the Doctrine of Essence, the logic of reflection develops the necessary connections, so that, for example, the reflection of 'ground' into 'appearance' and vice versa gives rise to 'actuality', which represents the dialectical resolution of the opposition between 'ground' and 'appearance'. The Doctrine of Essence demonstrates that the appearance of self-containedness in the Doctrine of Being is real and substantial because it is a self-containedness that is also self-determined.

When the self-containedness is filled out and fully developed by the self-determination that it enfolds, then there must be outward manifestations that reveal the truth of this fully developed totality. Here Hegel uses a logic of development to show that the self-containedness and self-determination of the previous two doctrines can be maintained, while explaining the development of outward manifestations which give us a 'handle', so to speak, on the truth of the previous two doctrines. In this fashion the Doctrine of the Notion uses a logic of development to bring out the fact that the dialectic is self-revealing.

A dialectic is only self-revealing to the extent that it is fully developed and this is why Hegel used the well-known metaphors: 'the owl of Minerva only takes flight at dusk', and the necessity for the world to become 'grey' to emphasize this point. It is only because philosophy had become fully developed and mature and because the world had reached the age of reason that Hegel believed he could immerse himself in the subject-matter and find the necessary inner connections by letting the logic of the subject-matter move his own mind. This in fact is the basis to his claim of objective knowledge. Instead of imposing his own subjective schema on the subject-matter, he claims to let the subject-matter speak for itself thus revealing its objective inner logic. Because the connections between the categories are necessary connections free from contingency, it is not he himself who makes the deductions, but rather he discovers 'the method by which the categories deduce themselves'.[1] This may sound mystifying, but is it really so strange to become so immersed in something that one can come to see the logic or form embedded in that something? Is this so different from a sculptor who claims that the form was in the wood or in the soapstone, and he or she simply helped it to emerge? No doubt there is room for endless debate on fine points, but the basic distinction that Hegel is trying to make is clear: does the investigator impose a logic on the subject-matter or does he or she discover a logic embedded in the subject-matter? Hegel claims to have done the latter, and this is why he thinks that his theory is objective.

Hegel's totality is all of creation, and the inner logic is the necessary structure of rational thought itself, the Absolute Idea, or God. Hegel believed that the universe is permeated by reason and by purpose, so that ultimately all of existence is grounded in rational necessity. The immediate appearances of the senses often seem to manifest nothing but accident and contingency. But the movement of the philosophic mind away from the imagistic thinking of sense perception finally reaches the lofty heights of pure abstraction where the necessary inner connections between the philosophical universals are revealed. The universe is seen by Hegel to be a coherent totality in which all things are interrelated in a self-contained whole. It contains the principle of its own existence and its own determination within itself, or, in other words, is grounded within itself, and this inner principle is called 'Absolute Idea' or 'God'. Hegel believed that human history had reached the age of reason. It was now possible for him to aid the Absolute Idea in revealing its inner logic. He, therefore, viewed his own philosophy as reflecting the rational system of the universe, which, having reached full development, was revealing itself. But how does dialectical reasoning reveal the inner logic of reality?

Dialectical logic starts with the simplest, most abstract and emptiest specification of the totality under consideration. The very emptiness and abstractness of the beginning forces thought to negate this emptiness and to fill it in with ever more concrete specifications. Each step in the dialectic is a necessary step impelled by negation and contradiction towards a more concrete (more determined and more specified) synthesis which in turn gives rise to new contradictions until the dialectical circle reaches closure. At this point there are no more contradictions to impel the logic forward, for we have returned to the starting-point, but now with a concreteness which fills the original emptiness with objective knowledge. Starting with the abstract, the dialectic traces the necessary inner connections of the totality until the way in which it determines itself is completely revealed. The dialectic traces the necessary inner structure and dynamic of the totality which makes the totality what it is, so that the necessity is relative to the self-positing identity of the totality. In a successful dialectic all categories are grounded in necessity. Such and such a totality must have this particular inner logic. No relations are contingent in the sense that they might be otherwise. Thus, in the dialectic, the sequence of categories is a necessary sequence with a necessary beginning, unfolding and ending. No category can be simply introduced or posited by the theorist; rather the motion inherent in the subject-matter must show the necessity of each derivation in the logic.

As I have already mentioned, Hegel's system involves three basic dialectics: the dialectical logic, the dialectic of spirit and the dialectic of nature. Though the dialectic of spirit and the dialectic of nature are less pure, and therefore less rigorous, than the dialectical logic, Hegel sees no problem in completely subsuming them to the logic, since they simply represent the same logic only unfolding in the realm of human consciousness and in the realm of nature instead of in the realm of reason itself, i.e. philosophy. Hegel' failure to see anything problematic in the relation of the three dialectics severely weakens his philosophical system, since he does not recognize the tension between the pure logic and the more empirical and contingent concepts of the natural and historical sicences. As a result, in these latter two sciences, the dialectic acts more on analogy with *The Logic* than as a train of reasoning arising from the subject-matter itself. In these cases the dialectic is especially unconvincing and often appears as an alien or contrived imposition, which, far from arising from the specificity of the realm under consideration, rests upon the metaphysical assumption that reason rules the universe. The dialectic of nature, for example, does not reduce all of nature to a single rigorous dialectic as a necessary unfolding of an initial contradiction. There is no dialectic of nature in this sense. Instead Hegel's dialectic of nature tries to show that the natural sciences as existing in his day can be seen as emanations of dialectical reason. In other words, the results of natural science do not depend on the dialectic, but Hegel's idealism requires that he take great pains to show that whatever these results are, they are consistent with the Absolute and indeed represent one more case of the cunning of reason working through men without their knowledge.

Hegel is a major figure in the history of human thought because of his contributions to the understanding of dialectics. Dialectics opens the possibility of finding a more objective foundation for knowledge by bridging the gap between subject and object, which has always been the basic and seemingly insurmountable problem of philosophy. Though Hegel successfully develops the basic principles and forms of dialectical thought, his contributions to substantive knowledge of human history and society are disappointingly thin. This is because of his largely religious and metaphysical ontology which entraps the dialectic within a totality where its real scientific possibilities cannot be developed. For Hegel dialectical thought entailed absolute idealism which put the divine spirit working through reason at the centre of the universe. By trying to explain everything from the point of view of the Absolute Idea, he in fact explained little about concrete history and social life. As a result his system is ultimately more akin to a religion than to science.

Hegel wrote at a time when what he called 'civil society' and what others have called 'market society' or 'capitalism' was still in its infancy. The development of reason in this world, which Hegel saw coming to fruition with the enlightenment and his own philosophy, had a definite material base. As Max Weber and others have shown, modern rationalism is largely a product of market society and the development of reification. Reason was appearing more in the world, but it was not the kind that Hegel's theory called for. Hegel's reason was more akin to the organic reason of medieval thought or even the reason of the unified interrelated universe of oriental philosophy, than to the calculating reason of profit-oriented market man. Although the rule of reason was in actuality the rule of capital or civil society, capitalism was still sufficiently undeveloped that Hegel did not see this and preferred to project 'old world philosophy' onto this new rationality, and contain civil society between the family and the state where it is firmly subsumed to divine reason and the rational will. Hegel could not foresee that civil society would come to play the role of his 'God' in shaping the destinies of modern man, and that this same civil society would be the source of an alienation so grounded in material and human institutions that no mere philosophy could overcome it.

Hegel's ontology involves a double displacement. First, he confuses the rule of capital in the world with the rule of reason. This   s easy to do since capital was still in its infancy and th   not yet clearly dominant in human affairs. Second, he sees the reason which arises from the commodification of human life, not as the reason of calculating economic man, but as divine reason which finally humanizes the universe. Hegel envisions a world ruled by the reason of divine harmony on the threshold of a world about to be ruled by capital where reason primarily takes the form of the calculations of possessive individuals. He envisions a world where alienation comes to an end on the threshold of a world where alientation becomes deeply embedded in the material structures of everyday life. In fact Hegel marks the culmination of idealist philosophy which sees some combination of divinities or abstract ideas as ruling the world. The secularization and rationalization of the world in the nineteenth and twentieth centuries makes it impossible for mainstream philosophy to produce any longer the great metaphysical and speculative systems of traditional philosophy. Hegel's philosophy is only possible in a world where capitalism is developing but is not yet too developed. It is basically a religious solution to the problem of alienation, a type of solution which is only plausible in the early stages of capitalism. It is the most ambitious edifice of old world philosophy, and it is an appropriate final monument – more grand and more all-encompassing than any previous philosophy.

According to Hegel, dialectical thought is necessarily idealist and this is because the necessary inner connections of the universe only become revealed with the purest concepts of philosophy. But Hegel was wrong about this. In fact his dialectic was seriously flawed precisely because of its idealist ontology. He grounds our understanding of the universe in objective rational necessity, but fails to produce a theory with any significant explanatory power in relation to those concrete realities of greatest human concern – history and society. The centrality of pure philosophical universals in Hegel's philosophy was a source of both strengths and weaknesses. The strengths have to do with his success in presenting the basic principles and forms of dialectics and in constructing a dialectical logic. The weaknesses relate to the lack of explanatory power of the dialectic and its divorce from empirical reality. From the point of view of social science and natural science, Hegel's dialectic appears to be an alien construction that, far from grounding the knowledge of history and nature in rational necessity, seems to impose a metaphysical contrivance upon social and natural science.

The basic problem with Hegel's dialectic is that his dialectical totality, which is in the first instance the entire universe of human experience, does not permit the dialectic to make the contributions to knowledge of which it is capable. Such a theoretical object or object of knowledge forces the dialectic to be idealist since only the most abstract philosophical ideas can really encompass the universe. A materialist dialectic of the universe is unlikely, since matter *per se* does not seem to have a necessary inner logic out of which the entire universe *including all of human history* can be shown to unfold. And yet, I shall argue later, a materialist dialectic (but not of the universe) can help us ground our knowledge of history and society on a firmer foundation, which can bring together social science and dialectics in a way that fulfils the original promise of dialectics – the promise to provide an objective ground to our knowledge of society. The explanatory power of the dialectic is severely hampered by Hegel's totality. Supposedly all of nature and history can be generated out of rational necessity. But as Hegel moves from *The Logic* and the Absolute Idea towards the concreteness of history, it is not clear how the lower levels of analysis where greater contingency occurs relate to the higher levels – the move between levels of necessity is not clearly specified. Further, even at the level of the historical concrete, it is still the idea that prevails; the concrete is never examined in itself and in its historical specificity and concrete development. The materiality and complexity of history is absorbed into the most abstract idea which periodizes history into a series of *'zeitgeisten'*. In his effort to ground everything in rational necessity, Hegel does not give contingency its due. Instead of immersing himself in the materiality of history and finding a dialectic there, he imposes a 'made-in-heaven' dialectic on history which cannot help but have very little explanatory power. Hegel's dialectic is only at home with his idealist ontology in a formalistic and one-sided way. The dialectic can only realize its potential by forming an objective foundation for social science, but this requires a materialist foundation.

2 THE DIALECTIC OF CAPITAL

Uno devoted the later part of his life to exploring the inner logic of Marx's *Capital* with the aim of discovering the necessary inner connections of the law of value. The logic that he arrived at by immersing himself in Marxian political economy was later seen, by his student Sekine, to be close in structure to Hegel's *Logic*. Let me examine the parallel that Sekine develops between the logic of a purely capitalist society and Hegel's logic of absolute reason:

Dialectic of 'Capital'	*Hegel's 'Logic'*

I. The Doctrine of Circulation
    A. The commodity-form
    B. The money-form
    C. The capital-form
	I. The Doctrine of Being
	    A. Quality
	    B. Quantity
	    C. Measure

II. The Doctrine of Production
    A. The production-process of capital
    B. The circulation-process of capital
    C. The reproduction-process of capital
	II. The Doctrine of Essence
	    A. Ground
	    B. Appearance
	    C. Actuality

III. The Doctrine of Distribution
    A. The theory of profit
    B. The theory of rent
    C. The theory of interest
	III. The Doctrine of the Notion
	    A. The subjective notion
	    B. The objective notion
	    C. The idea.

The dialectic of capital starts with the Doctrine of Circulation which examines the fundamental circulation-forms of capitalism in their discrete immediateness. The commodity must be the starting-point because it is the most abstract, universal and all-encompassing concept of capitalism, or, in the words of Marx, it is 'the cell-form' which contains the basic contradiction of the dialectic of capital. Just as the basic contradiction of Hegel's dialectic is between 'Being' and 'Nothing' so the fundamental contradiction of the dialectic of capital is between 'value' and 'use-value'. An analysis of the commodity shows that it is a unity of contradictory aspects: value representing its social homogeneity in relation to other commodities and use-value representing its material heterogeneity. Using a logic of transition Sekine shows that the commodity-form necessarily generates the money-form and that the two together necessarily generate the capital-form. Analysis of the commodity-form demonstrates that it cannot stand on its own because the commodity-form cannot universalize itself without the money-form which represents an externalization of value. Analysis of the money-form shows that it cannot firmly establish itself without the capital-form M–C–M' which represents a synthesis of the commodity-form and the money-form. Only in the circulation-form M–C–M' does value free itself from use-value constraints so that its motion becomes self-contained. It this way the Doctrine of Circulation uses a logic of transition to establish the self-containedness of capital as a circulation-form or value-form.

The Doctrine of Production uses a logic of reflection to show that the circulation-forms can subsume an underlying labour and production process in order to create a specifically capitalist process of value formation and augmentation. Here the contradiction between value and use-value takes the form of a contradiction between historically specific value augmentation and universal use-value production. 'In this case the contradiction cannot be overcome by suppressing particular use-values in order to release value, but by letting the form of value wholly absorb or internalize the production of use-values itself.'[2] The Doctrine of Production demonstrates that the self-contained circulation-form M–C–M' becomes self-determining once its source of value expansion is internal to its own motion.

In the Doctrine of Distribution the contradiction between value and use-value takes the form of a contradiction 'between the unifying principle of the capitalist market and its necessarily heterogeneous ingredients'.[3] Here the logic of development is used to reconcile the motion of value with the necessary diversity of use-values in a purely capitalist society. In the Doctrine of Production value formation and augmentation is constrained by use-values without concern for the technologies associated with particular types of use-values.[4] In the Doctrine of Distribution the unity of circulation and production established in the previous two doctrines maintains itself while capital differentiates itself into heterogeneous forms required by the market. Thus, for example, capital is differentiated into branches of industry with distinct organic compositions, and into commercial and interest-bearing capital, while at the same time this differentiation is unified through the average rate of profit.

In the Doctrine of Distribution the economic forms which lie on the surface, namely profit, rent and interest, constitute a 'holy trinity' which completely mislead our understanding without the previous doctrines which bring out the necessary inner connections of capitalism. For example, 'since the rate of profit is a mercantile form indifferent to the productive base of society, it automatically effaces the trace of any specific mode of production and establishes the universal relation of equality among the traders of the market'.[5] Rent makes it appear that a thing, land, produces value; and interest is the most fetishized form of all since it makes capital appear to create value automatically by itself. But the Doctrine of Distribution demonstrates that these outward fetishized forms are simply the outward manifestation of a self-contained and self-determined inner logic. Therefore the Doctrine of Distribution shows that capital is self-revealing, not in the sense that it tends to become transparent, but in the sense that in fully developed capitalism it is possible to make the connections between its outward manifestations and its inner logic.

Although the basic contradiction of the dialectic of capital is between value and use-value, this contradiction takes different forms in the distinct logics of the three doctrines. Our starting assumption is a fully developed and fully purified capitalism. Given a purely capitalist society, how does it work? The fact that it is possible to construct a rigorous dialectic of such a society proves that it has a necessary inner logic. The three doctrines look at the same thing – a purely capitalist society – from three different points of view with distinct logics. At the same time these three logics are unified in a dialectical totality.

The Doctrine of Circulation looks at commodities, money and capital as they first appear on the surface of pure capitalism – i.e. as discrete entities. It demonstrates that these entities have a necessary inner connection because they are all value-forms differentiated as circulation-forms. Though the circulation-forms constitute a logically self-contained totality, they cannot really be self-contained without being grounded in a historically possible mode of production.

All societies require a labour and production process in order to survive. In order to take root in history, the circulation-forms must therefore subsume a labour and production process or, in other words, in order to be really self-contained (i.e. to not be simply logically self-contained but to exist historically), the circulation-forms must also be self-determining. The Doctrine of Production is not deduced from the Doctrine of Circulation. Instead M–C–M is now looked at from the point of view of how it is possible for a social totality to operate according to

M–C–M'. The key is the subsumption of the labour and production process, and this, of course, requires the commodification of labour-power. The Doctrine of Production looks at the interpenetration of the production process and the circulation process in order to specify fully the reproduction process of capital. The logic involved is not the movement between discrete entities, but is the interpenetration of the circulation process with the production process.

Finally a purely capitalist society is market-governed so that in order to complete the dialectic it is necessary to consider more concretely how the market can fully govern socioeconomic life. This requires the Doctrine of Distribution which explores the ways in which the law of value manages technology, land, trade and money. In this case the logic involves the overcoming of obstacles that are apparently alien to the market so that capital can return to itself and operate itself according to its own market principles. The theory of profit shows how capital manages technological differentiation and innovation according to commodity-economic logic. The theory of rent shows how land is managed by the law of value. The theory of interest shows how capital becomes an automatically interest-bearing force once it manages itself according to market principles. Thus the three doctrines follow each other in a logical sequence which moves from the abstract to the concrete in reaching closure with the full synthesis of the inner logic of a purely capitalist society.

The dialectic of capital constitutes a self-contained, self-determined and self-revealing dialectical totality with a necessary beginning, a necessary unfolding and a necessary closure. Such a dialectic is possible because capitalism is sufficiently self-purifying that we can let this purification complete itself in theory arriving at concepts that are purified of contingency just as are Hegel's philosophical universals. In a purely capitalist society, all production is production of commodities by commodified labour-power. Reification is total and the market completely governs socioeconomic life. The result is that pure economic categories are at the same time social categories. The inner logic of capital is theorized without artificially abstracting from social reality and thereby reducing the economic to the purely material – technical.

The starting-point or the given is a purely capitalist society, and the dialectic of capital reveals its inner logic. Sekine does not impose a logic on the subject-matter from the outside. Instead he discovers the logic which is embedded in the subject-matter and lets that logic guide his theorization. To the extent that he is successful in letting the logic emerge from the subject-matter, the theory that traces that logic can be said to be objective. The theory is objective because the knowing subject does not add anything from his own imagination but is instead entirely guided by the logic of the object of knowledge. This of course is not possible with all objects of knowledge since a prerequisite for such a method to be successful is an inner logic which is tending to reveal itself, or which can be fully brought to light.

Before I go on to the next section, more needs to be said about the self-revealing character of the capitalist dialectical totality. I do not mean by this that in its maturity capitalism becomes completely transparent, but rather that as it becomes fully developed, the economic relations of capitalism become sufficiently purified in the sense of sloughing off pre-capitalist and extra-economic contingencies, that it becomes possible to theorize the inner logic of capitalism. The dialectical logic of the theory then becomes the expression of the inner logic of capital without the need for any concepts or logic brought to bear from the outside. At the same time as the inner logic is self-revealing in this sense, capitalism is necessarily opaque. The very reification and fetishism of commodities that makes a dialectic possible, also makes the inner logic of capital not immediately transparent in its outer appearances. A part of the self-revelation of capitalism is the revelation of the necessary opaqueness of an ecomonic system which subsumes real economic life to commodity-economic principles. Thus to say that mature capitalism tends to reveal itself does not at all imply transparency in the sense that an immediate reading of its appearances will spontaneously reveal its inner workings.

That capitalism tends to reveal itself is evidenced by the fact that political economy develops as a science only with the development of capitalism. Abstract labour, for example, only becomes sufficiently manifest to be conceptualized with capitalism. Adam Smith was the first economist to conceive labour in general as the source of wealth in general. Ricardo went further than Smith in developing a consistent labour theory of value only he failed to grasp fully the specific form of value creating labour and of surplus value. Capitalism reached its fullest maturity in

England in the 1860s, and it was here that Marx was first able to place political economy on firm scientific foundations. 'Classical political economy stumbles approximately onto the true state of affairs, but without consciously formulating it. It is unable to do this as long as it stays within its bourgeois skin.'[6] By the 1860s the proletariat and the socialist movement were sufficiently well developed that Marx was able quite definitely to get outside the bourgeois skin that limited Smith and Ricardo. It is no accident that the development of political economy parallels the development of capitalism, and this is because the self-purifying and self-abstracting tendencies of capitalist reification make it possible for theorists to arrive at ever more general, abstract and pure concepts which at the same time accurately grasp the inner essential workings of the capitalist economy.

3   DIALECTICAL MATERIALISM

In explicating the dialectical character of the theory of a purely capitalist society, I have focused on the similarities between Hegel's dialectic and the dialectic of capital. Now in order to bring out the materialist character of the dialectic of capital, it is necessary to focus on some of the differences between it and Hegel's dialectic.

With Hegel the material sensuous world is the manifestation of the reason and wisdom of the Absolute. But the Absolute can only be so rigorously theorized because in the pure concepts of metaphysics no trace of sensuous materiality remains that could introduce elements of contingency. Materiality does not disappear altogether, but is inactivated as a passive substrate so that it cannot interfere with the necessary inner connections of the metaphysical ideas. But because Hegel's 'Nothing' (in the basic 'Being'/'Nothing' contradiction) does not represent this passive materiality but instead total void, *The Logic* becomes trapped within absolute idealism.[7] There is no principle internal to the dialectic which would permit Hegel to move to more empirical or historical levels of analysis by reactivating materiality while remaining grounded in the logic. Consequently the notorious inadequacy of his dialectic of nature, which, instead of reintroducing materiality into the dialectic, imposes an alien logic onto the activity of natural science. Because Hegel's 'Nothing' is a mere shadow or ghost of 'Being', 'Being' meets no opposition from 'Nothing', but this means that 'Being' must revolve around itself without any possibility of breaking out and making any real contact with materiality. Thus the inadequacy of the dialectic of nature is closely related to the original inadequacy of the 'Being'/ 'Nothing' couplet in the *Logic*.

The dialectic of capital does not have this problem since unlike Hegel's 'Nothing', 'use-value' is material and substantial. The theory of a purely capitalist society neutralizes and pacifies use-values so that the law of value can display its necessary logic. The logic of capital or pure theory provides a framework of necessary relations which act to guide the analysis of contingencies which arise in stage theory and historical theory. Since use-values by themselves are heterogeneous and discreet, they do not possess their own logic. It is possible to arrive at an inner logic at the level of pure theory because reification neutralizes or deactivates use-values, but where use-values are reactivated at more concrete levels of analysis the inner logic becomes increasingly disrupted by contingency.

Implied by what I have just argued is an important difference between necessity in Hegel's dialectic and in the dialectic of capital. With Hegel's dialectic, rational necessity permeates the universe so that even contingency is rationally necessary. Nothing escapes the cunning of reason whose hold on the world is truly absolute. The 'cunning of capital' is different. It only takes hold of the world to the extent that the production of use-values can be completely governed by the commodity-economic principle or by the market. In fact it turns out that only a certain range and certain types of use-values can be capitalistically managed through the market alone, so that capitalism is historically limited and only achieves a partial hold on historical reality. The cunning of capital is therefore not so all-powerful and there is an outside into which it does not reach. The necessity of the law of value is only absolute over socioeconomic life in a purely capitalist society. At lower levels of analysis it is impinged on by contingencies or even by necessity (in the sense of structural tendencies) that arises outside itself. Pure theory, then, provides an objective foundation for social science, but it does not encompass all of social science within its own logic. The cunning of capital does not have a stranglehold on the world the way the cunning of reason does for Hegel.

All dialectics are teleological in the sense that they must achieve closure, but the dialectic of capital is not teleological in the same sense as Hegel's dialectic. The teleology of the dialectic of capital involves the overcoming of the contradiction between value and use-value. This is achieved in a purely capitalist society where the self-realization of capital is allowed to complete itself. To refer to the content of the dialectic of capital as the law of value is then accurate because the entire theory involves various metamorphoses of value as it completes its motion in subsuming all use-value obstacles, or, in other words, in subsuming the totality of socioeconomic life. The teleology in this case is logical and not historical, so that though the dialectic reaches closure with the commodification of capital in the form of interest, this says nothing about the historical destiny of capitalism. For the dialectic to be possible in the first place, there must be some tendency for capitalism to realize itself in history, but the actual course this takes and how it comes to an end is not a part of the dialectic. The subject/object of the dialectic of capital is capital. The dialectic of capital only shows how capitalism necessarily operates when it is allowed to be most fully itself. The historical genesis of capitalism or its historical demise must be studied at other levels of analysis and not at the level of pure theory. With Hegel, reason actually comes to realize itself completely in history; whereas with our dialectic, capital only partially realizes itself because of its limited ability to overcome the resistance of concrete use-values.

My interpretation of dialectical materialism indicates that Marx's much maligned 'copy theory' or 'reflection theory' of knowledge was on the right track. What makes the dialectic of capital objective is that it copies the self-reifying tendency of capitalism in arriving at the notion of a purely capitalist society and then copies the logic inherent in such a society. This does not imply that the law of value is a mere mental reflex since that would mean that capitalism was transparent. What I have in mind is a complex copy theory in which a tradition of discourse called 'political economy' develops with the development of capitalism. Smith and Ricardo partially discovered the inner logic of capital, but only partially because capitalism itself was only partially developed, because of their unfamiliarity with dialectics, because of their 'bourgeois skins', and for various other reasons. Marx was working within a tradition of discourse which he was able to advance because he escaped the above-mentioned limitations. The complex copy theory that I have in mind does not imply that Marx did not have to work very hard in arriving at his theory. Here it is necessary to separate the method of inquiry and the method of presentation. It was only by achieving total mastery of his subject-matter through arduous study that Marx was finally able to adopt a passive stance and let the logic inherent in capital manifest itself without his interference. Marx's discovery of reification was crucial to his understanding the self-synthesizing character of capitalism, and his knowledge of Hegel's dialectic was crucial to ordering the sequence of categories in *Capital*, even if he strays from a strict dialectical sequence.

Because Hegel's 'Nothing' provides no substantial opposition to 'Being', his dialectic as a whole is somewhat artificial in the sense that the categories could easily collapse into each other. This lack of differentiation in Hegel's dialectic, or this tendency for differentiation to collapse back into a simple unity, is not a problem with the materialist dialectic of the law of value, and this is because the economic categories are materially differentiated forms of value clarified by value really overcoming or absorbing use-value and not by a shadow-play between 'Being' and 'Nothing'.[8]

4 CONCLUSIONS

There is no end to the possible interpretations of 'dialectical materialism' if the concept is not derived from a theory which gives us objective knowledge and is at the same time both dialectical and materialist. I have indicated in outline that the theory of capital first developed by Marx in *Capital* is potentially such a theory. It is a theory which is about social relations which have become materialized and objectified through the self-expanding motion of capital. It is a theory which is dialectical in the sense that it traces the self-synthesizing inner logic of cpaital, and shows that a purely capitalist society is a self-contained, self-determining and self-revealing dialectical totality. Therefore the basis for the understanding of 'dialectical materialism' should be the dialectic of capital.

If the dialectic of capital is the basis of the concept 'dialectical materialism', there is reason to suspect that there may be no dialectic of history or of nature. No one has yet constructed a theory of the inner logic of nature with a necessary beginning, unfolding and closure. It seems unlikely that such a theory could be constructed unless nature becomes 'grey', but the idea of a fully developed universe may be absurd. It also seems unlikely that nature would turn out to have a single self-synthesizing inner logic. Furthermore, there is reason to suspect that there is no dialectic of history. What would be the necessary beginning and basic contradiction of such a dialectic? How could it reach closure? Would it not have to be written by the last humans just as humanity was coming to an end? No dialectic of history has ever been written. One almost hopes that none will be written, since the prospect of history becoming 'grey' is not appealing. It does not appear possible to write even a dialectic of feudalism much less of all human history. The dialectic of capital is possible because it is a piece of history delimited by reification to constitute a dialectical totality. This totality has the unique properties of being man-made and of being objectified in the sense that it is governed by the motion of commodities. It is an objectified, delimited, sociohistorical institution, which, though social, escapes human control and achieves a logic of its own. In Part I of this book, I tried to show how the law of value can serve as an objective foundation for the study of capitalism. In this chapter I have tried to show how the dialectic of capital can clarify the meaning of 'dialectical materialism' and the relation between Hegel and Marx. In the next chapter, I shall draw out some of the implications of this approach by critically analysing three of the most innovative and important theorists in the tradition of Western Marxism: Lukacs, Althusser and Colletti.

8   A Critical Analysis of Some Western Approaches to Dialectical Materialism

To Marxists 'dialectical materialism' has generally referred to the basic ontology and epistemology of Marxist theory. Neither Marx nor Engels gave a very well worked out or convincing account of 'dialectical materialism' with the consequence that from their day to this there has been almost continual controversy over the meaning and import of this basic concept. Since it is the most fundamental concept of Marxist philosophy, it is also the one over which the major schools of interpretation most clearly divide. At the one extreme are intepretations which argue that the universe is basically matter in motion, and that this motion occurs according to the basic principles of dialectics. At the other extreme, and increasingly in recent years, are schools of Marxist thought which tend either to reject dialectical materialism or to redefine it so that dialectics is sacrificed to materialism or materialism to dialectics.[1]

To explore the basic cleavages within Marxist philosophy, no issue is more decisive than the relation between Hegel and Marx, and more specifically the question of dialectics. Does Marx simply historicize and materialize the Hegelian dialectic by locating the prime mover in the historical unfolding of class struggle as opposed to Hegel's Absolute Idea? This position put forward by Lukacs in *History and Class Consciousness* is sharply disputed by Althusser who sees a radical break between the Hegelian and Marxian dialectic. According to Althusser the Marxian dialectic is not simply an inversion of the Hegelian; it is a distinct epistemology with only superficial similarities to Hegel's spiritual/expressive dialectic. Contrary to Althusser, Colletti does find dialectical logic in the Hegelian sense present in Marx's *Capital*, but cannot reconcile this with the general claim that *Capital* is a work of science. Colletti sees *Capital* as an effort to combine moral and critical philosophy with materialistic science, but for him these two do not combine very well so that the integrity of the theory is in continual jeopardy.

The early Lukacs, Althusser and Colletti all have important things to say about dialectical materialism, and all three have been influential. A critical evaluation of these three thinkers will enable me to develop a dialogue between some of the major debates over dialectical materialism within Western Marxism and the Japanese Uno School.

1 LUKACS: DIALECTICS AS REVOLUTIONARY PRACTICE

The essays collected together in Lukacs' *History and Class Consciousness* were written between 1918 and 1922. The underlying political motive of these philosophical essays is to attack the reformist and positivist tendencies in the theory of the Second International in favour of a Marxian epistemology that puts class struggle and revolution not only at the centre of Marxian politics but also at the centre of Marxian science and knowledge. Lukacs launches a sweeping attack against bourgeois thought and its manifestations within Marxism, because it essentially supports and confirms the capitalist status quo by separating thought from action, form from content, subject from object and individual from society. Lukacs argues that under the regime of bourgeois philosophy thought becomes compartmentalized and formalized as if the principle of divide and rule were applied to the mind in order to pacify the realm of ideas. Without cross-fertilization between ideas or between theory and practice, thought becomes sterile and impotent. A sort of *cordon sanitaire* is drawn around disturbing problems so that they can be dealt with in isolation and not be seen as symptoms of some larger disease that may ultimately indicate a radical anti-capitalist cure. In opposition to bourgeois thought, which is so reified and contemplative, Lukacs formulates the Marxian dialectic relying upon proletarian revolution to dissolve all the rigid separatenesses of bourgeois thought. Reality itself becomes fluid and can be completely grasped in thought in the process of being revolutionized in practice. In this way the revolutionary practice of the proletariat is the key to both the realization of communism and of knowledge, and the dialectic, which was essentially contemplative in Hegel's philosophy, becomes essentially activist in the hands of Marxism.

Lukacs sees 'deep affinities' between Marx and Hegel 'for both conceive of theory as the self-knowledge of reality'.[2] For Hegel, reality can attain knowledge of itself only to the extent that the unfolding of the Absolute Idea has been realized within concrete reality itself. The vehicle for this self-knowledge is philosophy or the philosopher, but the philosopher is essentially the instrument of the Absolute Idea which is the ultimate subject and object of history. It is the concretization of the dialectical unfolding of the Absolute that constitutes history. History is essentially the self-realization of the Absolute, and knowledge is the Absolute coming to know itself through its coming into full being. The problem with this approach, according to Lukacs, is that in the end Hegel's dialectic does not really 'overcome the duality of thought and being, of theory and practice, or subject and object'.[3] This is because the subject–object of history is the ahistorical, spiritual and essentially alien Absolute. 'Hegel was unable to penetrate to the real driving forces of history . . . he remained imprisoned in the Platonic and Kantian outlook, in the duality of thought and being, of form and matter, notwithstanding his very energetic efforts to break out.'[4] This is because the subject–object is located outside of history with the result that it is not human society that comes to know itself but the Absolute. Marx's great achievement and his essential difference from Hegel is his location of the subject–object within history so that the dialectic becomes thoroughly historicized.

Lukacs argues that for Marx history is a social process and is an outcome of human activity.[5] Pre-capitalist history is the unconscious product of human activity that is only partially socialized. The universalization of commodity production and exchange creates a society where man becomes a truly social being, and the development of the proletariat results in a class which can make history consciously. The proletariat, then, is the subject–object of history because:

for the proletariat the total knowledge of its class-situation was a vital necessity, a matter of life and death; because its class situation becomes comprehensible only if the whole of society can be understood and because this understanding is the inescapable precondition of its actions. . . . From its own point of view self-knowledge coincides with knowledge of the whole so that the proletariat is at one and the same time the subject and object of its own knowledge.[6]

In order to carry out its historical role successfully, the proletariat must understand history and its place in history. Thus for the proletariat self-knowledge coincides with the knowledge of history; knowledge of self (the proletariat) coincides with knowledge of the object (history). Since the historical role of the proletariat is to carry out a socialist revolution, it is only in the process of revolutionary transformation that knowledge of subject and object finally coincide and the proletariat finally realizes its destiny as subject–object of history.

The point of view of totality represented by the proletariat must continually struggle against the reification of capitalist society. Reification refers to a situation where man-made things come to dominate over the men who made them. With the generalization of commodity production, social relations come to be dominated by the motion of commodities in the market. In *Capital* Marx refers to cognitive misapprehensions that arise from this domination of things over men as 'fetishism of commodities'. Lukacs uses the term 'reification' to refer to the social and intellectual structures that arise in bourgeois society from the generalization of commodity production and exchange. Lukacs's 'reification' is a broader term than 'fetishism of commodities' because it includes misapprehensions arising from the commodity-form but also includes all social and intellectual structures arising from the objectification of social relations brought about by their subsumption to the commodity-form. For Lukacs reification is the key to understanding capitalist society, so much so that he can write:

It has often been claimed – and not without a certain justification – that the famous chapter in Hegel's *Logic* treating of Being, Non-being and Becoming contains the whole of his philosophy. It might be claimed with perhaps equal justification that the chapter dealing with the fetish character of the commodity contains within itself the whole of historical materialism and the whole self-knowledge of the proletariat seen as the knowledge of capitalist society (and of the societies that preceded it).[7]

or again; the problem of commodities must not be considered in isolation or even regarded as the central problem in economics, but as the central, structural problem of capitalist society in all its aspects. Only in this case can the structure of commodity-relations be made to yield a model of all the objective forms of bourgeois society together with all the subjective forms corresponding to them.[8]

Reification gives rise to the characteristic antinomies of bourgeois thought with subject being divorced from object, theory from practice, form from content, part from whole and the individual from society. With the rise of capitalism for the first time the economic structure of society becomes unified and dominant so that it serves as the material basis for a unified consciousness characterized by reification. The subsumption of human relations to the commodity-form makes them subject to economic calculation so that the process of capitalist rationalization is formalistic in the sense that the parts – firms or specialized disciplines – are subjected to precise rational calculation of details but the whole remains ruled by chance. Reason can achieve formal self-consistency and precision within each part, but since the part remains divorced from the whole which gives the part its substantial content, the result is formally rational parts embedded in a substantially non-rational whole. The divorce between form and content, part and whole produces a bifurcation in reason between formal and substantive reason.[9]

the contradiction that appears here between subjectivity and objectivity in modern rationalist formal systems, the entanglements and equivocations hidden in their concepts of subject and object, the conflict between their nature as systems created by 'us' and their fatalistic necessity distant from and alien to man is nothing but the logical and systematic formulation of the modern state of society.[10]

Thus the ideal of modern knowledge wavers between mathematics which is objective because man-made and physics which is objective because it grasps a natural reality which is objective precisely because it is distant from and not interfered with by human subjectivity (i.e. is not man-made).

For Lukacs there is no clear distinction between knowledge and class-consciousness. Only classes can know because only classes can adopt the point of view of totality. But for the bourgeoisie, knowledge of the contradictions of capitalism contradict their class interest which would like to see capitalism as an eternal system. The proletariat is in a privileged position to know because its class interests are in accord with the dialectic of history towards human emancipation. The proletariat is in a privileged position not only to know history but to know what to do in carrying out its historical role. For Lukacs there is no problem in the relation between theory and practice since the correct theory can directly determine the correct practice.

> Thus dialectical materialism is seen to offer the only approach to reality which can give action a direction. The self-knowledge, both subjective and objective, of the proletariat at a given point in its evolution is at the same time knowledge of the stage of development achieved by the whole society. . . . It is to know the direction that determines concretely the correct course of action at any given moment – in terms of the interest of the total process viz. the emancipation of the proletariat.[11]

Knowledge and self-knowledge become the same, the self-knowledge of the proletariat and the knowledge of the whole society become the same, and finally this total knowledge determines the correct course of action.

Even Engels failed to grasp the most vital interaction of dialectical materialism, 'namely the dialectical relation between subject and object in the historical process'.[12] For Lukacs this is central because the aim of the dialectical method is to change reality and this necessitates theoretical emphasis on a subject overcoming and remaking an alien object in the subject's own image.[13] Revolutionary change is so central that theory is subordinated to it, so much so that 'theory is essentially the intellectual expression of the revolutionary process itself'.[14] 'Praxis is central to the possibility of dialectics because 'the essence of praxis consists in annulling that indifference of form towards content that we found in the problem of the thing-in-itself." '[15] The divorce between theory and reality is overcome by making theory pragmatic.

Theory and reality are melted together by theory becoming pragmatic and by the fact that 'the objective forms of the objects are themselves transformed into a process, a flux'.[16] Theory is action-oriented so as not to deteriorate into the bourgeois ideology that is a product of reification:

> Every comtemplative, purely cognitive stance leads ultimately to a divided relationship to its object. . . . For every purely cognitive stance bears the stigma of immediacy, that is to say, it never ceases to be confronted by a whole series of ready-made objects that cannot be dissolved into processes. Its dialectical nature can survive only in the tendency towards praxis and in its orientation towards the actions of the proletariat.[17]

This is a very strong statement, for it claims that thought itself cannot dissolve ready-made objects into processes, and that this requires praxis. Ultimately it is only praxis that can make thought dialectical because otherwise the subject/object split undermines the dialectical process.

Lukacs's formulation of dialectical materialism is very appealing because there is a very strong activist, critical and utopian thrust in the Marxian tradition. The Marxism of the young Lukacs represents a longing for a unified world where there is no real separation between subject and object, self and other in the face of the radically atomized and fragmented world of capitalism. This vision of a more unified world is very attractive in a world that is so disunified. The appeal of Lukacs's interpretation of dialectical materialism is its thrust towards radical criticism, moral vision and revolutionary activism, but this appeal is achieved at the cost of undermining dialectical reasoning as a way of attaining objective knowledge. But Marxism must encompass both moral vision and science, and the romanticism of the young Lukacs arrives at a very one-sided Marxism – a critical revolutionary Marxism cut off from its scientific and materialist side. 'Dialectical materialism' falls apart into its two component concepts, and 'dialectics' is made triumphant by sacrificing 'materialism'.

Lukacs is quite correct in emphasizing the importance of the category 'totality' to dialectical thinking. The problem is his loose

usage of the concept sometimes to refer to all of history and
sometimes to refer primarily to capitalism and his tendency to
ignore problems in arriving at accurate and objective knowledge
of the 'totality'. Lukacs refers to history as a dialectical totality,
and yet he does not construct a dialectical theory of history with
its necessary unfolding of an original contradiction. The fact that
the only dialectic of history to be written has been idealist (Hegel)
suggests that history does not form itself into a totality which is at
once both self-determining and materialist. Instead of constructing a materialist dialectic of history that would give a scientific
grounding to his theory, he simply assumes history is a dialectic.
This enables him to see proletarian revolution as the outcome of a
teleology; and, since dialectical logic is a necessary unfolding,
proletarian revolution is necessary. But unfortunately there is
nothing scientific in all this. Instead moral vision and wish
fullfilment are dressed up in the language of dialectics.

One of Lukacs's major theoretical contributions is the recognition that reification is central to capitalism. But here again his
contribution is partially undermined by a loose and one-sided use
of the concept 'reification'. Instead of seeing that it is precisely
reification that makes it possible for Marx to construct a theory
of the laws of motion of capitalism which can serve as the
scientific grounding of Marxian social science, he only sees
reification as the central concept of a cultural totality that must be
overthrown. But reification has both of these aspects, and the two
aspects need to be kept distinct though not unrelated. Thus
because of reification, we can construct a dialectic of capital that
reveals the necessary inner connections of the capitalist mode of
production. Besides making a science of capital both necessary
and possible (science is necessary because capitalism is not
transparent), reification also is the material base of bourgeois
ideology, and hence the demystifying of reification can serve as a
basis for criticizing bouregeois ideology. But this critique of
capitalist ideology needs to be carefully derived from the dialectic
of capital so that it is grounded in Marxian social science.
Contrary to this approach, Lukacs ignores the law of value and
develops a critique of the bourgeois cultural totality based
entirely on the concept of reification. The result is a bifurcation
between cultural criticism and social science. The criticism of
bourgeois culture as a whole becomes very abstract and divorced
from history. It becomes easy then to reify 'bourgeois culture' and

turn it into an all-encompassing main enemy. To combat this moralistic and idealistic tendency, it is important to derive carefully the basic capitalist ideological forms from the dialectic of capital and then to historicize the content of capitalist ideology by moving through stage theory to historical analysis. Thus the abstract and formal 'bourgeois ideology' is filled in by analysing first mercantilist, liberal and imperialist ideologies, and then with historical/empirical analysis as, for example, ideology in Britain in the 1840s.

Besides understanding the role of 'reification' in both the dialectic of capital and ideological criticism, it is also important to understand the key role of this concept in thinking about the transition to socialism. Socialism is primarily the overcoming of reification in the sense that a society governed by the self-regulating market and hence by prices and profits is replaced by one in which society re-appropriates control over the economy. It becomes democratically organized to meet social needs. Both the dialectic of capital and ideological criticism can aid in understanding the nature of reification and in overcoming it at the level both of economic structures and processes and at the level of thought processes and cultural production.

According to Lukacs, 'theory is essentially the intellectual expression of the revolutionary process itself'.[18] Presumably the proletariat will attain knowledge as subject–object of history at the moment of revolution. In the process of revolution, reality itself becomes fluid; but if this is the case, then objectivity becomes a protean form that changes as we attempt to grasp it. At the moment that the proletariat arrives at knowledge of reality, reality itself dissolves into shapeless flux. At this point knowledge dissolves into 'making' resulting in extreme voluntarism.

It is true that theory and practice are related in Marxism, but it is inaccurate to call this relation 'dialectical' unless one is using the term very loosely to mean 'interaction'. To speak of 'the unity of theory and practice' as Lukacs does, tends to cover over the complex and complicated relationship between theory and practice. The theory of a purely capitalist society or the dialectic of capital frees itself from contingency because it copies the self-purifying and self-reifying tendencies of capitalism. At this level of abstraction, we can refer to necessity in the strong sense, as, for example, in the necessity for a general rate of profit to form. At the level of practice there is less necessity, and it is sometimes nearly swamped by contingency. Strategic theory must be based largely on experience and practical wisdom, and cannot have the same kind of necessity that we associate with the laws of motion of capital. The notion of a unity of theory and practice can lead to the celebration of the diversity of the concrete at the expense of theory, or it can lead to the celebration of the iron necessity of theoretical laws at the expense of the concrete. If Marxists attribute the same necessity to positions of political strategy as they do to economic laws, then they are committing the error of dogmatism. If, on the other hand, they eschew theory in favour of the concrete and spontaneism, they are giving up the commitment to rationalism and science that is so important in the Marxian tradition. The solution to this problem is the full development of the complex of mediations between various levels of theory and between these levels of theory and various kinds of practice.

2 ALTHUSSER: DIALECTICS AS COMPLEX STRUCTURE

The major preoccupation of Louis Althusser in his two most important and influential epistemological works, *For Marx* and *Reading Capital*, is to rid Marxism of the pernicious contamination of Hegelianism. It is Althusser's firm belief that Hegelian influences have undermined the scientificity of Marxism, so that the twin tasks of ridding Marxism of Hegelian influences and of establishing firm scientific foundations for Marxist theory nearly coincide.

According to Althusser, the Hegelian dialectic begins with 'an original simple unity' which divides because of negativity. The resulting contradiction is superseded in a succession of totalities representing an ever more concrete restoration of the original simple unity until the negativity is completely overcome in a final totality which realizes all the possibilities inherent in the original simple unity. Each totality is the supersession of the previous one because it represents the truth of the latter in a more developed form. Each totality or unity is a 'centred' or 'expressive' totality in the sense that the central idea or essence permeates the whole so that each part is simply a particular expression of this abstract essence. This means that within the Hegelian problematic there is no real otherness, autonomy or externality. There are no real breaks in history because each epoch simply represents the truth of the previous epoch raised to a higher level. Also within each totality, the parts as expression of the inner essence lack any substantial autonomy. As a result everything is internal to everything else, there is no substantial externality or even relative autonomy. History is a sort of circle with a simple beginning and an end which represents a return to the original unity only now with all the original potentialities realized. The Hegelian problematic is therefore both genetic and teleological in character. It is also a simple, centred, expressive totality because there is no real externality or autonomy of parts, but rather complex concreteness is reduced to the manifold expression of a simple inner essence.

For Althusser the Marxian theory of history stands in stark contrast to the Hegelian problematic. First, for Marx history has no beginning and no end; dialectical materialism is neither genetic nor teleological. Second, for Marx there are real breaks in history; the succession of modes of producton is not a supersession, but is instead a succession of distinct and different structural formations. Third, the Marxian totality is a complex structure of relative autonomous practices unified not by a centred abstract principle, but by a decentred structure-in-dominance. The Marxian totality is therefore a complex, structured totality that contains externality in the form of breaks in history and relative autonomy of parts within the totality.

The lack of autonomy in the Hegelian problematic applies also to the relation between knowledge and being. According to Althusser, with Hegel the real order follows the logical order, or in other words, the real concrete represents the concretization of the logical. The process of reality and the process of knowledge are parallel, so that knowledge is simply the self-consciousness of the present purified by philosophy. Hegel then represents the logical–historical method in its purest form. The logical and historical parallel one another, and the historical is the concretization of the logical. There is no break between the logical and the historical but instead an interpenetration.

The disjunction or relative autonomy that Althusser establishes between theory and history leads him to reject all reflection theories of knowledge which see knowledge as a direct reflection of reality or reality as a concretization of knowledge. 'We must completely reorganize the idea we have of knowledge, we must abandon the mirror myths of immediate vision and reading, and conceive knowledge as a production.'[19] For Althusser knowledge is a process of production, and the object of knowledge as a theoretical object must be clearly distinguished from the real object.

Althusser argues that classical epistemology loses itself in the fruitless task of searching for guarantees of the possibility of knowledge, when the appropriate question to ask is 'By what mechanism does the object of knowledge appropriate the real object?'[20] Althusser never answers this question, but he claims that by posing it, he is freeing us from the fruitless question of guarantees. According to Althusser, a scientific theory is one that is adequate to its object of knowledge and real object, but the criteria of validity are always internal to each scientific problematic.

A scientific problematic establishes itself by criticizing previous ideological problematics. It distances itself from these ideologies by showing both why and how they are one-sided or in other ways inadequate to the object of knowledge. Althusser claims that Marx's *Capital* is the founding work of a new science, and in order to understand the distinctiveness of this science, it is necessary to explore the 'epistemological breaks' that Marx makes with classical political economy and with Hegel. As a result of his studies, Althusser comes to the conclusion that Marx's *Capital* is the founding work of historical and social science much as Euclid's work founded the science of mathematics and the work of Galileo and Newton founded natural science. Marx's *Capital* is of such fundamental importance that 'the theoretical future of historical materialism depends today on deepening dialectical materialism, which itself depends on a rigorous critical study of *Capital*'.[21] I entirely agree with this statement, but Althusser himself does not carry out such a study in sufficient thoroughness. He examines the epistemological breaks between Marx and both Smith and Ricardo, but he does not examine the substance and adequacy of Marx's economic theory as a theory of the capitalist mode of production nor does he develop the relation between the object of knowledge (the theory of capital) and the real object (capitalist history). Failure to develop his theory in these directions has left his followers to flounder in a sea of confusions.

Dialectical materialism as interpreted by Althusser has very little left that could be called dialectical. Althusser's 'dialectical materialism' is simply the epistemology of historical materialism or of Marxian social science, and it is arrived at by criticizing the Hegelian problematic and by amalgamating various forms of French structuralism which are found to be latent in Marx. According to Althusser, the only thing that Marx took from Hegel is the idea that history is a process without a subject. The historical process is structured by the articulation of unevenly developing relatively autonomous practices unified by the structure-in-dominance and determined in the last instance by the economic. Dialectical materialism, then, simply refers to the epistemology of Althusserian structuralism. All that is left of Hegelian dialectics is the concept of 'process' but now altered to mean material–historical complexly structured process, and 'contradiction' now altered to mean 'real opposition' and conflict rather than 'dialectical' contradiction in the Hegelian sense.[22]

Despite all protestations to the contrary, Althusser is actually in many ways more Hegelian than Lukacs. The trend of Althusser's thinking is to move closer to the Hegelian emphasis on dialectics as a method of objective knowledge. A large part of Althusser's attack on the Hegelian problematic is directed at thinkers like Lukacs who use it to turn Marxism into a secular religion. Althusser brings to the fore the question of the objectivity and scientificity of Marxism. By asking many of the right questions, Althusser sets the stage for a reappropriation of dialectics as the method of objective knowledge, even though Althusser's own solution to the problem of objectivity is an eclectic amalgam that proves to be untenable.

Althusser correctly rejects Lukacs's view that history is one grand teleological dialectic. He argues that Marx completely rejected the view that history is teleological. History is not a dialectical unfolding with a necessary beginning and an inevitable end.

Althusser holds to the Hegelian view that a theory is true if it is adequate to its object. This leads him to examine carefully the theoretical object of Marx's *Capital*, which Althusser correctly sees as the founding work of a new science. His problems come when he tries to derive historical and dialectical materialism from a careful reading of *Capital*. According to Althusser, dialectical materialism is basically the method or epistemology of historical materialism. Like Lukacs, he sees dialectical materialism pertaining to history as a whole, only he sharply differentiates his interpretation of dialectical materialism from that of Lukacs by attacking Lukacs's expressive/spiritual problematic.

In an expressive problematic everything is internal to everything else so that there can be no real externality, differentiation or autonomy of the parts in relation to the whole. Such a totality is ultimately simple as opposed to complex because the unifying factor is a simple centre with the parts being no more than various forms of expressions of this centre. Thus separate categories are continually on the verge of collapsing into one another and losing their distinctiveness. This problematic is manifest in Lukacs in a variety of ways. His often-quoted 'unity of theory and practice' fuses together activities whose internal integrity is destroyed if their relative autonomy is not respected. His notion of the proletariat as subject–object of history collapses together knowledge, self-knowledge, history, class-consciousness and revolutionary praxis. Capitalism as a totality is often collapsed into history as a totality so that the distinctiveness of capitalism as a unique mode of production is often lost. What is characteristic of capitalism is the relative autonomy of the economic which forms the base relative to the political and ideological superstructure. But Lukacs tends to collapse economic categories together with political and ideological categories so that the distinctiveness of capitalism is lost. Lukacs uses the concept of reification as though it were the simple centre of the bourgeois cultural totality separating and estranging subject from object, form from content, time from space, part from whole so that the destruction of reification must result in collapsing together all of these antinomies of bourgeois thought. Following Luxemburg, Lukacs fuses the logical and the historical within Marxian political economy, though, as Althusser makes abundantly clear, Marx himself is quite explicit that the logical order and real order do not reflect each other and the sequence of categories in the theory of capital do not parallel history.

Clearly grasping the unscientific and even religious tendency of Lukacs's expressive problematic, Althusser substitutes an epistemology largely based on structuralist presuppositions. He still clings to the Hegelian idea that dialectics must pertain to knowledge in general or at least to sociohistorical knowledge, but rejects the expressive problematic of Hegel. He attempts to arrive at another method of achieving objective knowledge which he calls 'dialectical materialism' but which breaks quite significantly with Hegelian dialectics. History is no longer seen as a single totality but as a series of totalities which are distinct and not simply a series of unfoldings of an original genesis. Each totality or mode of production consists of structures within structures and processes within processes each relatively autonomous but all interrelated and unified by a structure-in-dominance. The idea of process is subordinated to the idea of structure; a process is simply the complex interraction of structures over time. The outcome of such a process is always 'overdetermined', meaning that it is the mutual support and overlapping of many structures that brings about the result. This is a step forward from Lukacs in offering a more materialist and scientific approach to understanding history.

Althusser's treatment of the economic, the political and the ideological as relatively autonomous structures guards against reductionist tendencies that would collapse the economic into the political and ideological or vice versa. Althusser is also very clear on the necessary relative autonomy of theoretical practice and on the need to separate the logical and the historical thus avoiding all crude reflection theories. He becomes confused though in relating the theory of capital to historical materialism in an effort to construct a general epistemology of history. That he fails fully to come to terms with the uniqueness of the capitalist mode of production is evidenced by his effort to arrive at a single epistemology for all of history. Further, his animosity to the Hegelian Marxism of the Lukacsian or Sartrean type blinds him to the actual dialectic present in Marx's *Capital* and to a serious consideration of dialectics as a method of objective knowledge. He is correct to deny that there is a teleological dialectic of history, but his tendency to counter Lukacs's epistemology of universal history with another epistemology, prevents him from considering the possibility that the dialectical part of Marxist theory is the theory of capital and only the theory of capital, that the materialist dialectic which provides the objective basis of historical materialism is precisely the theory of capital, that the theory of capital is a dialectic of objective knowledge in the Hegelian sense, and that the differences between Hegel's *Logic* and the theory of capital are due to the differences in the theoretical object in each case.

In opposition to Hegel, Althusser tries to establish objectivity by positing structures which govern 'both the development of the object and the development of the theoretical practice which produces knowledge of it'.[23] He asserts this but does not prove it or show us how theoretical practice actually relates to the object and the structure that governs both. A structure that governs both an object and knowledge of that object is dialectical in character, but because Althusser does not recognize this, he remains within a structuralist problematic which makes such relations ultimately inexplicable. Althusser's structuralism strives for objectivity by suppressing the subject; whereas the dialectic of capital achieves objectivity by showing how and why the subject becomes absorbed into the objective motions of capital in a purely capitalist society. The dialectic gives us a path to return from the abstract to the concrete by reactivating the subject; whereas Althusser's approach posits rigid structures which permanently swallow up the subject. There is no path back to the concreteness of history and class struggle.

Theorizing structures without subjects does not make for objectivity unless the structures have a necessary inner logic so that they must be this way and not some other way. Now the structures of capitalism have precisely such a logic and that is what makes an objective dialectic of capital possible, but Althusser ignores this in favour of a universal structuralist epistemology. The theoretical object of Marx's *Capital* is the capitalist mode of production, but in Althusser's schema it is not at all clear how we know that the theory is adequate to the object or how the abstract theoretical object relates to the actual history of capitalism.

Althusser attempts to achieve objectivity by substituting structure for dialectic, but this substitution is not convincing because it replaces the dialectical subject/object identity with a structural suppression of the subject. According to Althusser's approach, the concepts of Marx's *Capital* are not the constructs of the subject Marx, but are the distillates of a structure of theoretical practice which in the last instance is determined by the structure of the capitalist economy. Thus the theory of capital is a production without a producer. The relation between structure and theorist for Althusser is parallel to Hegel's relation between Absolute Idea and philosopher, only with Hegel the philosopher is a part of a necessary unfolding totality whereas Althusser's structures appear as historically specific given without any teleology or necessary logic. We can examine all of the various 'epistemological breaks' between Marx and his forebears indefinitely, but this does not establish the necessity or objectivity of Marx's theory. What is it about capitalism that permits us to have objective knowledge of it? Althusser never fully answers this question. It remains unclear just how the structure of capitalism establishes the objectivity of its theory and how Marx the theorist relates to this structure so that we can say for sure that his concepts are not simply subjectively constructed analytic constructs, but are necessary and objective.

Though Althusser's epistemology ultimately fails, he makes important strides towards establishing the objectivity and scientificity of Marxism especially in comparison to Lukacs. Most important is his focus on *Capital* as the founding work of a new science and his criticism of the theory of history based on an expressive problematic. That the place to look for the foundations of dialectical and historical materialism is *Capital* is a perspective the importance of which can scarcely be overstated. His rejection of any grand teleological dialectic of history is also extremely significant in contributing to a more scientific and more materialist approach to the study of history. Finally in some sense he is more Hegelian than Lukacs, because Hegelian dialectics above all is a method of arriving at objective knowledge, and though he rejects Hegelian dialectics, his attack on Lukacs's propagandistic and activist perversion of dialectics and his concern for objectivity and knowledge is at least a step towards the spirit of dialectics. Althusser's insistence on the relative autonomy of theoretical practice sets the stage for reestablishing the objectivity of Marxist theory on the firm foundation of the dialectic of capital.

3 COLLETTI: DIALECTICAL MATERIALISM AS DIALECTIC OF CAPITAL

In *Marxism and Hegel*, Lucio Colletti puts forward strong arguments against the orthodox Marxian interpretation of dialectical materialism. He claims that Hegel was 'the first and only dialectician of matter',[24] and that 'All the basic propositions of the "dialectic of matter" were originally formulated by Hegel and dialectical materialism has confined itself to transcribing those propositions from his texts.'[25] 'The consequence is that what Engels and all of "dialectical materialism" after him present as the highest and most developed form of materialism is none other than absolute idealism.'[26] In other words dialectics is inherently idealist so that 'dialectical materialism' is really a contradiction in terms.

Briefly, Colletti's argument runs like this. The basic principle of materialism is the heterogeneity of thought and being, and this principle combined with the principle of non-contraction is basic to all science. This realm of science in which the real opposition of material forces is studied is called by Hegel the realm of the intellect. In opposition to this realm, the realm of reason studies the necessary connections between pure concepts and arrives at a synthetic or concrete understanding of a self-determined totality by the logic of dialectical contradiction moving from the most abstract and empty specifications to more filled out and concrete specifications. Colletti argues that Hegel's reconciliation of reason and intellect results in the annihilation of the latter and with it the basic principle of materialism. If this line of argument is correct, then the conclusion follows that dialectical reason is necessarily opposed to materialism and science.

Colletti sees these irreconcilable principles of dialectics and materialism clung to in a succession of Marxist texts without any clear comprehension of the contradiction involved.

There is a continual tendency for the two sides of 'dialectical materialism' to split off from one another and develop into opposed intellectual tendencies or schools of thought. Works such as Lenin's *The Development of Capitalism in Russia* manifest the materialist and scientific side of Marxism; whereas works such as Lukacs's *History and Class Consciousness* represent the metaphysical and idealist side.[27]

In *Marxism and Hegel* Colletti tries to overcome the seeming antinomy embodied in 'dialectical materialism' by largely rejecting dialectics in favour of materialism. Kant replaces Hegel as the favoured philosophical ancestor. From Hegel Marx extracts.

a profound sense of the unity of logical process and real process, i.e., the principle of the *unity* of thought and being which in Hegel, however, was so imperious as to jeopardize from the very beginning their *real* distinction. From Kant . . . Marx clearly derives . . . the principle of real existence as something 'more' with respect to everything contained in the concept; a principle which, while it makes the process of reality irreducible to the logical process, also prevents us from forgetting that, if the concept is logically first, from another angle it is itself a resultant.[28]

Colletti attempts to illustrate this argument by an interpretation of Marx's *Capital* in which he argues that this work is both deductive and inductive, and that the logical sequence follows the real process of history very closely.

According to Colletti the method of the theory of capital is a logicodeductive method, which 'gradually penetrates the object in question, departing from the non-essential or generic aspects and going back to the fundamental or specific ones, from effects to causes, and (in short) from the most superficial phenomena to the real basis implicit in them'.[29] Starting with non-essential or generic aspects such as exchange-value and the commodity, Marx proceeds from these more superficial phenomena to capital and class which is the real basis. But this logicodeductive movement from the superficial to the real basis is at the same time an inductive movement following the course of history so that the:

> logical process itself is none other than the synthetic–rational résumé of the entire historical road that preceded the birth of modern capital . . . the *logical deduction* from money to capital represents the essence of the *historical movement* which preceded the birth of modern capital.[30]

Here Colletti falls into the logical–historical method. What remains of Hegel in this is a logicodeductive method, but this method is not very dialectical because the 'contradictions' that it analyses are not dialectical contradictions but are real oppositions historically specific to capitalism.[31] We are left, then, with an epistemology which is a slightly Hegelianized Kantianism.

Since writing *Marxism and Hegel*, Colletti has made a number of important changes in his position, and it is the *New Left Review* article 'Contradiction and Contrariety' that is most important to look at in this regard. After careful study of Marx's *Capital*, and especially of the implications of reification and fetishism, Colletti comes to the conclusion that the 'contradictions' of the theory of capital are not 'real oppositions' as he had thought before but are '*dialectical contradictions* in the full sense of the word'.[32]

In Marx's view, all the contradictions of capitalism are the outcome of the contradiction within the commodity between use-value and value, between useful or private labour and abstract social labour. The internal contradiction within the commodity is externalized as the contradiction between the commodity and money. The contradiction between the commodity and money develops in turn into the contradiction between capital and wage-labour, that is between the owner of money and the owner of that particular commodity, viz., labour-power, whose use-value has the property of being the source of exchange-value and hence of capital itself.[33]

The reification that makes the motion of commodities, money and capital dominate human society, makes it possible to theorize capital as a true dialectic:

> the process of hypostasization, the substantification of the abstract, the inversion of subject and predicate, far from being in Marx's eyes modes of Hegel's logic that were defective in reflecting reality, were in fact processes that he located . . . in the structure and mode of functioning of capitalist society itself.[34]

> Hegel separated human thought from man, turning it into an independent subject called the idea; for him it was no longer the thinking individual who thinks but the idea or Logos which thinks itself through man. . . . The effect of the world of commodities on real men has been similar. It has factually separated or abstracted from man his subjectivity . . . and has transformed it into a separate essence.[35]

Just as *Logos* is the subject–object of Hegel's dialectic of reason, so capital becomes the subject–object of the theory of capital. Capitalism is not simply a society of wealth-maximizing individuals, rather individuals are used by capital for its own self-expansion. Thus the capitalist mode of production is called by Colletti an 'inverted reality'.

Colletti concludes this *New Left Review* article by juxtaposing two statements which pose the fundamental question that Marxist philosphers must face. Firstly, he claims that 'The fundamental principle of materialism and of science . . . is the principle of non-contradiction. Reality cannot contain dialectical contradictions but only real oppositions, conflicts between forces, relations of contrariety.'[36] Secondly, he states that 'On the other hand, capitalist oppositions are, for Marx, dialectical contradictions and not real oppositions.'[37] According to Colletti this seeming contradiction confirms 'the existence of two aspects in Marx: that of the scientist and that of the philosopher. . . . The social sciences have not yet found a true foundation of their own. Hence I do not know whether the existence of these two aspects is fatal or advantageous.'[38]

4 CONCLUSIONS

Colletti does not see that because of reification the logic of capital can be constructed as a rigorous scientific dialectic. The inversion that Colletti speaks of makes such a dialectic possible. Now while it is true that in the natural sciences the principle of non-contradiction is fundamental, the dialectic of capital presents an objective basis for social science based on dialectical contradiction. The key to resolving Colletti's dilemma is to understand the necessity for levels of analysis. Because capitalism is an inverted reality it has the capability of remaking the world in its own image. This means that capitalism will tend to become more capitalist or will tend to purify itself. This tendency towards the realization of a purely capitalist society makes it possible to envision such a society and to theorize its necessary inner connections as a dialectic. Because of the total reification that exists at the level of pure theory, real opposition is suspended or neutralized by the law of value. So although we allow the motion of value to overcome all obstacles *in theory* in order to expose the necessary dynamics of capitalism, we know that real opposition is simply held implicit. As we move away from the theory of a purely capitalist society to stage theory or to historical theory, real opposition increasingly appears. Thus the dialectic of capital is pregnant with real opposition though at the level of pure theory real opposition is completely contained with a dialectical logic.

We have arrived at the solution to the problem. The dialectic of capital is at the same time a rigorous and objective theory based on dialectical contradiction and a materialist or scientific theory pregnant with real opposition. The self-purifying tendencies of capitalism mean that thought and being have a sufficient tendency to coincide so that a pure theory can be constructed by following the logic of capital, while the actual recalcitrance of concrete capitalism ever to become so pure, requires levels of analysis which recognize the very real contingencies inherent in conjunctural analysis that insist that we be mindful of the ultimate heterogeneity of being and thought. On the one hand, then, it is possible rigorously to theorize the laws of pure capitalism, and on the other hand, we must take into account various contingent circumstances that deflect or alter the working of those laws requiring us to mediate pure theory and historical analysis with stage theory. It is precisely because capitalism is an inverted reality that real opposition can be absorbed into dialectical contradiction so that the theory of a purely capitalist society can be an objective dialectic. With this discovery social science finds a true foundation of its own.

Colletti makes advances over both Lukacs and Althusser in grasping the uniqueness of the theory of capital. He sees it is not possible to construct a dialectical theory of history, but that the logic of capital is a dialectic logic. The result is that Colletti cannot reconcile the claim that *Capital* is a work of science with the fact that it contains a dialectical logic.

How then can the theory of capital be both scientific and dialectical? For Colletti the key to resolving this is the fetishism of commodities or reification, because it is with this key that we can understand that capitalism is an 'inverted reality'. The theory of capital is a scientific theory because its object is the real material world, but it is at the same time dialectical because the reality in this case is inverted. Having said this, Colletti still remains puzzled over just how we can have a theory that is at once both scientific and dialectical – a theory of this peculiar inverted reality. Colletti comes very close to the truth of the matter, for reification is indeed the key to understanding the theory of capital. His shortcomings stem from his tendency to accept the logical–historical method, his failure to grasp the precise relation between the logical and historical in the theory of capital, and a consequent connecting of the dialectic only with the critical–revolutionary implications of the theory.

Because capitalism is reified it is self-contained and self-purifying. This means that Uno and Sekine can arrive at an idea of pure capitalism not simply by constructing a Weberian ideal-type, but by extrapolating the inherent tendencies of capitalism itself. The result is a dialectical logic of pure capitalism. Sekine has demonstrated the very close correspondence between the sequence of categories in Hegel's *Logic* and the dialectic of capital. But there are differences, some of which I outlined in the previous chapter.

In Hegel's case the theoretical object is the necessary inner connections between abstract philosophical universals, and in Marx's it is the necessary inner connections of the reified economic concepts of capitalism. Marx's theoretical object is a historically specific material reality. Given this, how is dialectical contradiction able to overcome the real oppositions of materialism and of concrete history? In a purely capitalist society we let value completely subsume the use-value obstacles of real economic life. Within the dialectic of capital real opposition is overcome completely by the reifying force of the commodity-economic principle. Real opposition in the form, for example, of class struggle between capital and labour is implied by the theory, but it can be held implicit because of the assumption of the total sovereignty of value or, what is the same thing, total reification. But the complex unity of the dialectic of capital does not verge on collapsing back into a simple undifferentiated unity so characteristic of spiritual/expressive totalities precisely because real opposition is implicit in the theory and because the theory does ultimaely relate back to a historical material reality. Thus wages, rents and profits appear on the surface to be real oppositions, but precisely by piercing the reification of capitalism, Marx shows the necessary inner connections of these three categories and shows that ultimately they are different forms of value. Hegel's dialectic is the self-relation of thought, whereas Marx's dialectic is *the self-relation of thought aided by the self-relatedness of a reified material–social reality*. For this reason the dialectic of capital is not a spiritual totality but is materialist instead.

Here I return to Althusser to show both the partial truth and the errors in his attack on all reflection theories of knowledge. Althusser's attack on crude reflection theory has some positive aspects. It is this theory in conjunction with the logical–historical method that has produced so much havoc throughout the history of Marxist theory. The problem is that he makes too much of the opposition between reflection theory and his own production theory of knowledge. Any constructivist theory of knowledge must fall into subjectivism unless the object can be made to do the constructing. But if the object constructs the knowledge of itself, the result is a sort of reflection theory which may not be so crude as the ones Althusser is attacking but which nonetheless shares some of their common features. In fact dialectics must always involve some form of reflection theory – perhaps a complex reflection theory as in the case of the dialectic of capital.

Now it is quite true that the theory of capital is not arrived at by thought concentrating itself (Hegel) nor by the knowing subject abstracting from the real concrete. Political economy only becomes possible with the development of capitalism, and as capitalism develops so does political economy. It is roughly accurate to say that capitalism produces knowledge of itself without denigrating the creative genius of Marx. From the point of view of objective knowledge, it is not necessary to know the creative processes that Marx went through in arriving at his theory; all we need know are the grounds for claiming objectivity. In this case it is that the theory correctly copies the necessary inner connections of capitalism. How is this possible? Capitalism is a self-purifying and self-abstracting economic system. Because the economic relations become more pure and abstract in reality, reality aids the mind in completing these processes (which are never completed in reality) so that the necessary inner connections between categories can be revealed.

Althusser is of course correct to say that theory moves from the abstract-in-thought to the concrete-in-thought and not the real concrete. But he fails to grasp the unique relation between theory and history peculiar to capitalism: namely that history, because of its reification in the case of capitalism, can aid in the development of its own self-understanding. Althusser's failure here leads him to overgeneralize an objectivity that is only possible with capitalism. Instead of grasping the dialectical logic of capital and making that the objective base of historical materialism, he creates a universal structuralist epistemology which tries to attain objectivity in general by removing the subject. But it is only the reified economic life of capitalism that can absorb the subject into the objective motions of capital and even this is only achieved at the level of pure theory. Furthermore, Althusser's failure to understand the specificity of the relation between the theoretical and historical (or logical and real) in capitalism, leads him to fail to see the connection between the theory of capitalist society and the history of capitalism. Again failing to grasp the specificity of capitalism, his movement is from theory in general to history in general, or more concretely from mode of production to social formation, but this has led to the kind of confusion typified by 'the mode of production debates'.

Let me conclude by briefly summarizing the contributions and flaws of Lukacs, Althusser and Colletti to our understanding of dialectical materialism. Lukacs correctly understands the importance of the category 'totality' and the idea of subject–object identity for dialectical thinking. He also grasps the key importance of reification for understanding capitalism. But he fails because history is the wrong totality to choose, because the proletariat is the wrong subject–object and because reification is seen as the centre of a cultural totality and not the basis for a rigorous and objective economic theory. Althusser correctly grasps that *Capital* is the founding work of a new science, but he completely fails to grasp the sense in which the method of this science is dialectical and that the dialectic of capital is its objective foundation. Colletti correctly understands that only Marx's *Capital* is both dialectical and materialist, but he fails to reconcile philosophically dialectics with materialism leaving us with more questions than answers. The work of Uno and Sekine finally clarifies our understanding of dialectical materialism by grounding it in the dialectic of capital. The inescapable conclusion is that if 'dialectical materialism' is to have any definite grounding in substantive knowledge, it must refer to the dialectic of capital. The dialectic of capital is the only theory that is both materialist and dialectical. This is so because of the peculiar objectified and reified character of the social reality of capitalism. With the dialectic of capital social science has at last achieved a firm philosophical foundation.

Part III
Historical Materialism

9 Some Basic Concepts of Historical Materialism

Chapter 5 was entitled 'The Historical Analysis of Capitalism', and it explored historiographic issues of capitalism from the point of view of guidelines offered by pure theory and stage theory. Because the study of capitalist history is guided by pure theory and stage theory, it falls within the science of political economy. But historical materialism must include the study of pre-capitalist and post-capitalist modes of production which do not have a pure theory or stage theory of their own and which fall outside political economy. It is my contention that historical materialism is simply a materialist approach to the study of history. It is not the science of history, but instead is simply one of many approaches to the study of history.[1] What makes it a strong approach is the backing it receives from the science of political economy. In this chapter I shall therefore explore the relation between political economy and historical materialism, and I shall develop some of the implications of this relationship for basic concepts of historical materialism.

Part I of this book presented political economy or the science of the capitalist mode of production. Part II argued that dialectical materialism should be interpreted as the reconstructed logic of the science of political economy. To be more precise, the theory of a purely capitalist society is the only example of a scientific theory which is both dialectical and materialist. Furthermore, the coming together of dialectics and materialism depends crucially on the total reification of a purely capitalist society, and this implies that pure capitalism is the only theoretical object which can be both rigorously dialectical and materialist. No one ever successfully constructed a complete dialectical theory of nature or of history. If there is no dialectic of history, that means that history cannot be grasped by a single dialectical theory which establishes 'the laws of motion of history'. The study of history cannot be an independent science based on the dialectic of history the way political economy is a science based on the dialectic of capital. The interpretation of dialectical materialism in Part II shows that political economy must constitute the substantive grounding of Marxist theory. Therefore historical materialism is derivative of political economy and not the other way around. In other words, the science of the capitalist mode of production is not simply the sub-theory of one mode of production within a larger theory of modes of production in general. Instead the theory of the capitalist mode of production is fundamental, and it is this theory which serves as a guide to the study of all other modes. The Uno/Sekine approach to historical materialism that I have adopted here makes clear and precise what Marx meant by the metaphorical expression that 'human anatomy is the key to the anatomy of the ape'.

The sequence of presentation in this book is essential to the argument. Part I sets forth political economy as the science of capitalism objectively grounded in the dialectic of capital. Part II shows why the dialectic of capital is the only materialist dialectic, and why, therefore, the dialectic of capital should serve as the objective grounding of political economy. Part III will develop the relationship between political economy and historical materialism by arguing that historical materialism is simply the study of history in the light of the knowledge established by political economy.

In this chapter I shall mainly focus on the light that pure theory sheds on some traditional concepts of historical materialism. I shall not focus on the relation between the other two levels of analysis and historical materialism, nor shall I attempt to be exhaustive in my analysis of the basic principles of historical materialism. My impression is that the Japanese Uno School has not done a great deal of work in this area. Uno referred to the basic principles of historical materialism as 'ideological hypotheses' to distinguish them from the scientific principles of pure theory. It seems to me that there is still work to be done on precisely what these principles are and how they are supported by political economy. This chapter only offers a first small step in clearing the ground for future theorizing.

In the next chapter I shall look at history as it extends into the future – the question of the transition to socialism. In so far as theory is action-oriented and normative, I call it 'ideology'. Marxist ideology is concerned with criticizing capitalism and developing strategies to bring about democratic socialism. In order to make a meaningful start in discussing the relation between the science of political economy and Marxist ideology, I shall limit myself primarily to some general guidelines derived from pure theory. I shall not address the question of how all three levels of political economy clarify the transition to socialism or how historical materialism generally contributes to this clarification.

1 WHAT IS HISTORICAL MATERIALISM?

In my view what is most fundamental to answering this question is the clarification of the relation between political economy and historical materialism. It is especially important to understand that historical materialism is an approach and not a science. It is very common, if not orthodox, to claim that historical materialism is the science of history, but if we take this claim seriously, it is likely to lead us down the path of economism or theoreticism.

In Stalin's view historical materialism is the science of history which sets forth the laws of development of society similarly to the way biology does for living things.[2] Like many other interpreters, Stalin seems to derive his laws of development primarily from Marx's *1858 Preface to A Contribution to the Critique of Political Economy.* But this is a very condensed and abbreviated statement, the meaning and scientific status of which is unclear. What precisely are the forces and relations of production, how do they interrelate and to what extent can we explain history by this interrelation? Stalin puts forward the economistic position that this relation is the key to understanding history. The basic law of social development is the contradiction between forces and relations of production. Forces of production give rise to relations of production which at first foster the development of those forces. But when the forces pass a certain level of development the relations become a fetter on any further development of the forces. Eventually this produces a revolutionary situation where finally the fetters are burst asunder and a new mode of production is established. The economistic shortcomings of this law of historical development have been sufficiently commented upon by others for me to abstain from further critique.[3]

Althusser also sees historical materialism as the science of history, but he attempts to overcome Stalin's economistic emphasis on forces and relations of production by defining mode of production as a complex articulation of the economic, political and ideological. But since 'mode of production' is still the central concept of a science, Althusser is prone to commit theoreticist errors.[4] In other words, in his effort to turn the study of history into a scientific theory, theory is made to perform tasks that it cannot, and the actual study of concrete history is slighted. Later I shall argue that although the concept of 'mode of production' does have a role to play in historical materialism, it does not play the role of being the central explanatory concept of a scientific theory.

It is extremely important to emphasize that historical materialism is an approach guided by a science and is not itself a science. Even the study of capitalist history which falls within the science of political economy is only *guided* by more abstract levels of theory. Theory acts as a guide to historical research, but I emphasize the independent importance of concrete historical research. There is no general theory of capitalist history, and we cannot collapse theory and history together into a unified theoretical history. If there is no theoretical history within the science of political economy, there are even less grounds for such history with pre- and post-capitalist modes of production. Here theory still acts as a guide, but it is one step further removed than in the case of capitalist history. How then does political economy and especially the theory of a purely capitalist society act as a guide to the study of pre- and post-capitalist modes of production?

The theory of a purely capitalist society theorizes the most complex, developed and advanced economic society. With pre-capitalist societies the economic does not emerge as a separate realm or as a dominant realm. It is only when the labour and production process comes to be governed by the self-regulating market that the economic becomes clearly differentiated from the political and ideological. With a purely capitalist society the economic not only becomes purified of the non-economic and the contingent, but also it comes to dominate society since, as passive reflexes, the political and ideological play no role in actively governing society.

The fact that it is possible to have a purely economic society but not a purely political or ideological society suggests that the economic is more basic. This is also supported by common sense since it is necessary to eat before philosophizing or politicizing. It follows that the way a society is organized to produce and reproduce its material life is likely to explain a lot about that society and in some sense be basic to understanding it. With pure capitalism the production and reproduction of material life is entirely economic in the sense that the norms of material life which exist in all societies operate according to purely economic principles only in a purely capitalist society.[5] All societies have a labour and production process, but it is only with pure capitalism that this process can be operated without political and ideological supports. There are general norms of material life which operate in all societies, but we only understand their full economic significance in the theory of a purely capitalist society. This theory brings to light the general norms of economic life common to all societies by showing their particular realization in the most fully developed economic society, pure capitalism. What are some of these norms and how does pure theory bring them out?

All societies, in order to be viable, must find some stable way to combine available labour-power, technology and natural resources to meet basic social needs. All societies do this by a mode of dividing labour and the product of labour. Viability also requires that direct producers are guaranteed at least subsistence. Where society produces in excess of subsistence, it is possible for a class structure to develop in which a dominant class appropriates the surplus. An excess over subsistence is also a necessary condition for technological advance, since technological innovations involve a deduction from present consumption for the sake of improved productivity in the future. These are a few of the general principles or norms of economic life that in pure theory are converted by commodity-economic logic into laws of motion of capitalism. Now these norms cannot form the basis of a transhistorical science of economics. In fact they can only be understood as purely economic norms in pure theory where they operate commodity-economically. In pre-capitalist modes of production, they are often operated according to an undifferentiated amalgam of economic, political and ideological forces. The pure economic operation of these norms in pure capitalism can help to guide our historical materialist studies where they are always impure.

It follows from what I have been arguing that there is no

independent science of history, but instead historical materialism is an approach to the study of history guided by general principles which are clarified by pure theory. The law of value applies to the capitalist mode of production and not to pre-capitalist modes, but at the same time as it theorizes the necessary inner connections of pure capitalism, it reveals general principles common to the reproduction of material life in all societies. It also clearly differentiates the economic from the political and the ideological, so that the economic can be used as an analytic category in connection with modes of production where it is not clearly differentiated by the operation of the mode itself. Finally it is important to clarify the guiding principles of historical materialism in reference to the objectively grounded law of value and not from other texts such as *The German Ideology* or the *1858 Preface*. The theory of a purely capitalist society provides an objective ground for the principles of historical materialism, whereas, when supported by other texts, such principles must remain asertions that, however much they are supported by argumentation, will lack the objective support and clarifying precision of the dialectic of capital. In the following four sections I shall look at some of the basic concepts of historical materialism, and show the difference that the Uno/Sekine approach makes in their interpretation. In particular I shall emphasize the differences that flow from viewing these concepts not as central explanatory concepts of a science, but as guiding principles or sets of principles for a tradition of historical research.

2   MODE OF PRODUCTION

In recent years there has been so much debate over this key concept, that there is now a body of literature referred to as 'the mode of production debate'.[6] In my view, much of this debate would not have occurred had Western Marxists had the benefit of an exposure to the approach being outlined here. In fact the debate stems primarily from the Althusserian problematic with its emphasis on a science of history.

Althusser attempts to establish the objectivity of historical materialism by claiming that history is a 'process without a subject'. Althusser's approach completely absorbs the subject into structures, so that it has often been called 'structuralist'. It is defensible to place a strong emphasis on the need to theorize structures in historical studies, but surely the universal suppression of subjectivity is going too far. The result will not be Althusser's goal of objective knowledge, but instead an overly abstract and mechanistic history. As I have previously argued, it is only with the total reification of pure capitalism that we get social processes where the subject is neutralized.

Unlike Uno and Sekine, Althusser and especially Balibar do not find the objective grounding of the concepts of historical materialism in the law of value; instead their impulse is to create a transhistorical conception of 'mode of production' consisting of a small number of elements which recombine in various permutations and combinations to constitute various modes of production.[7] 'Mode of production' becomes the key concept of the science of historical materialism, but this concept is itself an analytic construct without an objective grounding.

With the Althusserian approach 'mode of production' is made to carry more explanatory weight than it can possibly bear. Is a mode of production a particular articulation of relatively autonomous economic, political and ideological practices? Is it instead defined by a particular articulation of forces and relations of production which of course must themselves be defined? Or perhaps we should define 'mode of production' by class structure? Finally if we want to be really synthetic, we could perhaps combine all three of these approaches in a subtle, multidimensional, overdetermined, interarticulated whole! These debates show that it is crucial for this key concept, which defines the theoretical object, to have a clear and precise meaning. But, since the concept is not grounded in the dialectic of capital, there is no objective basis for clarifying it.

Even if a clear definition of 'mode of production' could be established, the problem of how to relate this 'abstract-formal' theoretical object to concrete history remains. The Althusserians approach this problem by pairing 'mode of production' with 'social formation'. According to Poulantzas, the real concrete is a collection of social formations articulated with one another, and each social formation is an articulation of several modes of production unified by a dominant one. But the Althusserians have never achieved a clear articulation of several modes of production within a social formation or several social formations with each other.

Foster-Carter argues that the emphasis on 'mode of production' has sometimes created economism and formalism. These tendencies can be superseded, according to Foster-Carter, by substituting the notion of a 'mode of reproduction'.[8] According to Foster-Carter, if we think about the reproduction of the social totality, we will avoid the one-sided emphasis on the economic implied by 'mode of production'. Moreover, if we think about the reproduction of the *concrete* social totality, we avoid the formalism and theoreticism of the split between the abstract-formal mode of production and the concrete social formation. The problem with Foster-Carter's approach is that it falls back into the logical–historical method which makes it difficult to distinguish the difference between the expanded reproduction of a purely capitalist society and the reproduction of Nazism in Germany in 1938. It is an approach which sounds appealing because it tries to integrate everything into one reproducing totality. The appeal cannot be followed by a very impressive performance since in trying to explain everything very little is explained. A great deal could be said about the uses and abuses of the concept 'reproduction', but I shall avoid the temptation of pursuing this point further, since these critical remarks are merely a preface to my analysis.

Another consequence of the modes of production debate has been a tendency to fetishize 'the boundary-problem', that is, the problem of defining precise boundaries separating one mode of production from another. For example, what is the precise difference between feudalism, petty commodity production, capitalism and socialism? Are there more modes of production such as a 'neocolonial mode of production'? If each mode is a particular articulation of the economic, political and ideological, then how precisely do we define each one? Having defined each one separately what happens when their boundaries intermesh or interface as they do when articulated together in particular social formations? This can become especially complicated in instances like the transition from feudalism to capitalism, where several modes of production may interpenetrate. The way to sort out such a debate is not to insist that modes of production be constructed like rigid boxes with precise boundaries, but instead to use the clear picture of capitalism provided by pure theory and the image of mercantilism provided by stage theory to establish which historical changes are most crucial to the development of capitalism.

In my view the only clear and precise use of 'mode of production' is when referring to a purely capitalist society. In this one case, society really is a mode of production in the fullest sense. The economic is self-contained and dominant, subsuming all of social life. When 'mode of production' is used as a concept of historical materialism to refer to different historical periods, it should be used on analogy with this one clear and precise case. The concept 'mode of production' is not so much a scientific concept as a package of research maxims. To refer to feudalism as a 'mode of production' signals to the reader that a materialist approach is being adopted, and that feudalism is going to be examined as a way of organizing the reproduction of material life. Using 'mode of production' should imply that the study of history is going to be guided by the general materialist principles supported by the science of political economy and especially by pure theory.

'Mode of production' is more a classificatory concept than an explanatory concept. It is used to differentiate different types of economies existing in different historical epochs. For this purpose, it is useful to arrive at criteria of differentiation. Generally, three basic definitions have been used. First, a mode of production is defined as a particular articulation of the economic, the political and the ideological. Second, it is defined as an articulation of a particular set of forces and relations of production. Third, modes of production are differentiated according to differences in class structure. It seems to me that a mode of production can and should be looked at in all these ways, but the most useful general criterion and the one Marx himself most frequently used is class structure. If we think for a moment about what differentiates slavery, feudalism, capitalism and socialism most clearly and simply it is class structure. Class structure, as a mode of appropriating the surplus, is simpler and clearer than the other criteria. The distinction between forces and relations of production is not so clear. The distinction between slavery and feudalism for example has not usually been specified in these terms. Articulation of the economic, political and ideological is far too complicated in general to serve as a criterion of classification. The definition that seems most in keeping with common usage and is simplest and clearest is that a mode of production is a world-historic type of surplus appropriation. Where there is no class structure as in many tribal economies or as in socialism, forces and relations of production may be used to identify modes of production.

The distinction that the Althusserians make between mode of

production and social formation tends to break down when analysing pre-capitalist modes of production. Feudalism has no tendency to purify itself towards economic laws of motion of feudalism. So in specifying the feudal mode of production, we are essentially abstracting and generalizing from history with the guidance of the principles of historical materialism. When we look at the history of feudalism, we see that it takes many forms, and though we may abstract from these forms in order to arrive at a more general type, feudalism itself has no tendency to do this. Unlike capitalism which is self-abstracting, with feudalism it is we who do the abstracting though guided by principles derived from the theory of a purely capitalist society. It is possible to argue as Anderson does that one form of feudalism is the purest and most classical form, but this is not because feudalism itself has a tendency to create this form; it is instead because of a judgment that feudalism is a synthesis of slave and barbarian modes of production.[9] Then the classical form is the one that most clearly synthesizes the slave and barbarian modes in a balanced way.

'Mode of production' is not a hardened scientific concept. It is simply used for purposes of classification within a materialist approach to history. The concept should be used in a way that improves our understanding of history. At more concrete levels of analysis there is no definite limit to the types of modes of production or to their number. Feudalism may, for example, be seen as a collection of modes of production which have a 'family resemblance' while not having any dominant feature in common. My proposal that modes be differentiated according to class structure refers only to the classical world-historic types. These major types are insufficient to understand the diversity that exists when we look at history more concretely. Modes of production should not be rigid boxes stultifying the study of history, rather they should be conceptualized by using materialist principles to aid historical research.

3   FORCES AND RELATIONS OF PRODUCTION

Basing their ideas on Marx's *1858 Preface*, some Marxists have argued that the relation between forces and relations of production is fundamental to historical materialism. The forces of production give rise to a particular set of relations of production which in turn foster the further development of the forces of production until the relations of production become a fetter and are finally burst asunder. One of the problems with this emphasis is that the range of debate over even the meaning of 'forces and relations of production' would suggest that these are inherently vague concepts. When we move beyond the problem of meaning, the debate becomes even more pronounced with some arguing for the primacy of the forces of production and some for the primacy of the relations of production. Part of the confusion has to do with how class structure relates to forces and relations of production. Perhaps we can resolve some of these debates and confusions by referring to the theory of a purely capitalist society.

Marx does not use these two terms consistently and never engages in any systematic explication of them. Although these two concepts are not explicitly used in the dialectic of capital, they are implicit and hence can be clarified in reference to it.[10] The relevant point of reference is crisis theory with its alternating widening and deepening phases of capital accumulation. During the widening phase, capital accumulates on the basis of a more or less fixed organization of productive technology or 'productive forces'. Corresponding to the productive forces is a particular value relation between capital and labour which we may refer to as 'relations of production'. As the productive forces expand they dry up the reservoir of surplus population resulting in increased wages. But this threatens not only to de-commodify labour-power but to undermine the rate of profit. When the rate of profit is undermined, capital tends to disappear and to be converted into money. In short the capital–labour production relation is burst asunder and capital is faced with the threat of imminent demise. The resolution of the crisis requires the reorganization of productive forces on a more productive basis coupled with a renewed capital–labour production relation which will allow renewed accumulation.

This example demonstrates that the classical and orthodox interpretation of the relation between forces and relations of production holds in a purely capitalist society. By the same token, in societies that are not totally reified and commodified, we may question the explanatory power of these two concepts, and that is because the automatism resulting from reification is dissolved into politics, ideology and class power. Once this occurs it even becomes difficult to distinguish clearly between forces and

relations of production. 'Forces of production' may be given a
strict technological definition, but then the concept is separated
from the concept 'productivity' because the same complement of
tools can produce very different levels of productivity depending
upon how the users of the tools are organized and motivated. If
that is the case, relations of production directly enter into the level
of productivity. The choice seems to be between crude technological determinism or breaking down the distinction between
the two concepts.

On the other hand, it is no doubt useful to consider the
structural limitations associated with forms of technology and
levels of productivity. Thus although I disagree with Cohen's
general interpretation of forces and relations of production, I
agree with his conclusion that capitalism is only consistent with a
certain range of productivity and forms of technological organization. This is primarily because of the special requirements
needed for the commodification of labour-power. The commodification of labour-power is inconsistent with situations
where productivity is low, where most production is agrarian,
where the labour and production process is relatively rigid or
where most labour is skilled. These are precapitalist conditions of
production, but there are also post-capitalist forces of production
which are incompatible with the continued commodification of
labour-power. This is where automation replaces workers, or
where services come to replace commodity production as the
dominant economic activity, or where labour becomes skilled, or
where the types of use-values that are prevalent are highly
complex and social or are one-of-a-kind complex systems like
communications systems. It follows that capitalist market relations of production are only suitable for a certain range of
development of productivity. It should be clear that at levels of
productivity that are too low or are too high, it is not possible to
maintain the commodification of labour-power.

It is apparent that something like the relation that Marx
outlined in the *1858 Preface* exists in a purely capitalist society
where the forces of production are a particular technical organization of capital and the relations of production refer to the
capital–labour value relation. This tight fit occurs because in a
purely economic society the motion of value subsumes all use-
value production to the operation of the commodity–economic
principle. In non-capitalist modes of production this relationship

would not necessarily hold and the relations of production would necessarily include politics since in the absence of market regulation some sort of political/ideological regulation is essential. Furthermore, at low levels of productivity where the division of labour is simple, the productive forces do not require any particular set of production relations except that a society without a surplus may not have a class structure. However, once there is an agrarian society with a surplus, any number of variations in relations of production may accompany such forces of production. Generally the relations of production will involve a class structure, but not necessarily. Thus besides the diverse relations of production associated with primitive communism, various class forms of relation of production including slavery, feudalism and various types of tribute modes are all consistent with agrarian societies with low productivity but some surplus. It follows that in so far as the relations of production control and coordinate the forces of production, the relations of production, outside of pure capitalism, will always include class domination where it exists and will always include superstructural elements.

The relation between forces and relations of production is only purely economic in a purely capitalist society. Otherwise it is a rather vague distinction with the relations of production including all manner of superstructural elements and not necessarily being very distinct from forces of production. Although the distinction may be given precise meaning and be made useful in the study of some concrete piece of history, we cannot in general understand the movement from one mode of production to another as the forces of production bursting asunder the relations of production, with the possible exception of the transition from capitalism to socialism (even in this case it would seem rather crude and determinist). When we look at slavery and feudalism, it is not at all clear what constitutes the forces and relations of production. Of course, it is always possible in retrospect to define them in such a way that they are functional for each other and then at some point become dysfunctional, but this is not likely to add much to our understanding of historical change. In fact depending upon what we mean by 'forces and relations of production' it is entirely possible for the relations of production to 'burst asunder' the forces of production.[11]

The inescapable conclusion is that there is no general historical law that can be formulated as a relation between forces and relations of production. The distinction may be useful in shedding light on a mode of production, when its meaning is specified in relation to the dialectic of capital. This is because it is only with pure capitalism that the distinction has a determinant and purely economic meaning. Heretofore this distinction has often been used as a mechanistic gloss on history with scientific pretensions rather than as a concept that really helps to explain historical events. It does not contribute much to our understanding of the transition from feudalism to capitalism to claim that the development of feudal forces of production past a certain point bursts asunder feudal relations of production forcing them to be replaced by capitalist relations of production.

4   BASE AND SUPERSTRUCTURE

In recent years the base/superstructure distinction has been one of the most maligned and rejected concepts of historical materialism.[12] This is because of the very strong reaction against economism and reductionism. Nevertheless, despite all the reaction against it, the base/superstructure distinction, properly understood, is of fundamental importance to historical materialism.

In Chapter 6 I argued that the base/superstructure metaphor only holds at the level of pure theory. At this level the political and ideological are passive reflexes of the economic base. The fact that this metaphor only strictly holds at the level of pure theory does not leave us in a pluralistic and agnostic position with respect to other levels and non-capitalist modes of production. The economic, political and ideological are not simply three variables which may stand in any relation to each other. For example, in no mode of production would the ideological be the substructure and the economic the superstructure. Pure capitalism demonstrates that the reproduction of society's material life can be managed purely economically, and that this is the tendency in the most advanced organization of material life. The theory of a purely capitalist society demonstrates that there are general norms of economic life common to all societies, and that the reproduction of material life must always be understood first and foremost in economic terms. This does not mean, however, that the political and ideological are always passive reflexes. In historical materialist explanation the economic will always be basic in grasping the general features of a mode of production, but in many cases the economic is only *analytically* separable from the political and ideological. The political and ideological may play an active role in the very constitution of the economic. Furthermore, they may play a dominant role in the explanation of particular historical events as opposed to the characterization of world-historic modes of production where they must always be secondary.

The base/superstructure metaphor has been rejected because it has been abused by being used too literally and too universally. I have argued that the metaphor is literally accurate only in the case of pure capitalism. Beyond this it can serve as a rough approximation in guiding the study of pre- and post-capitalist societies. This metaphor is important because it underscores the fact that we do have a rigorous theory of the economic base of capitalism (the law of value), and that this theory can serve as an important source of guidelines when studying the reproduction of material life in other modes of production. In a sense the economic is the base in all modes of production, as long as we understand by this that it is more basic than the state and ideology and not that the latter two are passive reflexes. With this interpretation, the concepts of base and superstructure are central and crucial to historical materialism. Pure theory or the theory of the capitalist base, gives us a clear and precise comprehension of the economic, and without this we cannot clearly grasp modes of production where the economic can only be analytically separated from the political and ideological. Historical materialism assumes that what is fundamental to the understanding of any society is its material viability and reproduction of this viability. When we speak of material reproduction this must always centrally involve the economic even if it is mixed with non-economic elements. The base/superstructure metaphor is important because it expresses this basic perspective of historical materialism.

5   CLASS ANTAGONISM

While the base/superstructure principle has been attacked in recent years, the principle of class antagonism has often been too uncritically embraced. Sometimes the principle of class struggle has been so elevated that it is fetishized. In these cases the primacy of class struggle becomes the central if not the single principle of historical materialism. Historical materialism, then, is simply an approach which understands history in class struggle terms. Now it is no doubt true that class struggle plays an important role in explaining many major historical changes, but it is also clear that it cannot explain everything. Furthermore, if 'class' is to bear all the weight of historical explanation, it becomes crucial that this concept have a clear and precise meaning that is objectively grounded.

'Class' is a term that has many meanings, but generally it refers to some kind of social stratification. Is a struggle between landlords and tenants over the rent paid for apartments a class struggle? Is the struggle between merchants and consumers over the price of meat a class struggle? Is a struggle between creditors and debtors over the rate of interest a class struggle? The meaning of 'class' may be stretched in various ways for various purposes, but historical materialism will be more coherent if there is a stable and core meaning to the concept that can serve as a reference-point. It is my contention that this core meaning can be objectively grounded in the dialectic of capital.

The theory of a purely capitalist society presents a purely economic and objectively grounded conception of class. It shows that a class society can operate purely economically without any reliance upon extra-economic force. Because they are purely economic, the concepts of 'capital' and 'labour' are clear and precise conceptions of class. Capital owns and operates the means of production and labour sells its labour-power to capital in return for a living wage. Besides reproducing the value of its own labour-power, labour produces a surplus value which is appropriated by capital. The dialectic of capital demonstrates that the dynamic between capital and labour is central to capitalism, and that one class creates all the surplus and the other appropriates it. It is clear that surplus appropriation is basic to defining class and class structure.

The major world-historic modes of production are most frequently classified according to differences in surplus appropriation or class structure.[13] Each mode of production has a dominant type of surplus accumulation, though it may also have several sub-types. In non-capitalist modes of production, classes are never purely economic since politics must be involved in any economy that is not completely self-regulating. But class should still be identified according to criteria based on the paradigm case, the pure classes of capitalism, capital and labour. As long as there is this clear and precise core of meaning, it is possible consciously to move away from it without producing confusion. It is not necessary always to use 'class' in a strict and rigid way. Within the capitalist mode of production, the struggle between creditors and debtors may, for example, be called a 'class struggle' as long as we are clear about how it relates to the dominant capital/labour struggle and to the distribution or redistribution of surplus value. Besides classes, in the strict sense of the term, there may be other class-like or quasi-class formations that play an important role in history. In order to explain some phenomena, the most important division of labour will be the class division, but in others the division of labour based on gender or race may be more important. We are not likely to arrive at a good grasp of history if we cling to an overly rigid conception of 'class' that ignores the importance of other social groupings.

As with the other concepts of historical materialism, 'class' and 'class struggle' are general principles to guide historical research. As concepts they receive their objective grounding in the theory of a purely capitalist society, and this gives them a core of determinant and stable meaning. This core meaning then serves as a reference-point as the concepts of pure theory are converted into principles which serve to guide a materialist approach to historical research.

6 CONCLUSIONS

In this chapter I have argued that historical materialism is not the science of history, and that, indeed, there is no science of history. There is, however, a science of political economy grounded in the law of value as articulated in pure theory. The dialectic of capital generates an interpretation of dialectical materialism, which demonstrates that there is no dialectic of history that can serve to ground the theory of history as an independent science. Historical materialism is simply a general approach to the study of history, superior to other approaches because it is guided by the objective dialectic of capital. By clearly and precisely theorizing the most advanced economic society, the dialectic of capital serves to ground and clarify orienting concepts and guiding principles for a materialist approach to historical research.

Some of the traditional concepts of historical materialism have been dogmatized because they have been treated as though they were central explanatory concepts of a scientific theory. We cannot create a successful approach to the understanding of history by extracting some concepts from a number of Marx's texts like the *1858 Preface*. Our reference-point must be pure theory; and what we generate is not a science of history but some guidelines for a materialist approach. In this chapter I have tried to indicate a few of guidelines that can be generated by some of their uses and the limitations on this use. I have done this mostly by reconsidering some traditional concepts.

The most fundamental contribution of pure theory to historical materialism is a precise concept of the economic and of the general economic principles common to all societies. This establishes a basic framework for understanding the importance of a society's material life and how to conceptualize its reproduction. The concept 'mode of production' cannot be successfully made into a hardened scientific concept capable of explaining all modes of production in terms of the variations of a few central variables. 'Mode of production' only has a clear and precise meaning with the theory of a purely capitalist society because it is the only case where the economic is self-contained and self-determining. Outside of this instance, 'mode of production' is a classificatory concept and a sort of package of research norms indicating that a materialist approach is being used. 'Base and superstructure' have roughly the same logical status as 'mode of production'. They are only literally accurate at the level of pure theory, but they serve as an important guideline to a study of history that places primary emphasis on the economic. Though the contrast between forces and relations of production can also be grounded in pure theory, this pair of concepts requires the most caution and has perhaps been the most abused of the traditional concepts of historical materialism. Even more than 'mode of production' this pair cannot serve as adequate central explanatory concepts of a science of history.

Finally nearly all Marxists would agree that 'class structure' and 'class antagonism' are concepts of fundamental importance to historical materialism. The disputes over the meaning of these concepts are best settled in reference to pure theory. Having done this, I note that the only pure classes are capital and labour in a purely capitalist society, and that at a historical level class phenomena are often somewhat muddled. Thus though we have a precise conception of class, it is not necessary that we insist on its strict usage in all cases as long as we are fully aware of what we are doing. Often it will be fruitful to look at the social division of labour as a whole in order to avoid 'class reductionism'.

I close with this paradoxical observation. Historical material-ism will become more scientific as fewer Marxists try to turn it into a science of history.

10 Transition to Socialism

A principle concern of historical materialism has always been the transition to socialism. In this chapter I want to argue that the demise of capitalism does not automatically lead to socialism and that socialism is only one of the possible post-capitalist formations. Since socialism is not produced by any sort of objective laws, the subjective factor becomes crucial. In other words, the achievement of socialism depends very much on what men and women do around the world, which in turn depends to some extent on what they understand by 'capitalism' and 'socialism'. A clear grasp of 'capitalism' and 'socialism' will expedite the strategic thinking of how to move from one to the other. In this chapter I want to argue for the importance of grounding our strategic thinking in the dialectic of capital because it presents a clear and precise conception of 'capital', and because such a conception is the basis for gaining clarity on the 'negation' of capital or socialism.

Like every other chapter in this book, my concern in this one is not to present a completed theory of the transition to socialism, but instead to set forth some considerations which can guide the construction of such a theory. The starting-point must be some exploration of the basic principles of socialism, what these principles are and how to derive them. Second, in order to move from the present towards socialism, clarity about the current conjuncture is essential. In order to begin this task, I shall briefly discuss some of the features of our present global situation, and while doing this I shall also indicate the importance of the political and ideological dimensions and the inapplicability of the law of value. Third, well-worked out transformative strategy requires careful study of previous efforts to bring about socialism. Learning the lessons of past history is crucial in avoiding the repetition of errors and in learning from experience what works best. Although I shall not undertake this task in this book, it is not because I do not think it is important. On the contrary, it is too important and too big a task to fit into this book. In summation, then, an effective transformative strategy must combine clarity on the fundamental principles of socialism, clarity on the current conjuncture and clarity on the lessons to be learned from the past. In this chapter I shall focus on the basic principles of socialism and shall touch upon theorizing the current conjuncture.

However, there are other considerations when reflecting upon mainstream Marxist thinking about the transition to socialism. The Uno School's radical break with the logical–historical method has important implications for the relation between theory and practice. I shall analyse some of these implications in this chapter. Let me proceed, then, with the most basic question: what is socialism?

1 WHAT IS SOCIALISM?

Is socialism primarily a utopia to be filled out by our subjective wishes and hopes? Marx and Engels avoided drawing up utopian blueprints and rejected the idea that socialism is utopia; instead they wrote of socialism in terms of basic principles. They argued that socialism is a realistic possibility because capitalism creates both the material preconditions and the human agency to bring it about. Their principles were not the product of their imaginations, but were seen to represent the positive or progressive 'negation' of capitalism (i.e. the supersession of capitalism). Socialism preserves the social productivity achieved by capitalism while advancing the possibilities of a much fuller realization of the human potential.

If the basic principles of socialism are derived from the negation of capitalism, then they cannot be more determinant than the concept of capitalism. Depending upon what are seen to be the central features of capitalism, different principles of socialism will be emphasized. Some of the features that are typically emphasized include: the end of alienation, the end of exploitation, the end of oppression, the end of the repressive state, the end of the division of labour, the end of reification, the end of economic insecurity and crisis, the end of placing profits before people. Or viewed positively a socialist society is: planned, democratic, humanistic, internationalist, egalitarian, free, affluent, just and communitarian. In general a thinker's conception of socialism if related to his or her conception of capitalism and is no more clear and precise than the latter.

The theory of a purely capitalist society presents a clear and determinant conception of capitalism. The negation (supersession) of a purely capitalist society should therefore yield clear and determinant principles of socialism. In all pre-capitalist modes of production extra-economic force enters into the reproduction of material life. The total reification of pure capitalism makes it possible for material life to be reproduced without any intervention of extra-economic force. In the case of pure capitalism socioeconomic life is governed entirely by the self-regulating market. Because pure capitalism does not rely upon extra-economic force, it represents an advance over pre-capitalist modes of production. In order for socialism to represent an advance over capitalism, it must not revert to reliance upon extra-economic force.

The control over socioeconomic life which with capitalism is vested in the market must be re-appropriated by society. But the only way for society to reassert control over its economic life without reliance on extra-economic force is for that control to be thoroughly democratized. The commodity-economic principle or the market principle must be replaced by the human principle (production for profit replaced by production for human need). Human beings must be treated as ends and not means, and the fullest realization of each human being become society's goal. But a direct corollary of this principle of humanism is the principle of democracy, since it is the only alternative to force, coercion and manipulation. The two basic principles of socialism are therefore humanism and democracy. These are the two principles that follow necessarily and most directly from the positive or progressive de-reification of capitalism. Instead of being market-governed, economic life is governed by humanity for humanity. This necessitates democracy, not in the legalistic and formalistic sense of bourgeois democracy, but in the sense of the democratization of all social institutions. Further principles such as freedom, equality, community and distributive justice may be derived from the two basic ones.

Using these two principles as a guide, it is possible to think through the kinds of changes necessary to bring about socialism. For example, it is often asked, what will induce people to work in a socialist society where there is no reliance on the whip of economic insecurity or on extra-economic force. I agree with the cogent answer given by Marx: 'work becomes life's prime want'. In order for work to become an avenue of self-fulfilment rather than of self-negation many changes have to occur in society. It is the task of a socialist movement or party to think through these changes concretely.

The basic principles of socialism can be further clarified and elaborated, but it is important to fix these two basic principles as a basis for mobilizing people, for thinking through transformative strategies and for evaluating the success of past and present efforts to bring about socialism. These two principles may never be completely realized in any historical society. It is hard to imagine a completely democratic and completely humanistic society; and yet it is these principles that should be the stars that orient us. Societies that call themselves 'socialist' should be evaluated according to how seriously they strive to realize these two principles. Even in this early period of the world-historic phase of transition away from capitalism, the primitive socialist regimes that exist should not be called 'socialist' unless they show signs of moving in the direction of democracy and humanism.

There are basically two kinds of post-capitalist societies: those that rely heavily on top-down coercion and manipulation and those that do not. The first kind I shall refer to as 'statist' and the second as 'socialist'. This is a very important distinction to make because many states that call themselves 'socialist' are in fact statist. All existing socialist states are defective when it comes to democracy, but if they even show some signs of moving in the direction of democracy and of being concerned about increasing democracy, they may be considered as at least 'primitive' socialist societies. As E. O. Wright has suggested, there may also be various types of statist and socialist societies as well as hybrids.[1] Socialism is only one possible future and is only more likely than other futures to the extent that human beings often bring about that which is both possible and desirable.

Previously I discussed the subsumption of the general norms of economic life to the laws of motion of capitalism in a purely capitalist society. According to Shumei Ohuchi, one way of further clarifying and expanding on the principles of democracy and humanism is to consider carefully how the general norms can be freed in a progressive sense from the reified laws of capitalism.[2] To do this we need to think through what is implied by the

democratization of economic laws successively in the Doctrines
of Circulation, Production and Distribution. Thus, for example,
the Doctrine of Circulation might yield a conception of the
consumer's sovereignty (of course not in the formalistic sense of
bourgeois economic theory), the Doctrine of Production could
generate conceptions of workers' control and the Doctrine of
Distribution can generate notions of social control over profit,
rent and interest. We need to pose such questions as, how can
democratic institutions in a socialist society play the fine-tuning
role of the rate of interest in a purely capitalist society? In short
there is a need to think in concrete and institutional terms about
how to preserve the gains of capitalist society while reappropriat-
ing democratic control over our socioeconomic life.

In Chapter 6 I discussed the fictitious commodities, money,
labour-power and land, arguing that they pose severe problems to
capitalistic commodity-economic management. In the transition
to socialism, it is useful to consider how these fictitious commodities can be de-reified so that commodity-economic regulation can be replaced by regulation through democratic institutions and democratic and humanistic ethics. Since the commodification of labour-power is the key to capitalism, its de-
commodification through the initiative of labour-power itself
must be seen as the leading edge of socialism. This implies ethical
humanism where workers are no longer treated as means but as
ends in themselves. Humanism must also oppose war and all
forms of discrimination and oppression. As already suggested the
commodification of money needs to be replaced by real consumer
sovereignty or democracy. Finally the commodification of land
should be replaced by principles that regulate our relation with
nature in a harmonious fashion (i.e. according to ecologically
sound principles). If the de-reification of capitalism involves the
above aspects, then the movement for democratic socialism
would involve a confluence of the workers' movement, the peace
movement, the women's movement, the ecology movement and
all other movements which oppose oppression. It is extremely
important for such a general movement to begin to formulate
concrete democratic alternatives and an ethical theory based on
humanism.

Let me summarize the argument so far. The basic principles of
socialism are not the product of subjective imagination, but are
objectively grounded in the dialectic of capital. They are arrived

at by considering what is necessary in order to de-reify capitalism without resorting to extra-economic force. The two essential principles so derived are humanism and democracy. Humanism is the basic social ethic and democracy is the basic organizational principle of socialism.

2 THE CURRENT CONJUNCTURE

The basic principles of socialism are highly abstract. In order to move most effectively from our current situation towards socialism, it will be helpful to have a good grasp of the principle dynamics and contradictions of the current conjuncture. Such knowledge can help inform strategies of change so that socialists will deploy their energies most effectively. In this section I shall neither present a complete theory of the current conjuncture nor explore the strategic implications of such a theory. Instead, I shall adopt the more modest goal of how to approach the analysis of the current conjuncture, and I shall analyse some of its basic features.

The most important question is, how do we characterize the present dominant world economy? The answer to this question is crucial because it determines how we use the law of value and stage theory to understand our present situation. There are many Marxists who have used some variation of the law of value or of the theory of imperialism to theorize the post-World War II period. I have argued, however, that this is a phase of transition, and if I am correct about this, then it is not possible to construct a stage theory for the phase after World War I. In a phase of transition capitalist institutions persist, but they change their character and new post-capitalist institutions begin to emerge. If Marxists simply assume that full-blown capitalism still exists, then they are likely to apply the laws of motion of capitalism directly, and, as a result, fail to account for the novel, post-capitalist features of our present situation.

I argued earlier that the world-historic phase of transition away from capitalism had its symbolic beginning in 1917. This does not mean that capitalism suddenly ceased to exist in 1917, but instead that from this point on the law of value was in retreat and hence losing its hegemonic and self-regulating character. The effort to resurrect finance-capital between the wars was a failure resulting in fascism and war. The law of value no longer externalizes itself into a coherent dominant type of capital accumulation. Capital accumulation increasingly depends upon exogenous factors and hence cannot be explained by the law of value.

During the phase of transition, capitalists still pursue profits, workers are exploited and crises occur. But though it still exists and apparently operates, the market begins to atrophy and loses its self-regulating character. To the extent that the market ceases to be self-regulating, the law of value can no longer be hegemonic. The market may maintain its form while losing its capitalist content. A new dynamic is estlished. The market becomes less self-regulating, requiring more political and ideological supports, but the more it depends on supports the less self-regulating it becomes. The shrinking commodified sector depends more and more on a politicized de-commodified sector. Although prices still form in the market-place, they cannot be explained by the law of value.

Let me expand a little on what I mean by de-commodification. On the surface, it seems that more of the world economy is commodified than ever before. While it is true that more use-values are traded in the market than ever, not every use-value that is traded is a capitalistic commodity. As I previously pointed out, a capitalistic commodity is one that is capable of being supplied in any quantitity in response to shifts in demand, and it is widely and frequently traded in an impersonal market by large numbers of buyers and sellers. A space-station or a battleship is not likely to be a capitalistic commodity in the above sense. Where only one or a few of a type of use-value is produced for an identifiable buyer like the government, it cannot be a capitalistic commodity. Hence most of these use-values are produced by contract on a cost-plus basis. Value produces any use-value with indifference to any but quantitative and impersonal market criteria. Where qualitative and personal factors loom large, or where the use-value is too large, complex or social, the motion of value has difficulty operating. The motion of value has difficulty operating in these regions even when capitalism is young and vital. It is only in a purely capitalist society that the 'fictitious' commodities, labour, land and money become completely commodified. After the stage of imperialism, capitalism becomes increasingly ennervated; it can no longer stand on its own two feet. The fictitious commodities are the first to escape its grasp as the market for land, the money-market and the labour-market lose their self-regulating character.

The collapse of the gold standard after the stage of imperialism undermines the commodification of money. Our current sytem of managed currencies produces an artificial rate of interest. According to the law of value the price of land is equal to the rent divided by the rate of interest. But this assumes a separation between landed property and capital, and a rate of interest formed in a competitive market. But according to Sekine, capital and landed property become fused after the stage of imperialism, so that rent is absorbed into the surplus profit of finance-capital.[3] Furthermore, administered interest rates must give land an artificial price, undermining the self-regulating character of the land-market.

Essential to maintaining the commodification of labour-power is periodic crisis. But already with the stage of imperialism, periodic crises become less tolerable as a means of renewing the capital–labour production relation. World War I was the outcome of efforts to avoid the problems of excess capital by aggressive expansionism. The failure of finance-capital to re-establish a self-regulating labour-market between the wars led to the post-World War II system of powerful trade unions, managed currencies and managed demand. The development of the trade union movement is especially important in undermining the commodification of labour-power. The post-World War II system further atrophies the law of value and the market. In many cases, political units come to be more important economic actors than large firms. Crisis becomes even more intolerable so that a system of indebtedness builds which prevents the bankruptcy of large firms and large political units. The result of managed demand, managed currencies and debt expansion is inflation. When the state restricts credit to control inflation, the big corporations cut back production, laying off workers. Instead of using their money for accumulation, they now speculate in land (further destroying the capitalistic rational price of land), earn usurious interest rates or speculate in currencies (further destabilizing the international monetary order).

Reagan and Thatcher believe that the solution to these problems is to re-commodify the economy or in other words return to the self-regulating market. In order to criticize these policies effectively, socialists must be clear about why it is that the market has necessarily declined and why this is an irreversible process. If capital could always have its own way, as it does at the level of pure theory, there would never be political intervention in the economy. Political support is forced upon capital by the intractability of use-values, and the further away from the ideal use-values of pure capitalism that we move, the more capital requires political supports. As the dominant type of use-value production increasingly becomes for such things as space-stations, and as commodity production in general shrinks relative to the service sector, the forces of production can no longer be operated successfully by pure capitalist relations of production. Because they are contrary to the forces of production, policies to re-commodify can only have at best a superficial and short-term success. 'Free enterprise' is really not a viable alternative, and it can only appear to be so because of massive ideological and political supports. That some islands of the economy may seem to work effectively according to the principles of free enterprise, ignores the de-commodified sea which permits them to exist.

I have argued that the current conjuncture is a phase of transition, and that this means that neither the law of value nor stage theory is directly applicable. At the same time, we need to theorize the present with reference to the law of value and stage theory. This may seem like a subtle distinction. How, then, should we use the law of value and stage theory to help theorize the phase of transition?

By clarifying exactly what capitalism is, the theory of a purely capitalist society helps to distinguish the capitalist from the non-capitalist in the phase of transition. The basic value/use-value contradiction of the dialectic of capital serves to orient our analysis towards the use-value obstacles in the phase of transition that undermine the law of value. Understanding how the fictitious commodities, land, labour and money are commodified in a purely capitalist society helps in the analysis of their de-commodification in the phase of transition. Clarity on the relation between the economic, political and ideological at the level of pure theory is also useful in analysing the phase of transition. Similarly, clarity on 'class' can help analyse class phenomena in the present. Finally clarity about periodic crisis gained in pure theory can help us to understand the current crisis.

By clearly presenting the dynamics of finance-capital, the theory of imperialism can serve as a reference for understanding the failure of finance-capital between the two world wars. As the theory of the last stage of capitalism, it helps to analyse the movement away from capitalism where there is no hegemonic type of capital accumulation. In particular the failure of periodic crises to regulate the commodification of labour-power in the stage of imperialism can help us to understand the necessity for the Keynesian policies that developed after World War II.

The economic system that is dominant in the world today is moribund quasi-capitalism. It has many features of capitalism, but it also has many new features that are inadequately understood if we apply the laws of motion of capitalism directly. Some Marxists have debated over whether the current crisis should be understood according to the declining rate of profit, under-consumption or profit-squeeze. But this implies that it should be understood primarily according to some economic laws. It seems to me that this assumes that we are in a stage of capitalism and not a phase of transition. The present crisis does have a structural economic dynamic, but this dynamic also has essential political and ideological dimensions. The economic dynamic should not be analysed in isolation from the political and ideological factors, and it cannot be adequately understood by any version of the law of value.

Because of the influence of productivist readings of *Capital*, many Marxists have not paid much attention to money. Money was often seen to be the most determined and least determining factor of the capitalist economy. For Marxists it was not money that made the world go around, but rather it was the movement of production that caused money to go around. Though there is some truth to this simplistic posing of alternatives, productivists have a tendency to treat money as a kind of passive reflex of the realm of production. Sekine's *Dialectic of Capital* demonstrates that money plays a crucial and active role in the law of value. But because of productivist readings of *Capital*, Marxists have tended to ignore money even in periods of capitalist history where the law of value is hegemonic. This tradition unfortunately extends into the phase of transition away from capitalism, when the monetary system takes on increasing importance.

Socialists have often been defeated by the international monetary system, and yet there are few Marxist studies of it. The Left in general seems to have little understanding of the international monetary system and its importance. Time and again progressive governments have had to turn away from reform towards austerity in order to protect their currency or stop capital flight. The present socialist government in France is only the last in a long and not so glorious line. It seems that progressive governments must find ways to break from the international monetary system or at least protect themselves from its dictates that force them to turn away from reform. This requires that the socialist movement develop a stronger international dimension.

An important feature of the current international financial system is its debt expansion.[4] World debt has been increasing in geometric proportions. This debt system has little to do with the law of value, except to show the extent to which the movement of value (or perhaps pseudovalue would be more accurate) has become divorced from the requirements of economic life. Who gets the loans, how much they get and the terms of the loan has as much or more to do with politics and ideology as with economics. As I mentioned in the last chapter, when capital accumulation is undermined by the declining rate of profit in a crisis, capital tends to dissolve into money. In an economic system where stagnation or a kind of crisis is permanent then capital is continually dissolving into money and its entire existence is tenuous. Movements of money cut free from the requirements of accumulation are not only destabilizing but may lead to capricious, irrational and destructive uses relative to the needs of real economic life.

There is little market discipline of large firms because they cannot be allowed to go bankrupt for fear of jeopardizing the entire debt system. States are in an even better position to threaten the debt system because if they go bankrupt their assets cannot be so easily seized short of armed invasion. The most bankrupt countries still get loans in order to forestall bankruptcy. In this way debt expansion becomes a vicious circle.

Those Third World countries which are safest for capital tend to get the biggest loans. But 'safe for capital' generally means military dictatorship with fascist qualities. Wages are kept down by outlawing unions and strikes, while foreign capital is given very favourable investment terms. The military might necessary to impose such an order is costly and requires loans. The military might is also necessary to maintain stability while taxing the people to repay the loans. The debt economy is a truly reactionary system. It leads to the misallocation of resources on a global scale while fuelling militarism and bolstering reactionary regimes. The poor become poorer and more dependent on the rich. The reason that a regime like the Marcos regime in the Philippines gets so many loans is not because it is a model of democracy. Rather the United States is interested in maintaining its military base, its influence and the flow of interest payments. That the Marcos regime is a dictatorship matters little as long as it maintains 'stability' and its 'friendship' for the United States.

Along with the international expansion of debt has gone the international expansion of production. Capital seems to flow more freely on a global level than ever before, but this flow is not so much in response to the market as to political and ideological factors. To a large extent the location of productive investments follows the debt system. Those states that get large loans also tend to get capital investment. Investment especially flows to low-wage areas, 'free production zones' and to countries that provide tax advantages and other special enticements. The trade union movement is in a state of crisis because it has not kept pace with the internationalization of production. The internationalization of the trade union movement is a crucial step for the future prospects of democratic socialism. This challenge is now placed upon the agenda with a great deal of urgency.

The spectacular expansion of capital on a global scale after World War II was fuelled by debt expansion. Continued fear of a global depression has caused the debt expansion to take off with a frightening momentum of its own. The threat of runaway inflation has caused states to tighten credit and contract their economies. But this causes high unemployment with only a short-run reduction of inflation.[5] The combination of high unemployment and high inflation has been called 'stagflation'. Stagflation has been serious in even the most dynamic of the industrialized nations, but it has been truly disastrous for many Third World countries.

The law of value shows that capitalist crisis serves to replenish the industrial reserve army and to introduce new and more productive technology. With its austerity policies the modern state has no trouble replenishing the industrial reserve army, but how can the state bring about a renewal of fixed capital? The problem is that the technology which is in the wings now is so labour-saving that it may well complete the undermining of the commodification of labour-power which is already quite advanced. Much emphasis is placed upon the need for increased productivity in order to lift us out of the swamp of stagflation, but the prospects of automation raise the spectre of a truly intolerable level of unemployment.

The burgeoning service sector also contributes to the current crisis. Efforts to reduce its size in order to control inflation are bound to be only marginally successful. Since in the long run the production of commodities will be increasingly automated, people-to-people services will expand as a proportion of the economy even if much of the paper work and bureaucracy traditionally associated with the service sector is automated. Person-to-person services have always been difficult to manage capitalistically precisely because they are not reified or com-modified. Services can only be managed capitalistically to the extent that they are commodity-like and can be treated as if they were commodified. But if the more commodity-like and imper-sonal part of the service sector is automated, what will remain will increasingly be person-to-person services that are best managed other than commodity-economically (e.g. education and health care). Cutting back the service sector can only serve as a short-term palliative to inflation. The continued development of the need for person-to-person services as an ever larger portion of the economy points away from a 'free enterprise' solution to the current crisis.

That growth of the state sector which most bolsters the continuation of 'free enterprise' is the military sector.[6] The dependency of capitalism on this sector indicates the reactionary character of capitalism in the phase of transition. Increasingly capitalism depends upon the existence of repression and the production of the instruments of repression. Capitalism wants to buy security for itself through weaponry, but instead this only increases the insecurity. This sets up a convenient dynamic where the seeming insatiable need for security acts as a permanent stimulus to military spending, and military spending is the principle stimulus to the capitalist economy.

Military spending plays such a crucial role in the United States as a countercyclical tool that the phrase 'military Keynesianism' has been coined.[7] When the economy is in recession in the United States and an election year is approaching, the Red menace can easily be invoked to justify increased military spending which will lift the economy out of recession. In the post-World War II period militarism is closely tied to anti-communism. International crises such as the Greek civil war or the war in Korea were used as occasions to whip up anti-communist sentiment and get ever larger military appropriations passed by the U.S. Congress.[8] When it was clear that the Marshall Plan was not enough to get the world economy (especially Europe) back on its feet after World War II, the decision to re-arm provided the impetus.

Militarism also has a close tie with the debt economy since a lot of the international debt is generated to support and expand military apparatuses. Stronger military apparatuses are needed to impose ever harsher austerity policies on the people so that regimes can get further loans to pay off old debts piled up by previous military spending. A vicious circle is created in which the more poor nations get into debt, the more they need a strong army to impose austerity. As the crisis deepens, moribund capitalism comes to depend on militarism. At the same time as Reagan mouths free enterprise ideology, he proposes a manned space-station and the largest military budget ever to pull the economy out of a recession in an election year.

Part of the current crisis of moribund capitalism is the weakening of U.S. hegemony in the world economy. United States domination is increasingly challenged by Japan, Europe and the socialist countries. Since historically the international economy has generally been stabilized by one hegemonic power, in this period it is unclear how stability will be maintained. Since the United States is not likely to give up its position of domination gracefully, there is a real threat of war.

Last but not least the growing world-historic power of the workers' movement and the socialist movement on a global scale limits the options of moribund capitalism, shrinks the area of the world where capitalism can operate and occasionally makes real breakthroughs towards democratic socialism. This trend must be viewed over the long term because in the short term it develops very unevenly. 'Solidarity' may receive a set-back in Poland, but in the long term the so-called socialist states will democratize. The Sandinistas have been victorious in Nicaragua, but they may suffer set-backs due to U.S. power in the region. In the early 1970s the trade union movement saw a surge of militancy, but in the early 1980s the lack of internationalization, continuing austerity policies and other factors have dealt a set-back to the trade union movement. In the long term the popular democratic forces have gained strength and will continue to do so as the irrationality of dying capitalism forces them to reappropriate control over their lives and societies.

This brief analysis of some of the dimensions of the current crisis indicates that it is not like a periodic crisis explainable by the law of value. In the phase of transition, crises become serious threats to the entire system, unleashing revolutionary storms and undermining what remains of capitalism. As the law of value unravels, the global economy becomes more crisis-prone, and crises become more intolerable. Since the system has no tendency towards equilibrium, stability must be artificially maintained. But the effort artificially to maintain stability in a crisis-prone system creates a whole series of contradictions, some of which I have already discussed.

A further contradiction that needs mentioning is between the economic and the political. In Chapter 6 I argued that the basic capitalist ideological form is the legal subject and the basic capitalist political form is the *rechtsstaat*. If the material base of these superstructural forms, the market, becomes undermined in the phase of transition, then capitalist ideology will become more shrill and defensive as it loses its grounding, and the capitalist state will become less governable as it loses its legitimacy. The increased management of the economy by the state including austerity policies means that the state less and less appears to be a neutral legal instrumentality. Legal ideology in general goes into crisis because it is too formalistic to deal with the injustices of dying capitalism. The legal subject becomes a fiction that not only lacks a material base, but also can no longer even appear to serve fair play. The contradictions between the basic capitalist super-structural forms and the exigencies of moribund capital accumulation need to be studied in much more depth.

The foregoing analysis indicates that the current crisis cannot be understood by the law of value or by stage theory, and that political and ideological factors play a prominent role. What is needed is a structural analysis of the economic, political and ideological dynamics of the current conjuncture guided by pure theory and stage theory as reference-points that the present world is moving away from. This section has dealt with some of the complexities involved in both using and not using pure theory to understand the present. Suggested by this analysis, but not specifically focused upon, is the whole range of issues that have to do with the relation between theory and practice. It is to these issues that I turn next.

3   THEORY AND PRACTICE

The question of the relation between theory and practice is closely connected to the question of the relation between the logical and the historical. This is because by 'practice' Marxists mean primarily action aimed at bringing about socialism. But such practice is an effort to change the future course of history; it is history projected into the future. Practice is just a special kind of history. It follows that the logical–historical method has, as a corollary, the unity of theory and practice. Just as with the former, this latter doctrine has produced confusion and strategic errors throughout the history of Marxist theory and practice.

It is very common for Marxists to use the phrases 'the unity of theory and practice' or 'the dialectic of theory and practice', but the approach outlined in this book can lead to no such unquestioning acceptance of these slogans, and indeed must find them dubious. A critical analysis of these phrases, while revealing certain valid and positive impulses behind them, also reveals untenable conceptions that have not served Marxists at all well in their world-historic struggle for democratic socialism. I have criticized the 'logical–historical method' for its tendency to collapse history into theory or theory into history, and have given many examples showing that a too immediate and too close connection between theory and history destroy the integrity of each and results in either impoverishing theory or our understanding of history or both. I have demonstrated that there is neither a unity nor a dialectic between theory and history. However, I have shown that there is a connection between theory and history, but it is complex, involving the development of mediations and levels of analysis. There is no direct interaction between theory and history and there certainly is no unity or dialectic. This approach to theory and history also applies to theory and practice since practice is simply activist history or history with a view to its future alteration through conscious human agency. The relation between theory and practice is a direct corollary to the relation between theory and history.

In so far as 'the unity of theory and practice' refers to a future socialist society where the division of mental and manual labour is broken down, and the separation between theory and social life is reduced, I have no quarrel with it. However, Uno and Sekine's levels of analysis approach demonstrates that 'theory' is internally complex. There are different types and levels of theory. The theory of purely capitalist society is not unified with either history or practice. That theory which is closest to practice is strategic theory, but strategic theory is also that theory which is closest to being not-theory. Strategic theory as the theory aimed at bringing about socialism does not fall within political economy and therefore is not directly informed by the law of value. Because it develops primarily within the phase of transition away from capitalism, strategic theory falls within the purview of historical materialism. It is therefore an approach to change informed by political economy, but is not a part of the science of political economy. Furthermore, because strategic theory must be concerned with the particulars of a concrete conjuncture, experiential knowledge and practical wisdom play a major role. Theory and practice do form a kind of unity with strategic theory, because strategic theory is formualted at the juncture of theory and practice. However, it would be a monumental mistake to treat strategic theory as the paradigm case of 'theory' since it is a borderline case close to being not-theory. As practice approaches theory, it takes the form of an organized movement; and as theory approaches practice, it takes the form of experimential understanding informed by theory.

In order to be successful, theory must have a certain rigidity and practice must have a certain flexibility. If we collapse the two together, either the rigidity or flexibility must prevail. Stalin is a good example of imposing the rigidity of theory on practice, and Lukacs of dissolving theory into the exigencies of practice.

According to Stalin, historical materialism is a science like the natural sciences. It studies the laws of social development, and is capable of coming as precise a science as biology. Furthermore, the party of the proletariat should guide itself in its practice by making deductions from these laws. In this way socialism is 'converted from a dream of a better future for humanity into a science. Hence the bond between science and practical activity, between theory and practice, their unity, should be the guiding star of the party of the proletariat.'[9] This unity that Stalin writes of favours theory since practice is to be guided by 'deductions' from the science of historical materialism. Practice is dogmatized by imposing upon it the rigidities of theory.

In sharp contrast to Stalin, I have argued that historical materialism cannot be constituted as an independent science likely biology. Historical materialism is a materialist approach to the study of history grounded in political economy. Even political economy, which is a science capable of objective truths, cannot directly make use of even the laws of motion of a purely capitalist society for practical purposes. The law of value is not a developmental law at all, and we can only begin to consider developmental tendencies at the level of stage theory. But even stage theory cannot be directly applied to practical activity in the present conjuncture which is a phase of transition and not a stage of capitalism. The dialectical approach of Uno and Sekine precludes the direct application of the dialectic of capital as suggested by Stalin and his example of biology. Non-dialectical natural sciences can generate an applied science or engineering, but a dialectic cannot. The anology with natural science and engineering can lead to unfortunate forms of political practice which aim to impose a plan on human material in the way that an engineer imposes a blueprint on passive steel and concrete in making a bridge. With the Uno/Sekine approach, even the level of historical analysis within political economy can only serve as a guide to strategic thinking and cannot be applied directly to practical activity.

If Stalin tends to impose rigid theory on practice, Lukacs commits the opposite error of subsuming theory to practice. In *History and Class Consciousness* Lukacs writes:

> theory is essentially the intellectual expression of the re-volutionary process itself. In it every stage of the process becomes fixed so that it may be generalized, communicated, utilized and developed. Because the theory does nothing but arrest and make conscious each necessary step, it becomes at the same time the necessary premise of the following one.[10]

Lukacs sees Marxist theory as the direct expression of the revolutionary process with the aim of changing reality. The closeness of theory to practice is emphasized by the metaphor that pictures theory as the thought of the proletariat before each world-historic revolutionary step. Theory, then can be nothing but the self-conscious of the proletariat in the process of revolution. As I argued earlier, this formulation makes it difficult to distinguish between theory and practice at all, and in the end theory and knowledge seem to be reduced to 'making'.

The Uno/Sekine approach illustrates the incorrectness of Lukacs's claim that theory is the direct expression of the revoltutionary process. Pure theory copies and completes the self-reification of capitalism, and as a dialectic, it objectively grasps the necessary inner connections of capitalism for all times. The law of value does not change with each step in the unfolding revolutionary process. This is not to say that there is no connection between the dialectic of capital and history. It is no accident that the founding work of the dialectic of capital was written by Marx in England in the 1860s. It was only with the full development of industrial capitalism and with it the beginnings of a socialist movement that it became possible not only rigourously to theorize the material relations of capitalism but also to see these material relations as reified social relations. The fact that Marx was a socialist aided him in understanding reification and in therefore seeing capitalism as a historically limited mode of production. But the dialectic of capital is first and foremost an objectively true theory, although a class ideology may be derived from it. It may be that strategic theory is or ought to be the direct expression of the revolutionary process, but it is inaccurate and misleading to see the law of value in this way.

If theory is tied too closely to practice, both suffer as a consequence. If theory is made directly to govern practice, then practice takes on the rigidities of theory and will become overly dogmatic, failing to relate to the diverse subjectivities that it is trying to mobilize and to the diverse circumstances that must be taken into account in order to make the most of each situation as it develops. If practice is made directly to govern theory, then theory comes under the unbearable pressures of political immediacy and political expediency. Instead of striving for truth and objectivity, theory strives for political correctness however that may be defined in the existing conjuncture. In order to relate to each other most effectively, the separate identities of theoretical practice and political/ideological practice must be maintained. Otherwise theory can dogmatize practice, and practice can underine the truth and objectivity of theory. In the case of Lukacs and some critical theory, the spontaneism and subjectivity of practice is made to prevail over theory; and in the case of Stalinism, the rigidity of theory is made to prevail over practice. Thus critical theory and Stalinism are mirror images of each other, each using the looseness of the 'unity of theory and practice' for opposite but interdependent one-sided theories. My resolution involves grasping the separateness of both theory and practice, and the complex and complicated ways that they relate to one another.

Besides strategic theory, another kind of theory which is action-oriented is ethical theory. The basic principles of socialism arrived at by superseding capitalist reification are ethical principles. They are ethical because their purpose is to guide human behaviour towards a better society, but they are derived from an objective science.

The dialectic of capital is first and foremost an objective scientific theory which shows the inner workings of pure capitalism. But it is important to note that this theory is only possible because of the reification of capitalism, and reification itself makes the motion of things soveriegn over human beings. Reification is an objective state of affairs, but it not only subjects humanity to the violence of things, but subjects one class to another as commodities to be used for extracting profit. The idea of overcoming reification involves a moral point of view which may be called 'humanism'. If one thinks that human beings should be put before profits or that human beings should be treated as ends in themselves and not as means, then one must be opposed to the reification that is inherent to capitalism.

Although the idea of overcoming reification implies a moral point of view, it is not moralistic because it involves working towards a realistic possibility in the sense that the possibility, the need to realize it and the possibility of realizing it are derived from capitalism itself and not from anyone's subjective vision of the ideal society. Therefore though theory is not the direct expression of the revolutionary process, we see that even theory as objective science, in this case, does suggest the transformation of the reality it theorizes. Philosophers in the positivist tradition may find it difficult to see how a theory can at the same time be scientific and moral, but is this really so strange in the *social* sciences where we are concerned with both how societies work and how to make them work better?

The dialectic of capital is scientific because it traces the inner logic of a society that is materialized and objectified. The reification that makes this theory possible suggests the possibility of de-reification where humanity re-appropriates control over its own destiny. The basic principles of socialism must be ethical even though they are derived from an objective science, and this is because socialism depends upon the reassertion of the ethical. Socialism depends upon humanity acting instead of being acted upon; in this case action guided by ethical principles. The theory of the transition to socialism is both scientific and ethical. The ethical part is derived in part from the scientific and guides our thought about the most desirable course of action. Marxian social science not only serves as the basis for socialist ethics, but also helps us to understand the pattern of objective resistances that must be overcome in order to reach socialism. The theory of the transition to socialism cannot therefore be an 'engineering' precisely because of its ethical component which involves action, purpose and intention.

That capitalism cannot reach the perfection of the ideal environment of a purely capitalist society demonstrates that it can ever only have a partial hold on history and the real economic life of man, and that its continued expanded reproduction is therefore problematic. The dialectic of capital is the objective ground of Marxism, but the fact that it is possible to arrive at an obejctive dialectic of capital already implies the need to transform a human reality that can be so objectified. In this fashion an ethical standpoint of radical criticism can be directly derived from the very objectivity of the dialectic of capital.

The tradition of Marxist theory which is sometimes called 'critical theory' often argues that any theory that is objective or factual must reinforce the existing state of affairs.[11] As a result of this perspective, it follows that if we want to change reality, we must adopt a point of view of radical criticism as opposed to objectivism or scientism. Critical theory marks out its theoretical terrain in sharp opposition to positivism (and Stalinism) which is seen to epitomize reified theory which would reconfirm the existing order and either deny the possibility of significant change or understand change only according to a technological or technocratic model. Critical theorists reject the positivist paradigm because change is seen as a matter of applied science and 'engineering'. The attack by critical theoriests on technocratic thought arises from laudable motives, but in so whole-heartedly attacking objectivism and scientism and all such manifestations of reified thought, they tend to fall into the traps of voluntarism, spontanism, utopianism and idealism, and at the same time they destroy any basis for objectively grounding Marxist theory. If Marxists had to choose between theorizing that reinforced existing reality and theorizing that attempted to overthrow existing reality, then they must side with the critical theorists in favour of radical criticism. But these are not the only choices, and to see them as the only choices involves a partial acceptance of the subject/object split that lies at the base of reified thought. The need for theory to define itself entirely as radical criticism is a desparate effort at the level of thought to overcome the divorce between object and subject by dissolving the object through a thought process that radically subjectivizes it. All too often critical theory makes up for the lack of radical change at the level of history by ever more radical and voluntaristic criticism at the level of theory. For critical theorists the choice seems to be between scientific thought which necessarily objectifies or pacifies the subject, or radical criticism which subjectifies and dissolves the object.

Part of the error of critical theorists comes from their adhering too closely to the unity of theory and practice as proposed by Lukacs. I have already argued that for Lukacs this unity proceeds to the point where it becomes difficult even to distinguish between theory and practice. Theory seems to take on the same transformative qualities as practice—theory like practice directly changes the world. Thus theory like practice either conforms to the world or goes against the established order. Since science, in the view of the critical theorists, tries to conform to the world, they abandon science to the bourgeoisie and are essentially left with artistic rebellion.

In rejecting artistic rebellion as inadequate and limited, we are not then thrown to the other extreme of positivism with its technocratic models of change. To show that these are not the options, let me consider Popper's engineering paradigm. According to Popper, we have three choices: no change at all (let it be), piecemeal engineering, or utopian or holistic engineering. Popper rejects the possibility of no change, and he underscores the totalitarian horrors of holistic engineering, which leaves piecemeal engineering as the only reasonable approach.[12] Implicit in his critique of holistic engineering is a critique of Marxism, but according to my interpretation of Marxist theory, it is not prone to utopian engineering and that is because it rejects the engineering paradigm altogether. The dialectic of capital cannot directly generate an applied science precisely because of the separation it maintains between theory and practice. The dialectic of capital reveals the law of value. This understanding can serve as an objective foundation for stage theory, historical analysis and Marxian social science generally. By seeing through the reification that hides class domination, Marxist theory suggests the possibility and desirability of socialism and can therefore guide the building of a socialist movement. But, as I have argued, strategic theory is theory which is closest to practice and to being not-theory. It involves a significant experiential component and cannot in any way be deduced directly from higher levels of theory. In fact a dialectic is not like an axiomatic geometry at all – stage theory is not deduced from pure theory and historical theory is not deduced from stage theory. Each level of theory acts as a guide and framework for lower levels of theory, realizing that as we move from abstract theory to the real concrete, necessity becomes increasingly qualified and weakened by contingency and agency. Thus Marxist theory cannot directly generate an applied science or an engineering; it can only help to guide a socialist movement.

Furthermore, Marxist theory, as I interpret it, is not concerned with 'long-range forecasting' or with establishing the inevitability of socialism. The dialectic of capital can improve our study and understanding of history and thereby can improve our chance of constructing democratic socialism. By revealing exactly what capitalism is and how it operates in its inner essence, the dialectic of capital can serve to guide our understanding of the supersession of that system or socialism. Based on the dialectic of capital, we can see that socialism deserving of the name must be highly democratic, and that bureaucratic 'socialism' is not really socialism. By suggesting the need to overcome reification the dialectic of capital also suggests the idea of democratic socialism, but it only suggests it as a historical possibility. The dialectic cannot show that socialism is an inevitable or even likely outcome of capitalism; all it can show is that from the point of view of the realization of human potentials, it is a possible and desirable outcome. Nor can pure theory tell us exactly what a socialist society would look like; all it can do is indicate the general principles that would have to be realized in it. Historical experience demonstrates that democratic socialism is in fact difficult to establish and that though it is a force and movement in the world, it so far only exists in primitive and partial forms.

Though the unity of theory and practice is a crude and simplistic doctrine that breeds confusion, it is also incorrect to see theory and practice divorced from each other. In this section I have tried to explore the complex relations between theory and practice and to explore problems with the unity doctrine. I have also tried to show that Marxian scientific theory and moral theory are complementary, and that the opposition between positivism and critical theory can be transcended.

4   CONCLUSIONS

I want to end this chapter by briefly mentioning the important contributions that Laclau and Mouffe have made to strategic theory. According to them 'class reductionism' has produced serious theoretical and strategic errors in the Marxist movement, and instead of relying on narrow class rhetoric to mobilize people, we need to rely more on democratic and populist appeals.[13]

The dialectic of capital demonstrates that socialism is achieved primarily by democratizing capitalist society. Now the class composition of a democratic socialist movement will at least partially depend upon the extent to which the society in question is capitalist and upon how it is 'inserted' into the global economy. These same factors will also affect the extent to which it can actually achieve socialism. In the Chinese revolution it was necessary that the socialist movement be peasant-based, and it was also clear that given the level of development in China, the road to the full realization of democratic socialism would be a long one. In the case of advanced industrial countries, it is clear that the socialist movement will be based on working people broadly defined and on various oppressed groups all of whom are hurt by the prevailing economy and have a strong interest in democratizing the economy as well as the rest of society.

Theory acts as a distant guide, and the successes and failures of a past and present practice act as a closer guide to the socialist movement. A successful socialist movement must present realistic possibilities of democratic transformation, and it must appeal to those concerns that most move people in the here and now. It must offer solutions that will make a real and substantial difference to the lives of individuals. I whole-heartedly agree with Laclau and Mouffe when they advocate a 'war of position' whose strategy 'involves a plurality of democratic struggles, aiming to change the relation of forces at all levels of society . . .'.[14] We must elaborate a strategy that can 'unite all the fragments of the democratic movement'.[15] I believe that this requires Marxists to pay more attention to combating the hegemony of bourgeois ideology. In general the Left must also be much more practical in working out the paths of transition and at the same time display the sort of leadership and ethical vision that moves people to action.

The Uno/Sekine approach firmly establishes the scientificity of Marxian social science while avoiding abuses of that scientificity which have often led to dogmatism. As a stronger social science, Marxist theory is a better guide to practice. But also, realizing the limits of this science is an essential part of it, and it is this which enables us to use theory as a guide while avoiding dogmatism. The theory of pure capitalism establishes a more clear and precise idea of socialism, and this may serve to overcome some of the disunity on the Left. Understanding the transitional character of the current phase can lead to a better understanding of its basic character and dynamics. Seeing through the confusion connected to the slogan 'the unity of theory and practice' not only clarifies the relationship between theory and practice, but also supersedes points of contention that have, for example, divided critical theorists from more orthodox Marxism, or Marxist humanists from structuralists. This new approach lifts the pall of dogmatism that has always hung over Marxism and has deadened its creative life-affirming impulses. At the same time it does not fall back into eclecticism or skepticism, but instead offers an approach that has a firm foundation while being capable of being responsive to the conjunctural.

11 Conclusion

It should now be clear to the reader that the approach of Uno and Sekine is not simply one more contribution to the tradition of Marxian discourse, but instead constitutes a major reinterpretation. Political economy, dialectical materialism, historical materialism and their interrelations are understood differently from any of the perspectives that have been developed within Western Marxism. Furthermore, I have argued that the Unoist approach is superior to any that has been developed within the West not only in being more scientific but also in overcoming many of the unresolved oppositions and polarities that we find in the Western tradition.

According to the Japanese reconstruction, political economy is fundamental to Marxism, and the theory of a purely capitalist society or the law of value is fundamental to political economy. The fact that the theory of a purely capitalist society can be constructed as a rigorous dialectic provides Marxist theory with a firm and objective foundation. The law of value, however, cannot be directly applied to history in the way one might apply a law of nature to nature. Instead of generating an 'engineering', the dialectic of capital externalizes itself in history by developing the distinct levels of stage theory and historical analysis. The more abstract level of theory offers orienting concepts and guidelines for the more concrete level. Thus pure theory guides the construction of stage theory. Stage theory is not deduced from pure theory. The same can be said for the relation between stage theory and historical analysis. Dialectical materialism is derived from political economy in the sense that the dialectic of capital is the only substantive theory which is both dialectical and materialist. This means that the ontology, epistemology and methodology of Marxism are derived from analysing the logic of the dialectic of capital. In other words dialectical materialism is the reconstructed logic of a substantive scientific theory and not an independently constructed philosophical system. Though only the theory of

269

pure capitalism follows a rigorous dialectical logic, political economy as a whole follows a dialectical method in the sense that the more concrete levels of analysis represent an externalization of the dialectic in history.

Dialectical materialism demonstrates that historical materialism is not an independent science of history based on the laws of social development. Instead historical materialism is simply a materialist approach to understanding history based on the science of political economy. Thus it is the law of value that is the foundation of historical materialism and not some transhistorical and general laws of sociohistorical development. It is the theory of a purely capitalist society which clearly demarcates the economic class so that historical materialism becomes a strong hypothesis with clear and precise guiding principles and concepts. Historical materialism, then, is not a science but an approach derivative from the science of political economy.

That part of historical materialism which is concerned with the transition to socialism and the relation between theory and practice is rather myth-eaten and that is because of the prevalence of the logical–historical method throughout the history of Marxist discourse. Once we reject this method, it is possible to sort out the polarity between Marxism as science and as radical criticism. (In fact the science of political economy implies ethical humanism.) It also becomes clear that the slogan 'the unity of theory and practice' is a corollary of the logical–historical method, and as such has been a source of error and confusion. The most frequent tendencies towards error that flow from this slogan are to subsume practice to theory as with Stalin or to subsume theory to practice as with Lukacs. Those who simply emphasize the interaction between theory and practice reduce all theory and practice to the single case of strategic thought where there is a close interaction. The relation between theory and practice is complex because of multiple levels and types of both theory and practice. It is misleading to reduce this complexity to the simple unity of theory and practice. Some reflection on the complex relation between history and the theory of a purely capitalist society should be sufficient to indicate the crudeness of the idea of the unity of theory and practice.

The Uno/Sekine approach to Marxist theory enables us to resolve many recurring disputes in the tradition of Marxist discourse. No problem has so troubled this body of discourse than the relation between the logical and the historical. To escape the tendencies towards both economism and politicism that flow from the logical–historical method, we must reject the entire problematic associated with this method. The approach that I have outlined offers a new problematic based on levels of analysis which enables us to supersede many of the confusions and debates generated by the logical–historical method.

The Japanese approach that I have outlined also resolves the debate between 'traditionalists' and 'Neo-Ricardians'. Traditionalists were correct to defend the labour theory of value, but Neo-Ricardians were correct to reject the mathematical derivation of prices from values. The theory of a purely capitalist society provides a rigorous defence of the law of value while showing that prices and values are determined simultaneously in the capitalist market by technical data and 'the basic constraint'. Sekine's rigorous dialectical reformulation of Uno's theory of a purely capitalist society clarifies the precise meaning of the law of value and establishes its objective validity.

Stage theory helps to sort out many issues in the study of capitalist history, particularly issues surrounding the questions of underdevelopment and imperialism. Stage theory enables us to evaluate the strengths and weaknesses of the classical literature of imperialism, and also to see that underdevelopment cannot have any simple or exclusively economic explanation. Stage theory demonstrates the general necessity to mediate the law of value and historical studies with a distinct level of analysis. It shows us how to externalize the dialectic of capital in history by concretizing the basic value/use-value contradiction. Finally stage theory sheds light on the transition towards socialism and away from capitalism. The difficulties in trying to construct a stage theory of capitalism after 1917 and the clarity about precisely what capitalism is, gained at the level of pure theory, indicate that the period from 1917 to the present should be conceived of as a phase of transition. This frees Marxian analysis of the current conjuncture from inappropriate applications of the law of value or theory of imperialism.

The historical analysis of capitalism must be conceived as a distinct level of analysis and not a deduction from either stage theory or pure theory. Recently E. P. Thompson and others, in reacting against economism and reductionism, have rejected the law of value as a guide to historical studies. In some cases the reaction against theoreticism has gone so far that Marxian social science is reduced to little more than the concrete analysis of concrete situations. But it is a mistake to reject the guide offered to historical studies by the law of value and stage theory. The problem is not one of applying the law of value or not, but of understanding how to use it, including its limitations. From the point of view of the historical concrete, the law of value does not explain historical detail, but it does offer an invaluable guide in conceptualizing the flow of history. Not to see this is to discard Marx's greatest scientific achievement, *Capital*.

Part of the reason why economism is so widespread with orthodox Marxism is that Marx presented the law of value in *Capital* as a purely economic law without a corresponding analysis of capitalist ideology and politics. The Althusserians tried to correct this by including the political and ideological in their conception of the mode of production. But they never tried to improve upon Marx's *Capital*, and therefore never arrived at a precise theorization of the economic. Without this they could not precisely theorize the political and ideological. The political and ideological become semi-autonomous realms somehow articulated with each other and with the economic in a kind of uncomfortable limbo between the mode of production and social formation. The problems with this approach can be traced through the work of Poulantzas, which starts out attempting to be rigorously structuralist and ends up being historicist and even NeoGramscian.[1]

By developing the passive state and ideological forms at the level of pure theory, we do not start out with a purely economic law of value which then has the political and ideological added in *ad hoc* fashion at some more concrete level of analysis. By precisely specifying the relation between the economic, political and ideological at the level of pure theory, we have a clear guide for integrating these realms at more concrete levels of analysis. The logical-historical method has produced indescribable confusion around the analysis of the capitalist state and ideology. The levels of analysis approach can serve finally to move this body of literature out of the cave and into the sunlight.

The discovery that the theory of a purely capitalist society is both dialectical and materialist presents for the first time a firm basis for sorting out questions of Marxist epistemology which have often centred on dialectical materialism. There has always been a tendency to apply dialectical materialism to all of nature or all of history, but the only clear example of dialectical materialsim that we have is the dialectic of capital. The dialectic of capital provides an objective exemplar for clarifying the meaning of 'dialectical materialism' and for analysing the strengths and weaknesses of contributions from other thinkers such as Lukacs, Althusser and Colletti.

Dialectical materialism demonstrates that historical materialism must be derivative from political economy. Once we are clear that historical materialism is not a science but is simply an approach, we can focus our attention on the formulation of guiding principles. This approach is in sharp opposition to the one that tries to turn the concept 'mode of production' into the central explanatory concept of the science of history. The concept 'mode of production' cannot bear such explanatory weight and must therefore remain a confused and contested concept. Following Uno and Sekine, I do not try to construct the central concepts of an independent science, but I derive some guiding principles from political economy for the sake of developing a materialist approach to the study of history.

All of the muddles and confusions of the logical–historical method come to a head with strategic thought centred on the transition to socialism. It is here that the unity of theory and practice generates economistic and voluntarist mistakes that cost lives and unnecessary suffering. In Western Marxism the split between the scientism and positivism of orthodox Marxism and especially Stalinism stands in stark opposition to the idealism and voluntarism of critical theory. The approach I have developed supersedes this polarity by showing that Marxism includes both science and radical criticism. The science of political economy implies a moral point of view, namely humanism.

Furthermore, clear strategic thinking requires clarity about precisely what capitalism is, what socialism is and where we are located in the current conjuncture of world history. The approach I have outlined can establish this clarity. The meaning of capitalism becomes clear and precise at the level of the theory of pure capitalism, and the supersession of pure capitalism generates the basic principles of socialism. These principles demonstrate that crucial to the creation of socialism is the democratization of social life. But the concrete problems confronting democratization in the current conjuncture require not only the elaboration of a socialist ethic but also an analysis of the complex structures and dynamics that dominate this period of world history. Understanding that the present period cannot be adequately grasped by applying some mixture of the law of value and the theory of imperialism is the first step in coming to grips with the complex intermeshing of economic, political and ideological forces that we face in the 1980s. In the light of this understanding we can propose institutional alternatives to current institutional arrangements.

Finally it is clear that Marxian social science can only serve as a guide to a socialist movement or party. The transition to socialism cannot be achieved without a movement and/or party and this involves skills of leadership, communication and organization. It involves experience in working with people and it involves practical wisdom. The approach to Marxist theory that I have outlined is the basis for a more scientific and less dogmatic Marxian social science, and this can serve to make a socialist movement more enlightened and more successful. Furthermore, in strengthening the scientific grounding of Marxism while loosening up its body of thought, I present an approach that offers firm directions while being flexible in dealing with particulars. In superseding many traditional disputes and polarities this approach offers the possibility of a more unified Left – a unity based upon a clarity and agreement concerning the basic principles of socialism, while permitting much experimentation and diversity at the level of practice in the efforts to democratize the economy and all other areas of social life. This is a fresh approach that overcomes old and deep divisions while establishing greater clarity about the central thrust of our common project. It is time for Marxists to abandon old and stale rhetoric that is tied up with tiresome and petty in-fighting. This new approach opens up the possibility for a rebirth of Marxism as the creative life force that represents the interests of humanity for a better future.

Notes

NOTES TO CHAPTER ONE: INTRODUCTION

1. As the most recent hegemonic paradigm, I give more attention to Althusser and his followers than to other schools of thought, though other schools are certainly not neglected. My critical analysis of the Althusserian paradigm is scattered throughout the book and is not concentrated in one chapter in particular. Finally, although the Althusserian paradigm has declined for good reasons, some of which I highlight in my discussion, I have the highest respect for Althusser because of the scope of his undertaking and his lasting contributions to Marxist theory.

2. The only text available by Uno in English is *Principles of Political Economy: Theory of a Purely Capitalist Society*, trans. by T. Sekine (Sussex: Harvester Press, 1980). His student Sekine has a number of texts available. His immensely important *The Dialectic of Capital* is available from Yushindo Press in Tokyo (1984). He translated and contributed an important methodological essay to Uno's *Principles*. See also his 'The Necessity of the Law of Value', *Science and Society* (Fall 1980); 'Uno-Riron: a Japanese Contribution to Marxian Political Economy', *Journal of Economic Literature*, vol. XIII (1975); 'The Circular Motion of Capital', *Science and Society* (Fall 1981); ('The Law of Market Value'), *Science and Society* (Winter 1982–3). Makoto Itoh has written a number of articles and a book entitled *Value and Crisis: Essays on Marxian Economics in Japan* (New York: Monthly Review Press, 1980). See also the following articles by Canadian Unoists: B. Maclean, 'Kozo Uno's *Principles of Political Economy*', *Science and Society* (Summer 1981); C. Duncan, 'Under the Cloud of Capital: History Versus Theory', *Science and Society* (Fall 1983); R. Albritton, 'The Dialectic of Capital: a Japanese Contribution', *Capital and Class* (Spring 1984).

3. The School of Orthodox Marxism is much larger than the Uno School, but the Uno School is probably the second largest in the number of professors. There are also other significant schools of Marxian political economy such as the Civil Society School.

4. The appraisal that the Uno School has 'lost momentum' comes from S. Mawatari, 'The Uno School: a Marxian Approach in Japan', *The History of Political Economy Journal*, forthcoming.

5. Some of Itoh's work focuses on the current conjuncture as opposed to economic theory *per se*. Also Duncan's article 'Under the Cloud of Capital' focuses on the relation between the approach of Uno and that of E. P. Thompson.

6. According to Sekine, 'whoever carries Uno's tradition creatively in the future must first go beyond him in pure theory; for this latter is the core of Uno's contribution of which other parts are strictly derivative' (Uno, *Principles*, p. xvi.

NOTES TO CHAPTER TWO: THE UNO/SEKINE APPROACH AND MARX

1. For attacks on the law of value see I. Steedman, *Marx After Sraffa* (London: New Left Books, 1977) and B. Hindness *et al.*, *Marx's 'Capital' and Capitalism Today* (London: Routledge & Kegan Paul, 1977).
2. E. P. Thompson, *The Poverty of Theory and Other Essays* (New York: Monthly Review Press, 1978) and E. Laclau and C. Mouffe, 'Recasting Marxism: Hegemony and New Political Movements', *Socialist Review*, no. 66 (November–December 1982) carry out extended attacks on economism but from different points of view.
3. Uno uses 'commodity-economic principle' throughout his *Principles*. This means the principles by which the market becomes self-regulating once it is generalized and subsumes production. 'Commodity-economic principle', therefore, roughly means 'market principle'.
4. K. Marx, *Capital*, vol. III (Moscow: Progress, 1971) p. 831.
5. *Ibid.*, vol. II, pp. 108–9.
6. 'Intrinsically, it is not a question of the higher or lower degree of development of the social antagonisms that result from the natural laws of capitalist production. It is a question of these laws themselves, of these tendencies working with iron necessity towards inevitable results' (*ibid.*, vol. I, p. 19).
7. *Ibid.*, vol. I, p. 89.
8. Thompson, *Poverty of Theory*, p. 153.
9. K. Uno, 'Types of Economic Policies Under Capitalism', unpublished, partially translated manuscript; see also Uno, *Principles*, pp. 173, 179.
10. Besides Sekine's *Dialectic of Capital* the major source for this argument is Appendix I of Uno's *Principles* entitled 'An Essay on Uno's Dialectic of Capital'.
11. This will be discussed in Part II.
12. This will be discussed in later chapters.
13. For example, see R. Rosdolsky, *The Making of Marx's 'Capital'* (London: Pluto Press, 1977) and R. L. Meek, *Economics and Ideology and Other Essays* (London: Chapman & Hall, 1967) pp. 93–106.
14. K. Marx and F. Engels, *Collected Works*, vol. 16 (New York: International, 1980) p. 475.
15. *Ibid.*, p. 477.
16. K. Marx, *The Grundrisse* (Harmondsworth: Penguin, 1973) p. 101.
17. *Ibid.*
18. *Ibid.*
19. *Ibid.*, pp. 102–3.

20. *Ibid.*, p. 103.
21. *Ibid.*, p. 104.
22. *Ibid.*, p. 105.
23. *Ibid.*, p. 105.
24. *Ibid.*, p. 105.
25. The relation between political economy in the sense of the theory of capitalism and historical materialism as an approach to history generally will be explored in Part III.
26. *Ibid.*, p. 107.
27. *Ibid.*, p. 107.
28. *Ibid.*, p. 107.
29. *Ibid.*, p. 460.
30. *Ibid.*, p. 107.
31. *Ibid.*, p. 276.
32. *Ibid.*, p. 331.
33. Marx, *Capital*, vol. III, pp. 879–80.
34. Marx, *Grundrisse*, p. 156.
35. *Ibid.*, p. 157.
36. Marx, *Capital*, vol. II, pp. 108–9.
37. *Ibid.*
38. *Ibid.*, vol. I, p. 85.
39. For a much more condensed version without the explicit dialectics, see Uno's *Principles*.
40. K. Marx, *Capital*, vol. I, trans. by Ben Fowkes (Harmondsworth: Penguin, 1976) p. 1014.
41. Marx, *Capital*, vol. III (Progress), p. 175.
42. *Ibid.*, p. 831.
43. 'Of course the method of presentation must differ in form from that of inquiry. The latter has to appropriate the material in detail, to analyse its different form of development, to trace out their inner connexion. Only after this work is done, can the actual movement be adequately described. If this is done successfully, if the life of the subject-matter is ideally reflected as in a mirror, then it may appear as if we had before us a mere *a priori* construction' (*ibid.*, vol. I, p. 28).
44. *Ibid.*, p. 667.
45. L. Althusser, *Reading Capital* (London: New Left Books, 1970) pp. 11–71.
46. Marx, *Capital*, vol. III (Progress) p. 110.
47. *Ibid.*, ch. xiv.
48. *Ibid.*, pp. 436–8.

NOTES TO CHAPTER THREE: THEORY OF A PURELY CAPITALIST SOCIETY

1. Althusser, *Reading Capital*.
2. Sekine, *Dialectic of Capital*, vol. I (Tokyo: Yushindo Press, 1984).
3. With his distinction between 'capital in general' and 'many capitals'

Rosdolsky comes close to the concept of a 'purely capitalist society'. For example, he writes that the sequence of categories in Marxian political economy

> do not have the slightest relation to 'external considerations', or the conventional 'factors of production' theory of bourgeois economics. Rather, they are the product of the inner nature of the capitalist mode of production itself, of the historical and logical succession of the categories which constitute it, and which in fact required – at least temporarily – the dismemberment of the object of the analysis, especially at the outset, where 'the essential issue was to grasp the pure, specific economic forms and hence with not joining together things that do not belong together'. (p. 39)

The problem is that he combines the concept 'capital in general' with the logical–historical method so that the relation between the law of value and history remains unclear, and it is also unclear how one arrives at the concept 'capital in general'. Rodolsky remains so true to Marx, that he does not really advance these issues beyond Marx's formulations except possibly to focus our attention on them by emphasizing them within his book, *The Making of Marx's 'Capital'*.

4. See especially the articles by Jairus Banaji and Chris Arthur. Banaji firmly rejects the logical–historical method and does see the logic of Marx's *Capital* as dialectical, but unfortunately he has little real understanding of dialectics and he stays too close to Marx's text rather than immersing himself in the logic of capital. Thus he sees the movement from the category commodity to the category value as a movement from 'Being' to 'Essence'; whereas as Sekine convincingly demonstrates the category 'commodity' comes first only to locate the totality being theorized so that we move immediately to the basic contradiction inherent in the commodity which is between value and use-value and this parallels Hegel's 'Being' versus 'Nothing'. Furthermore, the Doctrine of Circulation parallels Hegel's Doctrine of Being, the Doctrine of Production parallels the Doctrine of Essence and the Doctrine of Distribution parallels the Doctrine of Notion. The circulation-forms are all unmediated as are Hegel's categories in the Doctrine of Being. Mediated categories only develop in the Doctrine of Production which is centred on the capital–labour production relation. Finally it is incorrect to describe the dialectical logic of capital as a continual oscillation between appearance and essence since these categories are only characteristic of the Doctrine of Production. Arthur tries to develop differences between formal logic and dialectical logic in interpreting value-form theory, but he does not actually develop the very close connection between the logic of the value-form and sections of Hegel's Doctrine of Being, nor does he explain the sense in which the logic of value-form theory is 'the logic of the concrete'. See Diane Elson (ed.), *Value: The Representation of Labour in Capitalism* (London: CSE Books, 1979).

5. David Levine understands that 'The opposition of value and use-value is the driving force which underlies the development of the entire system of economic relations' [*Economic Theory*, vol. I (London: Routledge & Kegan

Paul, 1978) p. 76]. Also he understands that 'Systematicity is not imposed upon the subject-matter but exists already implicit within it as its determining principle' [*Economic Studies* (London: Routledge & Kegan Paul, 1977) p. 15]. But Levine's reconstruction of Marx's *Capital*, though dialectical in many ways, falls short of being a self-conscious rigorously constructed dialectic. Furthermore, though his interpretation of value as 'the inner reflection, within the commodity, of the system of economic relations as a whole' is essentially accurate, he does not see that the labour theory of value can and should be made consistent with this conception of value. Instead he confines the labour theory of value to essentially its Ricardian form which sees value determined completely within the production process and treats circulation as superficial and epiphenomenal (*Economy Theory*, p. 5). Instead of trying to reformulate the labour theory of value to integrate circulation as an important constraint on value formation and augmentation, he abandons it, but this then runs the danger of placing too much emphasis on circulation since there is no counterweight. And this over emphasis on circulation could lead to a sort of Left version of Keynesian underconsumptionism.

6. Itoh, *Value and Crisis*, p. 45.
7. This is demonstrated by Sekine's *Dialectic of Capital* as a whole and there is also a methodological discussion of dialectics in the 'Introduction' to *Dialectic of Capital* and in 'An Essay on Uno's Dialectic of Capital' which is Appendix I to Uno's *Principles*.
8. Sekine, *Dialectic of Capital*, vol. I, unpublished manuscript (1982) f. 4.
9. Marx, *Capital*, vol. I (Progress) pp. 18–19; see also K. Marx and F. Engels, *Selected Correspondence* (Moscow: Progress, 1955) p. 177.
10. *Ibid.*, p. 19.
11. Sekine, *Dialectic of Capital*, 'Introduction', unpublished manuscript (1982) f. 18.
12. Marx, *Capital*, vol. I (Progress) p. 55.
13. This point is made forcefully in H. Watanabe, 'Logico-genetical Approximation to the Analysis of the Unfolding of the Value-form', *The Kezai Gaku*, Annual Report of the Economic Society, Tohoku University, Sendai, Japan.
14. Uno, *Principles*, p. 9.
15. Sekine, *Dialectic of Capital*, vol. I, unpublished manuscript (1982) f. 4.
16. See Ernest Mandel, *Marxist Economic Theory* (New York: Monthly Review Press, 1970).
17. See R. L. Meek, 'Karl Marx's Economic Method', in M. C. Howard and J. E. King (eds), *The Economics of Marx* (Harmondsworth: Penguin, 1976) pp. 114–28.
18. Sekine, *Dialectic of Capital*, vol. I, unpublished manuscript (1982) f. 19.
19. *Ibid.*, p. 24.
20. *Ibid.*, p. 12.
21. *Ibid.*, p. 5.
22. *Ibid.*, p. 41.
23. Marx and Engels, *Selected Correspondence*, p. 179. Though Marx is partially aware of the 'method of dialectic exposition', the three volumes of *Capital* lack explicit and full consciousness of the dialectical method.
24. Uno, *Principles*, p. 14.

25. Sekine, *Dialectic of Capital*, vol. I, unpublished manuscript, f. 201.
26. Sekine, *Dialectic of Capital* (Rosdolsky and Levine also emphasize this point).
27. Sekine, 'The Necessity of the Law of Value', p. 298.
28. Sekine, 'Uno-Riron', p. 864.
29. Sekine, 'The Necessity of the Law of Value', p. 303.
30. *Ibid.*, pp. 289–90.
31. *Ibid.*, p. 294.
32. For example, the debates between Wallerstein and Brenner or between Bettleheim and Emmanuel.
33. Uno, *Principles*, pp. 52–3.
34. Uno, *Principles*, p. 53.
35. Sekine, *Dialectic of Capital*, vol. II, unpublished manuscript (1982) f. 212.
36. Rosdolsky, *The Making of Marx's 'Capital'*, ch. 30; Ernest Mandel, *Late Capitalism* (London: New Left Books, 1975) ch. 1.
37. 'It is this confusion between the theory of circular flows and the theory of equilibrium that seems to me to constitute the real source of errors. By expressing all terms in value and not in actual labour expended, the reproduction schema exclude the possibility of disequilibrium of any sort' (Sekine, *Dialectic of Capital*, vol. II, p. 403).
38. *Ibid.*, p. 369.
39. *Ibid.*, p. 408.
40. *Ibid.*, p. 370.
41. *Ibid.*, p. 461.
42. A good example of this is D. J. Harris's book, *Capital Accumulation and Income Distribution* (Stanford University Press, 1978). To Harris's credit he recognizes the importance of value categories at a time when many theorists are rejecting them and he cautions us against 'attributing too much significance to the scheme itself in its purely formal aspect' (p. 250). However, Harris does go ahead and use the reproduction schema as his central tool of analysis by developing them into an equilibrium model in order to explore possible sources of disturbance and disequilibrium. The theory remains completely agnostic about what actually causes capitalist crises, and instead sees any potential disturbance as a possible cause of crisis. But, as I have argued, most disequilibriums are overcome by the price mechanism and it is only the commodities, fixed capital and labour-power that the price mechanism cannot so easily regulate that give rise to crises. Harris also recognizes the importance of supplementing his work with more concrete and historical analysis, but he leaps from the abstract to the concrete without any sense of levels of analysis so that he indiscriminately makes the following list of social and historical factors which may cause shifts in the all-important investment function: 'any change in method of production, as well as the accelerator–multiplier effect of investment itself and the effect of wars, but also the social mechanisms determining entry and mobility within the capitalist class, various methods of "primitive" accumulation, and the role of the state' (p. 268). On the one hand we have a highly formalistic and agnostic theory about the causes of capitalist crises, and on the other we have a 'grab-bag' of more concrete considerations. A more fruitful approach, as this book argues, is to clarify the necessary causes

of capitalist crises in a purely capitalist society and then develop a more concrete analysis by considering the typical predominant modes of capital accumulation and state policies in the major world-historic stages of capitalist development, and finally move to a more empirical/conjunctural level where very specific political, economic and ideological factors can be taken into account.

43. Professor Nagatani pointed out to me that the expression 'value category' can be misleading. This is because prices are introduced along with money in the early stages of the dialectic. Thus price categories exist alongside value categories from the beginning; however, they do not become substantially differentiated from value categories until the Doctrine of Distribution and the introduction of prices of production. When I use 'value category', then, it is with the above qualification.

44. Sekine, *Dialectic of Capital*, vol. II, p. 44.

45. *Ibid.*, pp. 43–4.

46. *Ibid.*, p. 37.

47. *Ibid.*, p. 119.

48. Sekine, 'The Necessity of the Law of Value', p. 299.

49. Sekine, *Dialectic of Capital*, vol. II, p. 3.

50. *Ibid.*

51. *Ibid.*, p. 129.

52. M. Lippi, *Value and Naturalism in Marx* (London: New Left Books, 1979) p. xx.

53. Steedman, *Marx After Sraffa*, p. 25.

54. I. Steedman, (ed.), *The Value Controversy* (London: New Left Books, 1981), p. 11.

55. *Ibid.*, p. 98.

56. For example, see G. Pilling, *Marx's 'Capital'* (London: Routledge & Kegan Paul, 1980). Anwar Shaikh's 'reiterative' method of solving the transformation problem is perhaps the most successful defence of the transformation problem as it stands in Marx's *Capital*. See A. Shaikh, 'Marx's Theory of Value and the Transformation Problem', in J. Schwartz (ed.), *The Subtle Anatomy of Capitalism* (Santa Monica, California: Goodyear, 1977).

57. Sekine, 'The Law of Market Value', pp. 420–44.

58. I. Steedman, 'Positive Profits with Negative Surplus Value', *Economic Journal* (1975) pp. 114–23. This article is used to support argumentation by Sraffian Marxists in *Value Controversy*.

59. Sekine, 'The Law of Market Value', pp. 432–3.

60. Sekine, *Dialectic of Capital*, vol. II, p. 110.

61. *Ibid.*, p. 104.

62. *Ibid.*, p. 104.

63. *Ibid.*, p. 104.

64. A briefer version is in Sekine, 'The Law of Market Value'.

65. Sekine, *Dialectic of Capital*, vol. I.

66. *Ibid.*, vol. II, pp. 222–4.

67. Uno, *Principles*, p. 112.

68. G. Hodgson, 'The Theory of the Falling Rate of Profit', *New Left Review*, no. 84 (Mar.–Apr. 1974), is a good example of the position that argues that the rate of profit has no more tendency to rise than to fall. Itoh notes in

Value and Crisis that a long-run tendency like the falling rate of profit cannot explain the periodicity of crisis (p. 127). John Weeks, in *Capital and Exploitation* (Princeton University Press, 1981), realizes that the theory of crisis must be rooted in the theory of accumulation and cannot depend entirely on the falling rate of profit taken by itself, and he also sees that it must have something to do with fixed capital. But his analysis runs aground because he fails to grasp the widening and deepening phases of accumulation and instead sees a continual investment in fixed capital and technical change that must devalue the old fixed capital so that 'The crisis was caused by the fall in the rate of profit, resulting from the implicit devaluation of means of production by technical change' (p. 212). But this conceptualization of crisis is inadequate so that he falls back on formulations that sound good but are actually quite empty such as: 'Crisis results from the uneven development of capital . . . capital as a whole comes into conflict with the mutual interaction of its decentralized parts' (p. 214).

69. E. O. Wright, in *Class, Crisis, and the State* (London: New Left Books, 1978), takes the first steps towards relating crisis theory to the stages of capitalist development. These are steps in the right direction, but his periodization of capitalist development is not rigorously posed or convincing, and at the level of stage theory political factors must be accounted for. Thus though it is accurate to argue that in the stage of imperialism capitalist crisis becomes more underconsumptionist, one has to go beyond this and investigate how crises themselves change in this stage and how their inability to solve certain problems solved by crisis in pure theory builds pressures towards imperialist war. Wright inadvertently falls into the economism of the logical–historical method when he tries to smooth the debate between the various interpretations of crisis theory by saying that the falling rate of profit theory is most applicable to the mid-nineteenth century, underconsumptionism is more applicable to the stage of imperialism and profit-squeeze is most applicable to the post-World War II period. This kind of application of economic models directly to history produces economism, and he still avoids answering the question of which account of crisis best fits the theory of a purely capitalist society. Also he really does not consider the possibility that the fundamental nature of crises may change in different stages of capitalist development.

70. This will be discussed more fully in Chapters 4 and 5.

NOTES TO CHAPTER FOUR: STAGE THEORY

1. For comments on stage theory, see Sekine, 'Uno-Riron', pp. 854–5, 869–70; Uno, *Principles*, pp. xiii–xiv, xxii–xxiii, xxvi–xxvii, 150–66, 173.
2. Sekine, *Dialectic of Capital*, p. 67.
3. For example, Marx writes: 'the more perishable a commodity is and the greater the absolute restriction of its time of circulation as a commodity on account of its physical properties, the less is it suited to be an object of capitalist production' [*Capital*, vol. II (Progress) p. 131] and 'a rational agriculture is incompatible with the capitalist system . . ., and needs either the hand of the small farmer . . . or the control of associated producers'

[*Capital*, vol. III (Progress) p. 121]. Although Marx believes that capitalism will be slow to penetrate agriculture and that it will generally be destructive when it does so, still Marx believes that a more or less capitalist agriculture will eventually develop at least some lines of production.

4. Some Japanese Unoists counterpose 'dominant mode of capital accumulation' to my 'concretization of the value/use-value contradiction', but this is because they do not fully understand the dialectical method made explicit by Sekine. The value/use-value contradiction is not meant in some narrow sense to refer only to the Doctrine of Circulation, but is the basic contradiction of the dialectic as a whole. This basic contradiction takes different forms in the different doctrines. In the Doctrine of Production the value/use-value contradiciton takes the form of a contradiction between historically specific circulation-forms and a universal labour and production process, and in the Doctrine of Distribution it takes the form of a contradiction between the heterogeneous forms of value required by the market and the hegemonic and unifying character of capital as a whole. I mean 'concretization of the value/use-value contraction' to be a summary expression of the dialectic as a whole. So in considering a stage it is not enough simply to concretize the circulation-forms. We need also to look at the way the production process and circulation process combine to form a reproduction process that assumes a dominant mode (concretization of the Doctrine of Production), and to examine the ways in which capital subsumes alien elements (e.g. land) and its own heterogeneity through the market (concretization of the Doctrine of Distribution). Understood in this fashion my 'concretization of the value/use-value contradiction' is broader and more all-inclusive than 'dominant mode of capital accumulation' which could be interpreted to refer mainly to the Doctrine of Production.

5. The implications of 'material-types' as opposed to 'ideal-types' and 'average-types' will be discussed in Section 3 below.

6. Uno, 'Types of Economic Policies Under Capitalism', pp. 48–9.

7. Sekine, *Dialectic of Capital*, vol. I, pp. 65–6.

8. *Ibid.*, p. 67.

9. *Ibid.*, p. 68.

10. *Ibid.*, p. 68.

11. Fred Block, *The Origins of International Economic Disorder* (Berkeley: University of California Press, 1977), p. 6.

12. Sekine, 'Uno-Riron', p. 854.

13. V. I. Lenin, *Imperialism: The Highest Stage of Capitalism* (New York: International, 1979), p. 61.

14. According to Mawatari there are studies in Japanese that show this to be the case. See Mawatari, 'The Uno School: a Marxian Approach in Japan'.

15. R. Hilferding, *Finance Capital* (London: Routledge & Kegan Paul, 1981) p. 297.

16. G. Arrighi, *The Geometry of Imperialism* (London: New Left Books, 1978) p. 17.

17. Marx, *Capital*, vol. III (Progress) pp. 436–8.

18. Hilferding, *Finance Capital*. This is the first English publication of this important work, and this no doubt is part of the reason why English-speaking theorists have given it so little attention.

19. For example, Hilferding does not distinguish between the functioning of banks in a purely capitalist society and the more concrete imperialist stage. He even goes so far as to claim that the more concrete 'finance-capital' is more abstract than 'industrial-capital'. He writes: 'capital assumes the form of finance capital, its supreme and most abstract expression' (*ibid.*, p. 21).

20. Hilferding fails to distinguish between the laws of motion of capital and the laws of the stage of imperialism thus confusing the type of necessity associated with the two levels of theory.

21. For example he discusses (*ibid.*) legisation which gave such a prominent role to the stock-market in the United States (p. 278), legislation against cartels (p. 412), the large economic territory of the United States (p. 329), the Monroe Doctrine (p. 327), immigration (p. 327).

22. *Ibid.*, p. 366.

23. *Ibid.*, p. 367.

24. *Ibid.*, p. 366.

25. See A. Brewer, *Marxist Theories of Imperialism* (London: Routledge & Kegan Paul, 1980) p. 87, and A. Hussain, 'Hilferding's *Finance Capital*', *Bulletin of the Conference of Socialist Economists* (March 1967) p. 1.

26. Hilferding, *Finance Capital*, p. 313.

27. *Ibid.*, p. 21.

28. Lenin, *Imperialism*, pp. 16–17.

29. *Ibid.*, p. 61.

30. R. Luxemburg, *The Accumulation of Capital* (London: Routledge & Kegan Paul, 1963); R. Luxemburg, *The Accumulation of Capital: An Anti-Critique* and N. Bukharin, *Imperialism and the Accumulation of Capital* (New York: Monthly Review Press, 1972).

31. Luxemburg, *Accumulation of Capital*, p. 348.

32. *Ibid.*, p. 359.

33. Luxemburg and Bukharin, *Anti-Critique*, p. 76.

34. *Ibid.*

35. Luxemburg, *Accumulation of Capital*, p. 371.

36. *Ibid.*, p. 416.

37. *Ibid.*, p. 446.

38. For example, see Brewer, *Marxist Theories of Imperialism*, pp. 75–6.

39. Bukharin, *Imperialism and the Accumulation of Capital.*, p. 241.

40. *Ibid.*, p. 260.

41. *Ibid.*, pp. 265–7.

42. Paul Baran and P. Sweezy, *Monopoly Capital* (New York: Monthly Review Press, 1966) written largely during a period of reaction is one of the most important and influential books on Marxian economics produced by the American Left. Also it was one of the earliest works of the post-World War II Marxian renaissance.

43. Baran and Sweezy, *Monopoly Capital*, p. 114.

44. *Ibid.*, p. 219.

45. A. Emmanuel, *Unequal Exchange* (New York: Monthly Review Press, 1972), p. 64.

46. C. Palloix, 'Multinational Firms and the Process of Internationalization', unpublished translation, p. 25.

47. *Ibid.* (emphasis added)

48. Wright, *Class, Crisis, and the State*, pp. 168–9.
49. Fine B. and L. Harris, *Rereading Capital* (London: Macmillan, 1979) pp. 109–10.
50. *Ibid.*, p. 112.

NOTES TO CHAPTER FIVE: THE HISTORICAL ANALYSIS OF CAPITALISM

1. Itoh's *Value and Crisis* and various articles written by him touch upon aspects of recent economic history such as the nature of contemporary inflation, but otherwise no work of the Uno School on capitalist history is available in English.
2. I. Wallerstein, *The Modern World System* (New York: Academic Press, 1974); Brenner, 'The Origins of Capitalist Development', *New Left Review*, no. 104. Wallerstein's approach is clearly inadequate because it places all the emphasis on the world market. Brenner's analysis is much stronger, but may err on the side of not focusing enough attention on the realm of circulation.
3. The notion of 'fictitious commodity' comes from Polanyi's *The Great Transformation*. This notion is used in the next chapter since it is especially with regard to the 'fictitious commodities' that the law of value is likely to need support from the superstructure.
4. For a historical analysis of the development of petty commodity production of cotton in Uganda, see M. Mamdani, *Politics and Class Formation in Uganda* (New York: Monthly Review Press, 1976).
5. Wallerstein, *The Modern World System*; Brenner, 'The Origins of Capitalist Development'.
6. Brenner, 'The Origins of Capitalist Development', p. 76.
7. *Ibid.*, p. 77.
8. For a much fuller discussion of Althusser, see Chapter 8.
9. See Thompson, *The Poverty of Theory*.
10. For example, see A. Foster-Carter, 'The Modes of Production Controversy', *New Left Review*, no. 107.
11. For example, see N. Poulantzas, *Political Power and Social Class* (London: New Left Books, 1973).
12. See N. Poulantzas, *State, Power and Socialism* (London: New Left Books, 1978).
13. For example, most 'discourse analysis' and 'deconstruction approaches'. See Laclau and Mouffe, 'Recasting Marxism'.
14. Hindness *et al.*, *Marx's 'Capital' and Capitalism Today*.
15. Laclau and Mouffe, 'Recasting Marxism', p. 94.
16. C. Palloix, 'The Internationalization of Capital' in H. Radice (ed.), *International Firms and Modern Imperialism* (Harmondsworth: Penguin, 1975) pp. 8, 25.
17. C. Palloix, 'The Self-expansion of Capital on a World Scale', *Review of Radical Political Economy*, vol. 9, no. 2 (summer 1977) p. 15.
18. Thompson, *Poverty of Theory*, pp. 59, 68.
19. G. Hodgson, 'The Theory of the Falling Rate of Profit', *New Left Review*, no. 84 (Mar–Apr 1974).

20. Marx, *Capital*, vol. III (Progress), p. 831.
21. Thompson, *Poverty of Theory*, p. 68.
22. *Ibid.*, p. 65.
23. *Ibid.*, p. 61.
24. *Ibid.*, p. 63.
25. Marx, *Capital*, vol. I (Progress), p. 19.
26. Thompson, *Poverty of Theory*, p. 153.
27. *Ibid.*, p. 155.
28. *Ibid.*, p. 163.
29. Adam Przeworski, 'Proletariat into Class: The Process of Class Formation from Karl Kautsky's *The Class Struggle* to Recent Controversies', *Politics and Society*, vol. 7, no. 4 (1977) p. 385.

NOTES TO CHAPTER SIX: THE THEORY OF THE CAPITALIST SUPERSTRUCTURE

1. Uno believed that the theory of the state should be formulated at the level of stage theory. Although the Japanese Uno School has not done much work on the theory of the state, most work that has been done has abstracted the capitalist state from the stage of liberalism which is closest to pure theory. But Uno did believe that it was possible to root legal theory at the level of pure theory. The pure theory of law would have three parts: civil law, criminal law and public law. Unfortunately Uno never expanded further on these ideas. In the approach I have developed, the state is only a legal form at the level of pure theory. The institutional and policy content of the state can begin to be theorized at the level of stage theory. It seems to me that this approach is not contrary to Uno, and it has the advantage of showing that the capitalist state in its inner essence is an ideological form – to be more precise a legal subjectivity made sovereign by means of a legal fiction. Furthermore, though the economic stands on its own at the level of pure theory, it is backed up by the passive reflexes of the basic superstructural forms. Because these forms become active and interventionist supports at more concrete levels of analysis, it is important to theorize the relation between the economic, political and ideological from the beginning. In this sense pure theory is not really complete without the accompanying theory of superstructural forms.
2. The German '*rechsstaat*' seems more accurate that the English 'legal state' or 'constitutional state' in describing the basic capitalist state form. The derivation of this form will be analysed later in the chapter.
3. Marx, *Capital*, vol. I (Progress) p. 88.
4. *Ibid.*, p. 89.
5. C. B. Macpherson, *The Political Theory of Possessive Individualism* (London: Oxford University Press, 1962); E.B. Pashukanis, *Law and Marxism: A General Theory* (London: Ink Links, 1978).
6. Pashukanis, *Law and Marxism*, p. 100.
7. Marx, *Capital*, vol. I (Progress) pp. 88–9.
8. Pashukanis, *Law and Marxism*, p. 80.
9. *Ibid.*, p. 100.

10. *Ibid.*, p. 152.
11. *Ibid.*, p. 45.
12. *Ibid.*, p. 82. Based on the form of the legal subject we can also derive the basic ethical form. Because legal subjects relate to each other externally and impersonally through exchange and because competition may push possessive individuals to exceed the laws of property, it is necessary that the law become inward and that the legal subjects also recognize each other as moral subjects or 'personalities of equal worth' (p. 151). According to Pashukanis, 'the rule governing transactions between commodity owners must penetrate the soul of every commodity owner, must be his inner law' (p. 154). To the extent that 'property must only change hands through mutual consent' is internalized, we have a moral law that says 'treat others as ends in themselves and not simply as means to your end'.
13. *Ibid.*, p. 103.
14. *Ibid.*, p. 113.
15. *Ibid.*, p. 14.
16. *Ibid.*, p. 104.
17. Marx, *Capital*, vol. I (Progress) p. 172.
18. The notion of 'class belonging' comes from E. Laclau, *Politics and Ideology in Marxist Theory* (London: New Left Books, 1977).
19. This notion 'the legal subject writ large' comes from S. Wolin, *Politics and Vision* (Boston: Little, Brown, 1960) p. 265.
20. Pashukanis, *Law and Marxism*, p. 14.
21. J. Locke, *Two Treatises of Government*, vol. 1, pp. 11, 106.
22. *Ibid.*, vol. 2, pp. 19, 222.
23. J. Shklar, *Legalism* (Harvard University Press, 1964).
24. Some thinkers in the Japanese Uno School think that the theory of the capitalist state should be abstracted from the liberal stage of capitalist development. But this approach fails to achieve the precision possible by grounding the superstructural forms at the level of pure theory.
25. The idea of 'fictitious commodity' comes from Polanyi, *The Great Transformation*. He has an unclear conception of money, but otherwise I generally agree with this characterization.
26. Sekine, *Dialectic of Capital*, vol. I, p. 461.

NOTES TO CHAPTER SEVEN: THE UNO/SEKINE APPROACH TO DIALECTICAL MATERIALISM

1. W. T. Stace, *The Philosophy of Hegel* (New York: Dover, 1955) p. 88.
2. Sekine, *Dialectic of Capital*, vol. I (Tokyo: Yushindo Press, 1984) p. 251.
3. *Ibid.*, vol. II, p. 40, unpublished manuscript (1982).
4. *Ibid.*, p. 47.
5. *Ibid.*, p. 31.
6. Marx, *Capital*, vol. I (Progress) p. 682.
7. Sekine, *Dialectic of Capital*, vol. I, pp. 49–50.
8. *Ibid.*

NOTES TO CHAPTER EIGHT: A CRITICAL ANALYSIS OF SOME WESTERN APPROACHES TO DIALECTICAL MATERIALISM

1. This tendency can be seen in the work of Della Volpe, Colletti and Althusser, which sacrifice dialectics to materialism, and in the work of Lukacs and critical theory which sacrifice materialism to dialectics.
2. G. Lukacs, *History and Class Consciousness* (London: Merlin, 1971) p. 16.
3. *Ibid.*, p. 16.
4. *Ibid.*, p. 17.
5. *Ibid.*, p. 19.
6. *Ibid.*, p. 20.
7. *Ibid.*, p. 170.
8. *Ibid.*, p. 83.
9. *Ibid.*, p. 102.
10. *Ibid.*, p. 120.
11. *Ibid.*, p. 23.
12. *Ibid.*, p. 19.
13. *Ibid.*, p. 3.
14. *Ibid.*, p. 126.
15. *Ibid.*, p. 3.
16. *Ibid.*, p. 180.
17. *Ibid.*, p. 205.
18. *Ibid.*, p. 3.
19. Althusser, *Reading Capital*, p. 24.
20. *Ibid.*, p. 61.
21. *Ibid.*, p. 77.
22. For the meaning of 'real opposition' see Colletti below.
23. L. Althusser, *For Marx* (New York: Vintage, 1969) pp. 198–9.
24. L. Colletti, *Marxism and Hegel* (London: New Left Books, 1973) p. 22.
25. *Ibid.*, p. 27.
26. *Ibid.*, p. 50.
27. *Ibid.*, p. 183.
28. *Ibid.*, p. 122.
29. *Ibid.*, p. 127.
30. *Ibid.*, pp. 128–9.
31. *Ibid.*, pp. 136–7.
32. L. Colletti, 'Contradiction and Contrariety', *New Left Review*, no. 93 (1975) p. 23.
33. *Ibid.*, p. 25.
34. *Ibid.*, p. 20.
35. L. Colletti, 'Some Comments on Marx's Theory of Value', in Schwartz (ed.), *Subtle Anatomy of Capitalism*, p. 464.
36. *Ibid.*, pp. 28–9.
37. *Ibid.*, p. 29.
38. *Ibid.*, p. 29.

NOTES TO CHAPTER NINE: SOME BASIC CONCEPTS OF HISTORICAL MATERIALISM

1. Sekine, 'Uno-Riron', p. 873.
2. B. Franklin (ed.), *The Essential Stalin* (London: Croom Helm, 1973) p. 312. In the only Unoist remarks on historical materialism available in English, Sekine also seems to derive the basic principles of historical materialism from the *1858 Preface*, but unlike Stalin he sees historical materialism as an ideological hypothesis with 'a scientifically substantiated core' ('Uno-Riron', p. 873). This is the approach that I have adopted in this chapter.
3. For example, see E. M. Wood, 'The Separation of the Economic and Political in Capitalism', *New Left Review*, no. 127 (1981); A. Levine and E. O. Wright, 'Rationality and Class Struggle', *New Left Review*, no. 123 (1980); R. Miller, in T. Ball and J. Farr (eds), *After Marx* (Cambridge University Press, 1984).
4. See Thompson, *Poverty of Theory*.
5. For 'norms of economic life', see Uno, *Principles*, p. 171.
6. Foster-Carter, 'The Modes of Production Controversy'; Brewer, *Marxist Theories of Imperialism*, ch. 11.
7. Althusser, *Reading Capital*, p. 317.
8. Foster-Carter, 'The Modes of Production Controversy', pp. 76–7.
9. P. Anderson, *Passages from Antiquity to Feudalism* (London: New Left Books, 1974).
10. This point was explained to me by Professor Nagatani at a seminar at Tohoku University in Sendai, Japan.
11. In *Passages from Antiquity to Feudalism*, Anderson writes:

> the characteristic figure of a crisis in a mode of production is not one in which vigorous (economic) forces of production burst triumphantly through retrograde (social) relations of production, and promptly establish a higher production and society on their ruins. On the contrary, the forces of production typically tend to stall and recede within the existent relations of production; these then must themselves first be radically changed and reordered before new forces of production can be created and combined for a globally new mode of production . . . the relations of production generally change prior to the forces of production in an epoch of transition. (p. 204)

12. See Laclau and Mouffe, 'Recasting Marxism', p. 91.
13. This includes primitive communism where there is no class because no surplus and socialism where the surplus is democratically appropriated to benefit the entire society.

NOTES TO CHAPTER TEN: TRANSITION TO SOCIALISM

1. E. O. Wright, 'Capitalism's Future', *Socialist Review*, no. 68 (March–April 1983).

2. From a discussion with Professor S. Ohuchi at Tohoku University, Sendai, Japan.
3. Sekine, *Dialectic of Capital*, vol. I, p. 93.
4. No single Marxian text fully analyses the dynamics of the debt economy, but a number of texts make important contributions. In particular see Cheryl Payer, *The Debt Trap* (New York: Monthly Review Press, 1974) and *The World Bank* (New York: Monthly Review Press, 1982); A. Sampson, *The Money-Lenders* (London: Coronet, 1981); Block, *Origins of International Economic Disorder*.
5. Block, *Origins of International Economic Disorder*, pp. 203–12.
6. Many books deal with the importance of militarism in the latest phase of dying capitalism, but one of the earliest and most influential is Baran and Sweezy's *Monopoly Capital*.
7. Block, *Origins of International Economic Disorder*, p. 107.
8. *Ibid.*, pp. 73, 83, 103.
9. Franklin (ed.), *The Essential Stalin*, p. 312.
10. Lukacs, *History and Class Consciousness*, p. 3.
11. See especially H. Marcuse, *One-Dimensional Man*.
12. Karl Popper, *The Poverty of Historicism* (New York: Harper & Row, 1964).
13. E. Laclau, *Politics and Ideology in Marxist Theory* (London: New Left Books, 1977).
14. Laclau and Mouffe, 'Recasting Marxism', p. 105.
15. *Ibid.*, p. 112.

NOTE TO CHAPTER ELEVEN: CONCLUSION

1. For a good discussion of the Gramscian elements in Poulantzas, see Robert Jessop, *The Capitalist State* (Oxford: Martin Robertson, 1982).

Bibliography

Albritton, R., 'The Dialectic of Capital: a Japanese Contribution', *Capital and Class*, vol. 22 (Spring 1984).

Althusser, L., *For Marx* (New York: Vintage, 1969).

Althusser, L., *Reading Capital* (London: New Left Books, 1970).

Althusser, L., *Lenin and Philosophy and Other Essays* (London: New Left Books, 1971).

Althusser, L., *Politics and History* (London: New Left Books, 1972).

Amin, Samir, *Accumulation on a World Scale* (New York: Monthly Review Press, 1974).

Anderson, Perry, *Lineages of the Absolutist State* (London: New Left Books, 1974).

Anderson, Perry, *Passages from Antiquity to Feudalism* (London: New Left Books, 1974).

Anderson, Perry, *Arguments within English Marxism* (London: New Left Books, 1980).

Anderson, Perry, *In the Tracks of Historical Materialism* (University of Chicago Press, 1984).

Aronowitz, Stanley, *The Crisis in Historical Materialism* (New York: Praeger, 1981).

Arrighi, Giovanni, *The Geometry of Imperialism* (London: New Left Books, 1978).

Bahro, R., *The Alternative in Eastern Europe* (London: New Left Books, 1978).

Ball, T. and Farr, J. (eds), *After Marx* (Cambridge University Press, 1984).

Baran, Paul, *The Political Economy of Growth* (New York: Monthly Review Press, 1957).

Baran, Paul and Sweezy, P., *Monopoly Capital* (New York: Monthly Review Press, 1966).

Beirne, P. and Quinney, R. (eds), *Marxism and Law* (New York: John Wiley, 1982).

Bleaney, M., *Underconsumption Theories* (New York: International, 1976).

Block, Fred, *The Origins of International Economic Disorder* (Berkeley: University of California Press, 1977).

Bohm-Bawerk, E., *Karl Marx and the Close of His System* (London: Merlin, 1949).

Brenner, R., 'The Origins of Capitalist Development', *New Left Review*, no. 104 (1977).

Brewer, Anthony, *Marxist Theories of Imperialism* (London: Routledge & Kegan Paul, 1980).

Bukharin, N., *Imperialism and World Economy* (London: Merlin, 1972).

291

Cleaver, H., *Reading Capital Politically* (Austin: University of Texas Press, 1979).

Cohen, G. A., *Karl Marx's Theory of History: A Defence* (Princeton University Press, 1978).

Colletti, Lucio, 'Contradiction and Contrariety', *New Left Review*, no. 93 (1975).

Colletti, Lucio, *From Rousseau to Lenin* (London: New Left Books, 1972).

Colletti, Lucio, *Marxism and Hegel* (London: New Left Books, 1973).

Colletti, Lucio, 'Some Comments on Marx's Theory of Value', in J. Schwartz (ed.), *The Subtle Anatomy of Capitalism* (Santa Monica, California: Goodyear, 1977).

de Brunhoff, S., *The State, Capital, and Economic Policy* (London: Pluto Press, 1978).

Duncan, C., 'Under the Cloud of Capital: History Versus Theory', *Science and Society*, vol. XLVII, no. 3 (Fall 1983).

Elson, D. (ed.), *Value: The Representation of Labour in Capitalism* (London: CSE Books, 1979).

Emmanuel, A., *Unequal Exchange* (New York: Monthly Review Press, 1972).

Fine, B. and Harris, L., *Rereading Capital* (London: Macmillan, 1979).

Foster-Carter, A., 'The Modes of Production Controversy', *New Left Review*, no. 107 (1978).

Frank, A. G., *Capitalism and Underdevelopment in Latin America* (New York: Monthly Review Press, 1967).

Franklin, B. (ed.), *The Essential Stalin* (London: Croom Helm, 1973).

Gordon, D., 'Up and Down the Long Rollercoaster', *U.S. Capitalism in Crisis*, Union of Radical Political Economists (1978).

Gough, Ian, *The Political Economy of the Welfare State* (London: Macmillan, 1979).

Harris, D. J., *Capital Accumulation and Income Distribution* (Stanford University Press, 1978).

Harvey, D., *The Limits to Capital* (University of Chicago Press, 1982).

Hegel, G. W. F., *Science of Logic*, trans. by A. V. Miller (London: Allen & Unwin, 1969).

Hegel, G. W. F., *Logic*, trans. by W. Wallace (Oxford University Press, 1975).

Hilferding, R., *Finance Capital* (London: Routledge & Kegan Paul, 1981).

Hindness, B., Cutler, A., Hirst, P. and Hussain, A., *Marx's 'Capital' and Capitalism Today*, 2 vols (London: Routledge & Kegan Paul, 1977).

Hodgson, G., 'The Theory of the Falling Rate of Profit', *New Left Review*, no. 84 (1974).

Horowitz, D. (ed.), *Marx and Modern Economics* (New York: Monthly Review Press, 1968).

Howard, M. C. and King, J. E. (eds), *The Economics of Marx* (Harmondsworth: Penguin, 1976).

Hunt, E. K. and J. Schwartz (eds), *A Critique of Economic Theory* (Harmondsworth: Penguin, 1972).

Hussain, A., 'Hilferding's *Finance Capital*', *Bulletin of the Conference of Socialist Economists* (March 1967).

Itoh, M., 'A Study of Marx's Theory of Value', *Science and Society* (Fall 1976).

Itoh, M., 'The Formation of Marx's Theory of Crisis', *Science and Society* (Summer 1978).

Itoh, M., *Value and Crisis: Essays on Marxian Economics in Japan* (New York: Monthly Review Press, 1980).

Itoh, M., 'On Marx's Theory of Accumulation: a Reply to Weeks', *Science and Society* (Spring 1981).

Jessop, Robert, *The Capitalist State* (Oxford: Martin Robertson, 1982).

Kaplan, B. (ed.), *Social Change in the Capitalist World Economy* (Beverly Hills: Sage, 1978).

Kemp, T., *Theories of Imperialism* (London: Dennis Dobson, 1967).

Laclau, E., *Politics and Ideology in Marxist Theory* (London: New Left Books, 1977).

Laclau, E. and C. Mouffe, 'Recasting Marxism: Hegemony and New Political Movements', *Socialist Review*, no. 66 (November–December 1982).

Larrain, J., *Marxism and Ideology* (London: Macmillan, 1983).

Lecourt, D., *Marxism and Epistemology* (London: New Left Books, 1975).

Lenin, V. I., *The Development of Capitalism in Russia* (Moscow: Progress, 1967).

Lenin, V. I., *Imperialism: The Highest Stage of Capitalism* (New York: International, 1939).

Levine, A. and E. O. Wright, 'Rationality and Class Struggle', *New Left Review*, no. 123 (1980).

Levine, D., *Economic Studies* (London: Routledge & Kegan Paul, 1977).

Levine, D., *Economic Theory*, vol. I (London: Routledge & Kegan Paul, 1978).

Lippi, M., *Value and Naturalism in Marx* (London: New Left Books, 1979).

Lukacs, G., *History and Class Consciousness* (London: Merlin, 1971).

Luxemburg, R., *The Accumulation of Capital* (London: Routledge & Kegan Paul, 1963).

Luxemburg, R. and N. Bukharin, *The Accumulation of Capital: An Anti-Critique* (New York: Monthly Review Press, 1972).

Maclean, B., 'Kozo Uno's *Principles of Political Economy*', *Science and Society* (Summer 1981).

Macpherson, C. B., *The Political Theory of Possessive Individualism* (London: Oxford University Press, 1962).

Mamdani, M., *Politics and Class Formation in Uganda* (New York: Monthly Review Press, 1976).

Mandel, E., *Marxist Economic Theory*, 2 vols (New York: Monthly Review Press, 1970).

Mandel, E., *Late Capitalism* (London: New Left Books, 1975).

Marcuse, H., *One-Dimensional Man* (Boston, Mass.: Beacon Press, 1964).

Marx, K., *Capital*, 3 vols (Moscow: Progress, 1971).

Marx, K., *The Gundrisse* (Harmondsworth: Penguin, 1973).

Marx, K., *Value: Studies by Marx* (London: New Park, 1976).

Marx, K., *Capital*, vol. I, trans. by Ben Fowkes (Harmondsworth: Penguin, 1976).

Marx, K., and F. Engels, *Selected Correspondence* (Moscow: Progress, 1955).

Marx, K., and F. Engels, *Collected Works*, vol. 16 (New York: International, 1980).

Mawatari, S., 'The Uno School: a Marxian Approach in Japan', *The History of Political Economy Journal*, forthcoming.

Meek, R. L., *Economics and Ideology and Other Essays* (London: Chapman & Hall, 1967).

Meek, R. L., 'Karl Marx's Economic Method', in M. C. Howard and J. E. King

294 *Bibliography*

(eds), *The Economics of Marx* (Harmondsworth: Penguin, 1976).

Mepham, J. and D. H. Ruben, *Issues in Marxist Philosophy*, vols I, III (Sussex: Harvester Press, 1979).

Miliband, R., *The State in Capitalist Society* (London: Weidenfeld & Nicolson, 1969).

Miller, R., in Ball and Farr (eds), *After Marx* (Cambridge University Press, 1984).

Neumann, F., *Behemoth* (London: Victor Gollancz, 1942).

O'Connor, J., *The Fiscal Crisis of the State* (New York: St. Martin's Press, 1973).

Offe, C., 'The Ungovernability of Liberal Democracies', *Studies in Political Economy*, no. 3 (Spring 1980).

Palloix, C., 'The Self-expansion of Capital on a World Scale', *Review of Radical Political Economy*, vol. 9, no. 2 (Summer 1977).

Palloix, C., 'The Internationalization of Capital', in H. Radice (ed.), *International Firms and Modern Imperialism* (Harmondsworth: Penguin, 1975).

Palloix, C., 'Multinational Firms and the Process of Internationalization', unpublished translation (1981).

Pashukanis, E. B., *Law and Marxism: A General Theory* (London: Ink Links, 1978).

Payer, C., *The Debt Trap* (New York: Monthly Review Press, 1974).

Payer, C., *The World Bank* (New York: Monthly Review Press, 1982).

Pilling, G., *Marx's 'Capital'* (London: Routledge & Kegan Paul, 1980).

Popper, K., *The Poverty of Historicism* (New York: Harper & Row, 1964).

Poulantzas, N., 'Internationalization of Capitalist Relations and the Nation State', *Economy and Society*, vol. 3, no. 2 (May 1974).

Poulantzas, N., *Political Power and Social Class* (London: New Left Books, 1973).

Poulantzas, N., *State, Power, and Socialism* (London: New Left Books, 1978).

Przeworski, Adam, 'Proletariat into Class . . .', *Politics and Society*, vol. 7, no. 4 (1977).

Rosdolsky, R., *The Making of Marx's 'Capital'* (London: Pluto Press, 1977).

Sahlins, M., *Stone Age Economics* (New York: Aldine, 1972).

Sampson, A., *The Money Lenders* (London: Coronet, 1981).

Sayer, D., *Marx's Method* (Sussex: Harvester Press, 1979).

Schwartz, J. (ed.), *The Subtle Anatomy of Capitalism* (Santa Monica, California: Goodyear, 1977).

Sekine, T., 'Uno-Riron: a Japanese Contribution to Marxian Political Economy', *Journal of Economic Literature*, vol. XIII (1975).

Sekine, T., 'The Necessity of the Law of Value', *Science and Society* (Fall 1980).

Sekine, T., 'The Circular Motion of Capital', *Science and Society* (Fall 1981).

Sekine, T., 'The Law of Market Value', *Science and Society* (Winter 1982–3).

Sekine, T., *The Dialectic of Capital*, vol. I (Tokyo: Yushindo Press, 1984).

Sekine, T., *The Dialectic of Capital*, vol. I and II, unpublished manuscript (1982).

Shaikh, A., 'Marx's Theory of Value and the Transformation Problem', in J. Schwartz (ed.), *The Subtle Anatomy of Capitalism* (Santa Monica, California: Goodyear, 1977).

Shklar, J., *Legalism* (Harvard University Press, 1964).

Sraffa, P., *The Production of Commodities by Means of Commodities* (Cambridge University Press, 1960).

Stace, W. T., *The Philosophy of Hegel* (New York: Dover, 1955).

Steedman, I., 'Positive Profits with Negative Surplus Value', *Economic Journal*, (1975) pp. 114–23.

Steedman, I., *Marx After Sraffa* (London: New Left Books, 1977).

Steedman, I. (ed.), *The Value Controversy* (London: New Left Books, 1981).

Sweezy, P. and C. Bettleheim, *On the Transition to Socialism* (New York: Monthly Review Press, 1971).

Taylor, C., *Hegel* (Cambridge University Press, 1975).

Thompson, E. P., *The Poverty of Theory and Other Essays* (New York: Monthly Review Press, 1978).

Uno, Kozo, *Principles of Political Economy: Theory of a Purely Capitalist Society*, trans. by T. Sekine (Sussex: Harvester Press, 1980).

Uno, K., 'Types of Economic Policies Under Capitalism', unpublished partially translated manuscript (1980).

Warren, Bill, *Imperialism: Pioneer of Capitalism* (London: New Left Books, 1980).

Wallerstein, I., *The Modern World System* (New York: Academic Press, 1974).

Wallerstein, I., 'The Rise and Future Demise of the World Capitalist System: Concepts for Comparative Analysis', *Comparative Studies in History and Society*, no. 16 (1974).

Watanabe, H., 'Logico-genetical Approximation to the Analysis of the Unfolding of the Value-form', *The Kezai Gaku*, Annual Report of the Economic Society, Tohoku University, Sendai, Japan (1983).

Weeks, John, 'The Process of Accumulation and the "Profit-Squeeze" Hypothesis', *Science and Society* (Fall 1979).

Weeks, John, *Capital and Exploitation* (Princeton University Press, 1981).

Wells, D., *Marxism and the Modern State* (Sussex: Harvester Press, 1981).

Wolin, S., *Politics and Vision* (Boston: Little, Brown, 1960).

Wood, E. M., 'The Separation of the Economic and Political in Capitalism', *New Left Review*, no. 127 (May–June 1981).

Wright, E. O., *Class, Crisis, and the State* (London: New Left Books, 1978).

Wright, E. O., 'Capitalism's Future', *Socialist Review*, no. 68 (March–April 1983).

Zeleny, J., *The Logic of Marx* (Oxford: Basil Blackwell, 1980).

Index

296